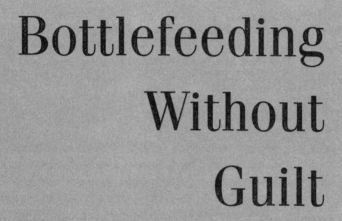

Bottlefeeding Without Guilt

A REASSURING GUIDE FOR LOVING PARENTS

Peggy Robin

Prima Publishing

PRIMA PUBLISHING and its colophon, which consists of the letter P over PRIMA, are trademarks of Prima Communications, Inc.

Library of Congress Cataloging-in-Publication Data

Robin, Peggy
  Bottle feeding without guilt: a reassuring guide for loving parents / Peggy Robin.
    p. cm.
  Includes index.
  ISBN 0-7615-0001-4
  1. Bottle feeding. I. Title
RJ216.R56 1995
849' .3–dc20

                                                                    95-885
                                                                    CIP

96 97 98 99 AA 10 9 8 7 6 5 4 3 2 1
Printed in the United States of America

How to Order:

Single copies may be ordered from Prima Publishing, P.O. Box 1260, Rocklin, CA 95677; telephone (916) 632-4400. Quantity discounts are also available. On your letterhead, include information concerning the intended use of the books and the number of books you wish to purchase.

For Karen and Claire,
who taught me that nurturing
is far more than what goes into a baby's mouth

Contents

Acknowledgments

The research material for this book came primarily from parents who responded to my notice in a Washington, D. C., parenting magazine seeking interviews with mothers who had bottlefed their babies. I thank them for telling me their stories and for giving me permission to tell those stories in this book. I must also express my gratitude to several hundred message-writers on various computer bulletin boards and electronic mail forums, who provided me with some of the most quotable lines in the book illustrating the phenomenal range of opinion currently being expressed about bottlefeeding and breastfeeding (from the most fervent evangelists of the breastfeeding gospel to the embattled defenders of the bottle.) But most of all, I must thank my husband, Bill Adler, Jr., who put me on-line and made it possible for me to listen in on all those fascinating dialogs and debates about infant feeding practices going on in cyberspace.

Thanks, too, to Jennifer Basye Sander and Alice Anderson at Prima Publishing for their encouragement and advice. Finally, I could never have written this book without the help of Fiona Lewsley, who gave me peace of mind that my children were receiving the very highest quality of care while I pounded away at the keyboard.

Why a Guide for Bottlefeeding Parents?

"I Felt Like I'd Failed as a Woman and a Mother"

It's two in the morning and the new baby is screaming. He's five days old and he's been trying to nurse but is frustrated and frantic. His parents are, too. The mother is still exhausted from a thirty-six hour labor that seemed to go nowhere, until a cesarean section brought an end to the agony. In her first day home from the hospital, during a hurried session with the lactation consultant on staff, this mother learned that it's all a matter of "correct positioning." If she could just get the baby's mouth onto her nipple in one perfect push, she and her baby would surely be able to experience the bliss of breastfeeding that all her friends have talked about. Meanwhile the father paces about, afraid to suggest bottles, afraid to advise her to keep on trying—afraid, in fact, to say anything, because his wife is so upset that she is likely to take whatever he says as a rebuke of her ability to mother her infant.

So the mother persists in trying to get the baby to "latch-on."* The baby cries. So does the mother. The pediatrician has warned her about danger signs that the baby is not getting enough milk. Her son needs to produce six to eight really wet diapers a day—but this baby has had only two. Worse still, the baby's cry has now dropped from a shrill, siren-like sound to a whimper, he's starting to act listless, and his eyes are looking dull. He could be getting dehydrated, a serious, possibly lethal consequence that the doctor has told the mother she must be sure to prevent.

She becomes scared enough about her baby's health to try a little formula—though she dearly wishes she didn't have to. Throughout her pregnancy she'd never considered the possibility that she'd end up using a manufactured product to feed her baby. That was for her mother's generation, for back in those days when even well-educated women were taken in by formula companies' slick advertising, a time when women's breasts were never seen except in the pages of *Playboy*, and only low-income women who couldn't afford formula or lived in isolated areas far from grocery stores were seen with babies at the breast.

The parents are not ready to go for the bottle yet. The lactation consultant from the hospital had warned them in no uncertain terms: "Any use of an artificial

---

*Latch-on is the term used when the baby's mouth is correctly positioned on the mother's nipple for effective sucking.

nipple in the first six weeks of life will cause *nipple confusion*. It may take the baby *months* to relearn the correct sucking pattern for successful breastfeeding." If parents feel they must turn to formula for any reason, she had suggested giving it to the baby by eye-dropper, or on a spoon, or in a cup. Dutifully, the new parents try all three of these methods. The feeding of just two ounces takes over an hour, with much spillage, and tears for all. The mother's vision of herself cuddling and holding her newborn during feedings, establishing an early bond of love and trust, is shattered. Her baby stares at her with wild confusion and hunger, wailing piteously all the while.

When the feeding is at last over, and the baby is mercifully asleep, the parents lie awake, wondering what to do. At last the mother speaks. "You know, I was bottlefed from the start, and I've always been healthy," she begins, almost in a whisper.

Relieved to have her bring it up first, the husband seconds the thought: "I was too, and so were all my younger brothers and sisters, and we had a great, close relationship with our mother. We never felt we missed out on any 'bonding' because we weren't breastfed. In fact, I remember how much fun it was to help my mom feed my baby brother. I didn't want to say anything because you seemed so intent on nursing, but I knew I would feel a loss if I never got to do any feeding."

So when dawn comes and the baby is awake, they break out the bottle kit that the husband's mother had given them (in what, at the time, had felt like an unwelcome present for the nursing-minded mother-to-be). They prepare the formula, and oh-so-tentatively slip the artificial nipple into the baby's mouth. Half a second later, both parents' faces are all smiles as they see that tiny mouth greedily sucking away, hear those tiny gurgles of satisfaction as the baby swallows the formula, and welcome the intense pleasure on his face as his appetite is at last sated. The parents let out a sigh of relief.

For the mother, this means no more cracked and bleeding nipples, less exhaustion, and no more painfully engorged and backache-inducing enlarged breasts. For the father, feelings of helplessness, of standing by uselessly while both his wife and baby suffer, are eased. The baby can finally enjoy a nutritionally complete and satisfying feeding each time, and the chance to sleep longer and more soundly on a full stomach. With that first bottle, both parents are flooded with a sense of the rightness of what they've decided, and have no doubt that they have made the best decision for their baby's physical and emotional health, as well as their own well-being.

A happy ending, right? This is how a book is supposed to end, not begin. That might have been the case if the parents could have held firm in their conviction that they'd done the right thing for their baby. But we live in an age in which personal choices have political implications (or so many believe). Nothing is so intimate anymore that it cannot be discussed on TV talk shows. Nothing is "nobody else's business" these days, and everyone is supposed to "share" their feelings—whether they wish to do so or not. The parents of a bottlefed baby will all too quickly discover that a great many others will take an interest in the feeding decision they have made in the privacy of their bedroom in the wee hours of the morning.

So the mother goes out with her baby one fine morning, the baby gets hungry, and the mother stops at a park bench and takes out a bottle for her newborn. Along comes an old friend who says, "Oh, I thought you were nursing." The mother explains her reasons for switching to bottles, only to see her friend shake her head in disapproval. "You gave up too fast," the friend comments. "You could have gone to La Leche League meetings. You could have learned the right way to do it."

After that encounter the mother proceeds to the grocery store to buy formula. A woman behind her in line comments on her purchase. "Don't you know breastmilk is much better for your baby?"

Later that afternoon the mother takes her baby to the pediatrician. "The baby's gaining weight nicely," the doctor reports, "but he'll be troubled by more colds, ear infections, and so on, than if he'd been breastfed."

On it goes. In the playgroup the new mother has joined, all the other mothers are nursing, and they make a point to tell her it's a shame she's depriving her baby of the comforts of the breast. And when her maternity leave is up, and she's back at her old job, the other women with children proudly tell her how much time and energy they used to put into pumping breastmilk for their babies, so they could have all the health benefits and extra cuddling that comes with breastfeeding. Though they may have complained about the difficulties of combining nursing with a full-time job, their underlying message comes through clearly: A mother who is truly unselfish and loving will accept the difficulties and put her children's best interests ahead of her career.

To top it all off, when she comes home at night and relaxes with a magazine or turns on the TV, she keeps seeing reports on how wonderful, how beneficial, how perfect breastmilk is for her baby, and what potential new dangers of formula are being investigated. Just as she's getting ready to crawl into bed at night, as she mixes one more bottle for her baby (who, by the way, is thriving and happy), she reads the back of the formula can: "Breastmilk is best . . . ."

After all this, how does she feel? GUILTY, GUILTY, GUILTY!

Speaking from Experience

I am a bottlefeeding mother, and I got fed up with all the comments, dirty looks, and unsolicited advice. Shortly after I began bottlefeeding my second child* I began to wonder if other new mothers feeding their babies with bottles were experiencing similar pressures and guilt-tripping over their decision. I also looked for answers to questions and problems I had with bottlefeeding. (For example, will my bottlefed child really suffer more from colds, flus, and infections? Will she be more prone than a breastfed child to asthma, eczema, obesity, behavior problems, and a host of other ills?) After a thorough search of my local library and bookstore, I could not find a single guide written specifically for the bottlefeeding parent. I found no shortage of books that dealt with the common problems of breastfeeding (over forty listed in *Books in Print*), but every one of them was meant to help the mother overcome each nursing problem as it happened; not a one was written for the mother who had already concluded that the better course of action for her and her baby would be to stop trying to force her aching breasts into her screaming baby's mouth.

I did find some general childcare books (such as Dr. Spock's *Baby and Child Care* and *Your Baby and Child* by Penelope Leach) that gave advice on cleaning bottles, preparing formula, and feeding it to the baby, but these books still implied, bottlefeeding is for mothers who haven't

---

*I breastfed my first child. Later on in this Introduction I will explain how it came to pass that I did not breastfeed the second time around.

made the same kind of commitment to their baby's welfare that breastfeeding mothers have. No one had written the book that I wished I had had on hand to help me with bottlefeeding my baby.

As a writer, I decided to take on the challenge. But first I wanted to assure myself that enough new parents felt the need for such a book. I began to ask around. Nearly all of my close friends had breastfed their babies for at least nine months, so I had a pretty small base to start from—mainly friends of mine who were parents by adoption, who had not had the option to breastfeed. Opinion was mixed among this group: Most said a book about bottlefeeding was a terrific idea, though a substantial minority said, in effect, "Bottlefeeding is so quick and easy, it doesn't require a guidebook." These parents (fortunately for them) did not feel as troubled as I was by the constant societal message that formula is second-best. They had sufficient confidence in the evidence supplied by their own eyes, ears, and touch, that their babies were not being deprived in any significant way.

I applaud their self-assurance. But I was more inspired than ever to do this book, so that those of us who have suffered guilt, and questioned our own commitment and feeding practices, could gain that same confidence and peace of mind. There should at least be one source in the lay literature that a bottlefeeding parent can cite to contradict that "friend" who keeps telling you, "Your baby would be so much better off on breastmilk instead of formula."

Having exhausted my circle of friends who bottlefed, I next turned to the media to contact a larger pool of bottlefeeding parents. I put the following notice in a bimonthly Washington, D.C.-area newspaper called *Washington Parent*:

> ## Author's Query
>
> I am writing a book about the infant feeding decision—bottle or breast—to be published by Prima Publishing in 1995. I would like to interview mothers who chose to bottlefeed their newborns, or who switched from breast to bottle within 3 months. I am especially interested in hearing from mothers who bottlefed one child but breastfed another, and mothers who received unsolicited advice, comments, or pressure about their decision not to breastfeed. Complete confidentiality assured.

I especially wanted to hear from parents like myself with both breastfeeding and bottlefeeding experience, because this group would best be able to evaluate and compare the two methods. Only this group, I concluded, had any business telling a new mother the pluses and minuses of each style of feeding.

The day the paper hit the street, the calls began pouring in. If I'd had any doubts about the need or interest of parents in a book on this subject, those doubts were gone by the third call. Nearly every caller began with words like these: "Oh, how I've wanted to talk about this to someone!" Or: "I've felt *so guilty!* I just wish I'd had a support group, or a book, or *someone* to tell me that what I was doing was okay." Or this: "When I'm out with my baby and the bottle, some people treat me as if I'm guilty of child abuse!"[1]

I'd clearly touched a raw nerve in a great many parents.

Speaking from the Experience of Others

Bottlefeeding Without Guilt presents the experiences of many parents, the good, the bad, the funny, and the more creative ways bottlefeeding parents have dealt with criticism and other bottlefeeding dilemmas. In addition to the phone interviews I conducted with sixty-four women who responded to my newspaper notice, I also became a frequent listener on the electronic information networks. My husband Bill, resident computer genius and on-line aficionado, kept me plugged into all conversations about breast versus bottle on four different computer networks: the Internet, Prodigy, Compuserve, and America On Line. Sometimes we started a "thread"—that is, we introduced a new discussion subtopic under a given subject heading—asking for comments from mothers who did not breastfeed. Other times we just listened in as the pro-breastfeeding militants heaped guilt (usually while denying that this was their intent) on "mothers who were not educated to the true benefits of this miracle fluid breastmilk" or "mothers who did not understand how truly harmful formula was" (although these anti-formula message-writers seldom produced any compelling research data to back up their assertions, beyond the opening line: "Studies show. . .") In the three-month period from October 1 to December 31, 1994, I collected well over 500 messages posted on-line by both parents and medical experts discussing the pros and cons, hows, whys, and why-nots of both bottlefeeding and breastfeeding.

I was more than a little surprised to note that the biggest battle zone between opposing camps on the electronic bulletin boards was not between advocates of the bottle versus advocates of the breast; indeed, these two groups had so little in common that there was seldom any direct give-and-take between them. The fairly constant attack-and-rebut pattern I followed was between zealots of breastfeeding who believe that *any* formula at all represents a threat to the baby's health, and more moderate advocates of breastfeeding who can tolerate the use of formula as an acceptable (if second-class) choice. That the lines should be so sharply drawn represents the present atmosphere of disapproval into which the non-nursing mother brings her baby and her bottles. A calm, supportive voice of defense is clearly called for—or so many of my interviewees have told me.

How I Became a Bottlefeeding Mother

I never thought I'd end up writing a book on bottlefeeding, because, in all honesty, I never dreamed I'd be bottlefeeding a child of mine. I want to admit up front that prior to the circumstances that led me to the bottle, I was one of those breastfeeding snobs. While I never publicly criticized another woman for using bottles, I certainly felt smug about the fact that I didn't need to.

When my first daughter was born, I had a hard time from the start getting her to nurse successfully. The first ten days I recall as a hellish blur of crying, worrying, hunger (for her), and pain (for me, from cracked and sore nipples, engorgement, breasts grossly swollen from a 34D to a 38H cup) and much frustration for both of us. But I had so deeply ingrained in me the dogma that bottlefeeding was BAD—a sign of laziness and lack of commitment on the mother's part, and a cause of lifelong health problems for the baby—that I just would not give up. I faithfully attended La Leche League meetings, was on the phone with the lactation consultant in my pediatrician's office about twice a day, made two office visits for breastfeeding instruction, and just kept at it until, by the tenth day, my baby and I finally got the hang of this nursing business.

From then on I was my baby's sole source of nutrition, until she was about five months old and began to eat solid food. I remained her source of liquid nutrition until she was seven months old. Looking back on my time as a nursing mother, I must report often feeling overcome by this nursing bliss that breastfeeding mothers sometimes gloat about. There was joy in the experience, unmatched by anything else in my life as a parent so far. But it certainly wasn't all the Garden of Eden for me. During the baby's growth spurts at about six-week intervals, my daughter would demand marathon nursings, for over an hour at a time, with barely an hour's interval between feedings—hardly time enough for me to take a shower or grab a bite to eat. I was often left exhausted, feeling like nothing so much as an overworked dairy farm.

While breastfeeding is often touted by its advocates as being both convenient and cheap, for me neither was true. My baby seemed able to settle down and suck comfortably only when fed in the same position in the same chair in the same room of my house. If I hoped to have a successful feeding, that meant I could not take my baby anywhere during her mealtimes. Many nursing mothers might be able to "whip it out" anywhere, on the road, in restaurants, in shopping malls, or at the playground, but they didn't have my squirmy, fussy, colicky baby.

Breastfeeding Isn't Free

I had never considered the expense of nursing. To overcome my initial difficulties with latching-on (that is, getting the baby correctly positioned on my breast), I needed several sessions with a lactation consultant. Fortunately, that cost was covered by my health insurance, but I learned during many interviews with new mothers that the lactation consultant's fee is more commonly an unreimbursed item. Then there was the cost of a rented electric breast-pump. I discovered that the surest way to tempt my new baby to nurse was to start each feeding session by pumping my breasts until I had a strong, steady stream of milk coming out before I put her to the breast. That way the baby did not have to endure that frustrated, empty sucking period while waiting for the milk to "let down" (the term for the start of the mother's milk flow).

Clothing was another unanticipated cost. Each nursing bra that I special-ordered from the *Motherwear Catalog* (since you don't find 38H bras just sitting around in your average maternity store!) cost $41.75, when you added shipping and handling. I also ruined quite a few blouses, tops, and jumpers through milk leaking, spraying, or dripping on my clothing during the first few weeks of nursing. My bed linens came through my nursing days permanently discolored from too-frequent washings, as every morning for the first eight weeks of lactation I awoke to find twin puddles of milk in the bed. The mattress pad took on a curdled milk smell and became unsalvageable.

There was also the additional expense of my own food while I was producing food for my baby, as well as the high price of prescription vitamin and calcium supplements—significantly more expensive than the over-the-counter variety.

I'm sure if I added it all up, nursing would still be cheaper than the cost of a year's supply of formula. I mention these outlays made for nursing's sake only to point out the misapprehension that many women are under that breastmilk is totally free.

Breastfeeding Isn't a Guarantee of Health

I quickly came to see that breastmilk had its own costs, but it took me far longer to question the almost universally held notion that breastmilk protects our children forever from allergies, asthma, colds, ear infections, and a host of other ailments. Although my breastfed daughter exhibited signs of eczema just two weeks after her birth, I assumed that her allergic condition would have been far worse if she'd been bottlefed. Four years later during a consultation with her allergist I was amazed to learn that not only did breastfeeding *not* confer on her any protection from allergies, but her sensitivity to certain foods may have been exacerbated by the presence of those foods in my diet, and therefore in the breastmilk she consumed.

Having seen her suffer through numerous colds and ear infections, I would caution any new nursing mother against overconfidence regarding her breastfed baby's ability to fight off contagion through assimilation of the mother's immunities via breastmilk. Put a new baby, even a breastfed one, in a room with an infected person and that baby is likely to get sick. Keep all cold-bearing visitors away, and your baby, bottlefed or breastfed, will more likely stay healthy.

When Bottlefeeding Is Best

Though my personal experience had done much to deflate the most overblown claims of breastfeeding's benefits, when pregnant with my second child I was still enough of a believer in its advantages to be determined to breastfeed again, for at least nine months. (I stopped breastfeeding my first child at seven months because of my desire to have a second child before I turned forty; I was approaching thirty-nine and did not resume my menstrual/ovulatory cycle until almost three months after weaning. More about breastfeeding's often-unwanted curtailment of fertility in chapter 1.)

Nothing in the first four days after my second daughter's birth made me question my ability to breastfeed again. My new baby quickly learned to latch on and was growing and daily producing the requisite number of wet diapers to indicate that she was getting enough milk from me. All was well and good.

Until the fifth day. About midday I started to feel strange, weak, light-headed. I thought it was just the exhaustion and difficulty of having a new baby and a two-and-a-half-year-old in the house. By six o'clock that evening, though, I felt on the verge of collapse. I had a searing pain in one breast, a fever of 103°, and a feeling that I might pass out at any second. I was too weak to talk to my doctor on the phone. My husband called my doctor and was told to get me to the emergency room. Upon admission I was diagnosed with a particularly acute case of mastitis, a breast infection, and was put on intravenous antibiotics.

The first question I asked upon my hospital admission was: "Will I still be able to nurse?"

Oh, yes, I was assured. In fact, I should use a breast-pump to keep the infected breast as empty of milk as possible. I was not permitted to keep my newborn overnight with me in the hospital—an odd rule—because, as one nurse put it, "the baby is not the patient, and we can't be responsible for her overnight." So for three days I pumped and stored milk in bottles in the hospital freezer. My husband brought the baby in during the day for me to try to breastfeed her, but after the doctor told me that the source of the infection was most likely bacteria (harmless to her) found in my baby's mouth, I became skittish about putting her back on my nipple. And feeding her on the infected breast was so excruciating I didn't try it more than once. The pain was so intense it made me afraid that the infection would spread to the other breast. It would be prudent, I figured, to feed her breastmilk in bottles—for a few days, at least. Even pumping on that breast sent shock waves through my body, though I managed to do it.

Meanwhile, my husband, who was doing the baby's night feedings on formula (since I had not stockpiled enough breastmilk before I had the mastitis attack), reported that the baby seemed to be taking to the bottle just fine, and didn't seem the least bit fussy or deprived. I felt reassured, but at the same time was determined to go back to nursing when my mastitis was cured.

When I got home I continued on a ten-day course of oral antibiotics. I was surprised that more than a month afterward I still felt shaky and weak. I did return to nursing, but my nipples remained sore, and the act of nursing was never comfortable or happy, for me or my baby. I continued to pump my milk (again paying for a hospital-quality rented pump) and fed it in bottles to the baby, still hoping to get back to actual breastfeeding when my breasts recovered. I tried nursing in short sessions about two or three times each day.

By the time my baby was six weeks old, I was finally beginning to feel better. But by then my daughter was so used to the milk (either expressed milk or formula) coming out of a bottle that she began refusing to stay at the breast for more than a minute at a time. She'd turn her head away and cry until I broke out a bottle. I felt frustrated and rejected. Why, if nursing was so wonderful, and why, if my breastmilk was so much better than that odious-smelling formula, didn't she prefer the real thing? But there was no denying what was happening: Though *I* was finally healthy enough to want to go back to nursing full time, my baby had another plan in mind.

I would have had to battle her over every feeding to get her to stay on the breast. There is no doubt that I could have done so, and also no doubt that to have done so would have meant an extended time of misery for her, for me, and for the rest of my family as well. I started to wonder whether breastfeeding was worth the fight. I started to look skeptically at all the claims for the superiority of breastfeeding over bottlefeeding.

By the time my baby was two months old she was completely on a formula diet. By that time, too, I had had more than my share of well-meaning but pushy people attempting to "educate" me about the wonders of breastfeeding and save my baby from a life sentence of ill health and emotional trauma, which, according to them, would be her fate.

I knew I didn't have to justify my decision to strangers on the street. To satisfy my own need for unbiased information about bottlefeeding, I started researching the experiences of other bottlefeeding parents and their babies. I suspected that there would be a wide variety of circumstances in which bottlefeeding was not merely acceptable but actually *superior* to breastfeeding (as, for example, when the mother must take a medication that taints breastmilk. More on this and other situations calling for bottle preference in chapter 1). I also expected to find the formula-using mothers I interviewed raising well-developed, emotionally secure children (much like my own second daughter), who had no greater incidence of colds, allergy, or asthma than breastfed children.

These, then, are my biases, stated frankly at the outset. (I wish that the authors of all the "breast is always best" literature would similarly inform the reader up front that they began *their* work with a strong preconception of what their research would reveal.) My method of contacting new parents through a newspaper notice admittedly steered me to a group who shared some of my own personal experiences and thus would end up reinforcing many of my ideas about bottlefeeding. However, I was also party to discussions—and sometimes intense debate—among a wide-ranging group of new parents, including medical experts, lactation consultants, and breastfeeding militants, who posted messages back and forth on several different national and international electronic mail (e-mail) forums. I listened respectfully and with an open mind to the anti-bottlefeeding points of view—and was astonished to find that *some* anti-bottlefeeders would respond with a tightly shut mind (and occasional terms of abuse*) to any suggestion that formula just *might*, in some cases, be a wise choice made by an informed and caring mother.

Supporting the Bottlefeeding Choice

I'd like to emphasize (though I know breastfeeding zealots will never believe me) that I am in no way opposed to breastfeeding, nor do I wish to see its practice diminished. My central goal in writing this book is to provide support and positive feedback to those parents who have weighed all the factors in their individual circumstances, who have

---

*In e-mail jargon, this is called "flaming" someone. It wasn't unusual for a pro-bottlefeeding message-writer to begin her posting with the forlorn plea, "I bottlefed my baby—no flames, please!—because . . . "

concluded that for *them*, all things considered, the bottle would work best. *Bottlefeeding Without Guilt* is about the freedom to choose, to make such a personal decision without being stigmatized, analyzed, or judged by strangers, and about the information—and misinformation—out there, influencing what we decide.

I chose breastfeeding for my first child and was on the whole satisfied with that choice. When breastfeeding works, it is indeed a glorious experience, with many benefits to both mother and child. I would never dream of telling a new mother intent on trying to breastfeed that she should consider the bottle. What I would like, ideally, is for those who have chosen breastfeeding to be equally respectful of the rights and feelings of those of us who, for whatever reasons that are personal and private to us, have chosen the bottle. In other words, stop the pressure and guilt-tripping, please!

On a more realistic note: I don't expect true breastfeeding zealots to be moved by the pleas of bottlefeeders. Too many of them see the issue as black and white, right versus wrong, and believe that the public has the right to influence women in their choices. Many see themselves as *morally obliged* to act, to protect our children from the bottle. (For examples of this attitude, see "Voices from the Breastfeeding Cult" in chapter 3.)

Bottlefeeding Without Guilt was written to provide bottlefeeding parents with some much-needed reassurance about the safety and nutritional completeness of formula, and to point out the many *positive* aspects of life as a bottlefeeding parent, which in the current climate of "breast is best" tend to be forgotten or downplayed.

Which Is Right for You?

If you are an expectant mother and you have not yet made your infant feeding decision, chapter 7 contains a quiz designed to help you determine whether your attitudes, physical condition, and work and home environment are more compatible with bottlefeeding or breastfeeding. The quiz is not intended to tell any woman what choice to make; it's meant to be a fun and interesting way to elicit your feelings and examine your reactions to certain aspects of infant care. If the numerical score at the end should conflict with what you end up deciding is the medically, personally, or morally correct choice, then by all means, throw the results out and do what you want to do!

You might find it revealing to take the quiz twice. First, before you read this book. Then, once you read about other women's breastfeeding and bottlefeeding experiences, take the quiz again, to see if your attitudes have changed. You might take the quiz while you are pregnant and again a week after the baby is born, to see whether the reality of having a baby to feed at all hours has affected your opinion.

A Brief History of Bottlefeeding

Throughout history there have been mothers who did not breastfeed their babies but prior to our modern age these mothers had to turn to other women to provide milk for their children. Generally speaking, in our Western world, only the richest women in any society could afford to have a servant act as a wet-nurse to a baby. Since nursing requires the infant-feeder to be available to the new baby for twenty minutes to an hour at a time, every two to three hours throughout the day and night, the wet-nurse would usually be wholly at the disposal of the baby's parents, often serving as a slave, serf, or chattel. Though in some cases she might be treated as a member of the family, just as often she could end up regarded as a feeding-thing, given little or no respect. Her own babies would be weaned early, left malnourished, or even abandoned.[2] Mothers of stillborn children would sometimes be recruited to wet-nurse the master's child, only to be shunted aside as soon as the child was weaned. Such a relationship was bound to be exploitative. Wet-nursing has all but died out in America, as the ideology that permits the exploitation of workers has given way to widespread belief in (or at least lip service to) the ideals of equality, justice, and workers' rights—battles largely waged and won in the mid-nineteenth to early twentieth centuries.

Women fortunate enough to survive childbirth and to be able to afford a wet-nurse could still have chosen to breastfeed, all or part of the time, and those who did so were generally credited with being exceptionally devoted mothers. Yet there seems to have been little disdain for upper-class woman who relied upon the services of the wet-nurse. If the mother was the mistress of a large household or estate, she was burdened with many obligations, social responsibilities, and demands on her time, and infant feeding was regarded as something that virtually any healthy peasant woman could readily provide. There was never anything sacred about the mother's own milk.[3]

Nor was breastfeeding generally regarded as being some wonderful, bond-enhancing experience for the mother.[4] In the days before such a thing as breastfeeding advocacy groups existed to point out the wonders of the breast, it is safe to say that for most women who nursed, breastfeeding was seen mainly as a chore, just another of the endless round of childrearing duties that was a woman's lot in life, her biological destiny. Any lifting of any part of the burden was a welcome thing in most women's lives—though few were privileged enough to find such relief. For the vast majority of women, life with a new baby meant having an infant at the breast almost constantly after the birth, until the child was old enough to feed itself table food and drink from a cup, at which point the mother would likely be pregnant again. A woman's fertile years could be entirely taken up with pregnancy, childbirth, and nursing. Only menopause brought relief.

Of course, during those past eras when nearly all but the richest women were destined to spend years of their lives nursing, help with breastfeeding problems was all around. Women then, just as now, were prone to nipple pain, mastitis, exhaustion after childbirth, inverted nipples, as well as myriad other difficulties that could make successful lactation difficult or impossible. But women tended to live with other women who had nursed and who could advise, encourage, and instruct. Back when it was commonplace for a household to include grandmothers, sisters, aunts, cousins, or other female relatives, reliable nursing advice was never far away. If the new mother was worn out, or needed time or help to build up her milk supply, there might well be a lactating sister, friend, or cousin to help out.

However, I do not wish to paint too rosy a picture of the past. Some breastfeeding literature treated certain nursing difficulties as a disease of our modern life, and suggested that the past was this ideal time of shared knowledge among women, and that with gentle and patient help from family members, women almost universally would be able to breastfeed with ease. But such a portrait distorts the historical record. What is often forgotten is how shockingly high infant mortality rates were in this not-so-rosy past.[5] Babies were extremely vulnerable in their first two years of life, and died from any number of untreatable diseases—high among them, a general wasting away, not specified to any cause. Novels and journals of the Victorian age and earlier are full of descriptions of babies being "sickly," not expected to live very long. There was a grim acceptance of the ephemeral, unpredictable nature of an infant's life. Women were routinely cautioned by male doctors or preachers not to become overly attached to their babies in early infancy, and not to grieve too long or too deeply should the baby die, for to do so would seem to challenge the mysterious workings of God.[6]

The woman who lost an infant might well become pregnant the following month, or might have eight or nine other children still alive; the end of one infant's life might not be the tragedy calling for the sort of medical investigation that is usually undertaken today. Even when doctors were able to determine the proximate cause of an infant's death, no public health authority collected statistics on causes of infant mortality for us to examine today. We cannot therefore assert with any accuracy what the relationship was between high infant death rates and the absence of a safe alternative to breastfeeding.

However, based on what is known about lactation today, we can make educated guesses about how certain breastfeeding difficulties may have affected infants in the days before formula existed. Take the commonly reported problem of inadequate milk production, which affects about five percent of new mothers.[7] These days, with the help of lactation consultants, a woman may be able to take steps to bring her milk supply to a sufficient level through use of specially designed nursing aids, such as the Supplemental Nursing System (described in more detail in chapter 1), or through use of an electric breastpump to stimulate the milk-producing ducts in her breasts. Until the mother's milk supply reaches the necessary level, the modern baby's diet can be supplemented with formula.

But imagine a time without a safe supply of formula, breastpumps, or widespread awareness of the medical warning signs that the baby is not receiving adequate fluids. When the breasts are not producing enough milk in response to normal sucking, the baby may spend hours latched on but receive little nourishment, and the mother might not even know that anything was seriously wrong. As weeks went by her baby might grow, but not at a normal pace. It would remain small and underdeveloped and prone to infection, until it eventually succumbed, most likely to some common germ that would have caused only a mild illness in a well-nourished child.

Within a few months it might appear to the parents that such a baby was unlikely to survive, and they would not invest much emotional interest in its future. Its death would be accepted as one of those things that happens in nature, like the runt of the litter not surviving among live-stock. If low milk supply affects five percent of women in present-day America—women who are well-nourished and have access to quality medical care—consider how much more common this must have been at a time when, for poor women (that is to say, the great majority of women), some degree of malnourishment was the norm.

The Era of the Bottle Arrives

Because of lack of data, we will never know how many babies may have died, or may have survived with lifelong health problems because of their mothers' breastfeeding difficulties; however, one fact in the history of breast and bottle is indisputable: Once a safe method of formula feeding became widely available in America, it was only a matter of a few decades, from the 1920s to the 1940s, before the practice of bottlefeeding became the majority choice in this country.

Through my research, I have identified five significant social and technological changes that contributed to the feasibility and popularity of the bottle over the breast:

1. Mass production of affordable refrigerators and their near universal use in homes, so that bottles of formula could be safely stored for later use.

2. The coming of the Second World War and the need for even mothers of young children to work outside the home, leaving their babies to be fed by others.

3. The urbanization of the nation, which meant that most women lived near enough to stores to make shopping for the components of infant formula convenient.

4. Greater education among women about hygiene so mothers could have confidence that they were correctly preparing and feeding a safe product to their babies.

5. Increased economic strength, so that even a young couple could afford their own house or apartment, and would no longer be expected to share the same house with grandmothers, aunts, or other female relatives who in earlier times served as a round-the-clock source of breastfeeding counsel and support.

What's remarkable about the shift from majority breastfed babies to majority bottlefed babies is that once all five of these factors were in place, breastfeeding was virtually abandoned by the middle class and came to be regarded as something practiced only by the very poor or those isolated on farms far from modern supermarkets. By 1956, the year that La Leche League was founded, only eighteen percent of American newborns were being breastfed. Several weeks after childbirth, the figure dropped to under ten percent.

Why, if breastfeeding is all the wonderful things its advocates claim it to be, was the practice so widely abandoned by new mothers? Breastfeeding proponents usually lay the blame unequivocally on corporate greed: The formula companies had discovered a lucrative target market and shamelessly exploited it, to the great detriment of both babies' and mothers' lives.[8] Doctors and hospitals, swayed by bonuses and gifts for participating in formula makers' plans, seduced unwitting postpartum women into accepting the bottle and not giving the breast a try. Everywhere Americans were swept up by the '40s and '50s fad for innovation, rocketry, scientific advances—and formula was pitched as "scientific" and "quantifiable." What was natural was "old-fashioned"; what was new and machine-made had to be better.

Advertising is also blamed for the switch. In the 1950s, the "art of persuasion" was at a fever pitch. TV was a powerful new medium that sent into almost every home commercials with their pretty, well-dressed housewives and their plump, pink-cheeked (never non-white!) babies and their bottles. Only a small percentage of mothers of infants worked outside the home, yet the modern woman, as her life was depicted on TV, had a busy, intensely scheduled day. She needed to be freed from the constraints of nursing so that she could keep a spotless house (no waxy yellow build-up on the bottlefeeding mother's floors!), pick up her breadwinner husband at the commuter train station each evening, chauffeur her older children to school and after-school activities, and volunteer at worthwhile causes such as the PTA.

Prudery of society is blamed as well. Exposing the female breast in public has never been acceptable among polite society in any of the Western cultures. In past ages when women nursed (except for the very poor, who were thought to have no shame) they confined themselves to their homes. Women's lives were thus severely circumscribed during their childbearing years. Though they worked hard throughout their lives at an endless round of chores, including childcare, they seldom traveled beyond the bounds of their own household or farm—especially when pregnant or nursing. This was reflected in the use of the term "confinement" to describe the time just before a woman gave birth until the time the baby was old enough to be taken out of the house. "Respectable" women did not nurse in public in earlier ages, because, as the nearly universally held proverb had it, "A woman's place was in the home."

With the advent of the bottlefeeding age, women were finally freed to go out into society with their babies. This represented a big step forward for women's freedom of movement—though they were, of course, still far from liberated, as there was no recognition of the right of a woman who still chose to breastfeed to take out her breast and do so in the presence of men. All over the country (to this day in many places), the simple act of nursing would leave a woman open to a charge of indecent exposure.

It is perhaps not so surprising given the near-universality of these attitudes in the late '40s and early '50s that bottle-feeding should have been so eagerly embraced. It would not take a conspiracy of corporate villains to see why a young woman with a new baby, alone in her new suburban subdivision house, far from her mother or grandmother, with enough disposable income to be able to buy formula, and living in a town in which to breastfeed in public is to invite arrest for indecent exposure, would with little hesitation choose the bottle over the breast.

Breastfeeders Organize

Breastfeeding advocates feel that women were deprived of information about the benefits of breastfeeding and often misled—perhaps deliberately—by male doctors as to the supposed health benefits of measurable, clean formula (implying that if only those '40s and '50s mothers had been properly educated, they would never have opted for the bottle). And that may indeed be the case. Since the late 1970s, breastfeeding support groups and advocates in the medical profession have worked so effectively to circulate information about the benefits of breastfeeding that the balance has shifted back to breastmilk for the majority (54 percent) of American newborns. Among educated women the percentage of those who breastfeed in the first weeks of the baby's life is now between 75 and 90 percent.[9]

How did this remarkable turnaround occur? Much credit belongs to the seven determined, energetic, and endlessly resourceful women who were the founders of the first organized breastfeeding support network, La Leche League (now officially, La Leche League International). These tireless advocates, Mary Ann Cahill, Edwina Froehlich, Mary Ann Kerwin, Viola Lennon, Marian Tompson, Betty Wagner, and Mary White, deserve mention by name for the inspiring job they have done of making women aware of the advantages of this feeding choice, in the 1950s when choices for women were especially limited, and when organizing and aggressive pursuit of a goal were often frowned upon as "unfeminine." La Leche League did more than any single entity to bring breastfeeding back into public approval as a right and fitting thing for a new mother to choose—if she wants to. (There is a substantial element within La Leche League that is disapproving of any choice *but* breastfeeding, and this militant minority and their impact is the subject of further discussion in chapter 3.)

A second, more amorphous influence leading to the resumption of widespread breastfeeding by American women was the revitalization of feminism in the mid- to late-1970s. The women's movement and its attendant "consciousness-raising groups" led many new mothers to a reexamination of the roles women play in our society. There was a growing clamor against barriers and restrictions on women's choices in all areas. Women must be free to make full use of their talents—whether to compete with men in the workplace and prove themselves through material success, or stay at home and raise children, or attempt to manage both family and career at the same time. Those who take on the challenge of working full time while having children should not be told how those children should be fed. A woman *can* work and breastfeed at the same time: This idea—shockingly radical when first introduced—has gradually won widespread acceptance.

The convenience of the portable and effective electric breastpump was the key. The pump has freed lactating working women much as the bottle had freed busy housewives of the generation before. Women's breasts were recognized as functional body parts, and it was a woman's right to use her breasts for this intended purpose, wherever she chose to, on the job or at home. Battle cries went up for breastfeeding rights, the right to feed a baby by breast and not be regarded as committing a sexual indecency, the right to have employers recognize their needs, to give them time and a place to feed the baby or express milk, to have on-site childcare available. These battles are ongoing, and feminist leaders (even those with no children or those who have personally chosen the bottle) will agree that there is still much work to be done to advance the acceptance of breastfeeding by women in all walks of life.

For the most part, breastfeeding advocates have won their battle for public acceptance. It is now nearly universally acknowledged among the medical community that breastmilk is the optimum choice of nutrition for a normally healthy baby of a normally healthy mother. Six states now have legislation protecting a woman's right to breastfeed in public[10] and many more states have bills pending. Some major corporations and government employers, such as Amoco Oil, the National Security Agency, and the Los Angeles Department of Water and Power, have adopted nursing-friendly personnel policies, to provide accommodation for mothers of breastfed babies to pump and store their milk, or make nursing visits to on-site daycare centers.

Breastfeeding advocates have won even more impressive victories on the international front. In 1981 the World Health Organization adopted a comprehensive code calling for the medical profession to give thoroughgoing preference and support for breastfeeding over formula, and calling for a ban on many marketing strategies for formula, such as hospital giveaways and most forms of advertising. Breastfeeding activists, led by the worldwide organization Infant Feeding Action Coalition (INFACT) waged a seven-year campaign against international foodstuffs manufacturer Nestle Corporation, the world's largest supplier of infant formula, that ended when Nestle agreed to abide by a stringent set of rules for marketing and distributing formula in Third World countries (more on both the WHO Code and the Nestle boycott in chapter 2).

These victories are all impressive, but anti-breastfeeding prejudice has not been entirely eradicated. Every year one can find a few outrages in the news: the story of the still-nursing three-year-old taken away from her mother for over a year because a family court judge finds the practice of breastfeeding beyond infancy to be a form of child sexual abuse; the nursing women at a public swimming pool in New Jersey who were told to leave; the firefighter who was allowed to bring her baby to work but was fired when she discreetly nursed her baby at her desk. There is still some work to be done in ensuring fair treatment of nursing mothers.

A Plea for Peace

Bottlefeeding women are generally pleased when breastfeeding advocates win their cases.[11] What is cause for discontent among bottlefeeders is the fact that with each victory there is a tendency among a certain segment of the breastfeeding movement toward smugness—the sense that breastfeeding must be gaining approval because it is the *only* right and acceptable way for a mother to feed her baby. It is wrong for the freedom of one group to turn into the stigmatization of another.

Is that really happening, or have I spent too long listening to the overheated sensibilities of bottlefeeding mothers with an inferiority complex?

Look over the sampling of quotes that follow and judge for yourself, based on what any number of bottlefeeding mothers have encountered themselves.

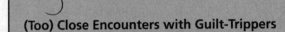

(Too) Close Encounters with Guilt-Trippers

[As a bottlefeeding mother] I experienced unbelievable prejudice and discrimination. One woman in my mothers' group told me I was ignorant. I cried . . . I was very emotional about it. The leader of my mothers' group said breastfeeding was an experience every woman really ought to have. Another woman said, if you can't breastfeed, you must be doing something wrong. They treated me and the other bottlefeeding mother [in the mothers' group] like a failure. She dropped out. . . . Twice in the grocery store strangers asked me if I was breastfeeding. Why do they ask, unless they are passing judgment on you? I'm not impervious to the media pressure for breastfeeding that's all around. . . . I still feel guilty. I wish there was a support group for bottlefeeding mothers!

—Kristin

Sharon from England posted this message on a parenting forum:

So many people made me feel like a criminal be-cause I wasn't breastfeeding. I would have, if Mother Nature had given me better equipment [this mother had inverted nipples, and though she followed the advice of three different lactation consultants, she was unable to solve the problem], but now I've heard that mothers with good nipples have just as many prob-lems—mastitis, bleeding nipples, etc. No thank you. If I ever decide to have another child, I will formula feed from the day she/he is born.

—Signed, Just-another-mom-who's-sick-of-being-labeled-a-bad-mom-because-she-didn't breastfeed

Some members of my husband's family are openly critical. If the baby gets a cold, they say it's because he's bottlefed.

—Penny

I felt very badly about it [bottlefeeding]. Friends criticized me. My closest friend said [about the trouble she was having producing enough milk], "That's ridiculous. Everybody's milk comes in." Everyone asks me, "Why aren't you nursing?"

—Judith

I experienced lots of pressure with my first child. I got lots of "Don't you know it [bottlefeeding] causes ear infections?". . . And then there were the put-downs of children who weren't breastfed. They didn't smell as nice, they didn't act as nice, and they weren't as smart. My daughter is a delightful, cheerful, healthy three-and-a-half-year-old who has been speaking in compound sentences since she was two . . . but the LLL [La Leche League] women kept telling me how much *smarter*, and *healthier* she would have been if I had been able to nurse her!

—Eva

I'm having a hard time finding a group of mothers I can feel comfortable with. When I'm around nursing moms, they treat me like I don't care as much about my baby. My friend had a similar story: She was approached in a mall with her baby and her bottles and her shopping bags, by a woman who said, "You're buying nice clothes for your baby but you don't care enough about her to breastfeed!"

—Cathy

"We All Turned Out Well"

We are not all intimidated by the "lactation police," those most outspoken members of the breastfeeding movement who relentlessly crusade against the bottle. Twelve of the letters or e-mail messages that I received expressed no guilt whatsoever. I put these comments in a file labeled "Pro Bottle and Proud." Here's a typical comment from Barbara, one of those hardy twelve: "I'm that odd person out—I rebelled. That everyone was doing it [breastfeeding] was reason for me not to. My mom had four bottlefed kids and we all turned out well. If it would have made a critical health difference to my kids, I would have breastfed, but I did a careful cost-benefit analysis [of all the pluses and minuses involved in her particular situation] and concluded that for me, the positives outweighed the negatives."

But the strongest expression of bottlefeeding support came from Jane who, cheering me on to do this book, wrote:

"Bottlefeeders of the world, unite! There is safety and support in numbers! We have been silent and isolated too long."

A Note on Names

The selections of quotes that appear clustered throughout the text are those of real mothers, and in some cases, fathers. All those I interviewed are identified by pseudonyms to preserve their anonymity, because to many of my respondents the decision to bottlefeed was a highly intimate, even agonizingly personal decision. When I cite a message posted publicly on an electronic forum I have also changed the name of the message-poster, to be evenhanded in the treatment of all my sources. Only those writers, medical experts, or other professional opinion-givers who specifically requested to have their words credited to them are identified by name in this book.

CHAPTER 1

Why the Bottle?

Breastfeeding guides like to take a reassuring tone: Every mother can breastfeed. La Leche League's *The Womanly Art of Breastfeeding* tells you in the first chapter: "Given the right support, mothers and babies have untold levels of strength and adaptability. Mothers throughout the ages have happily breastfed their babies, and you can do it, too."[1]

"Any woman can nurse her baby"—that promise appears on the flyleaf of the handbook *Nursing Your Baby* by Karen Pryor and Gale Pryor.[2]

Reality quickly sets in when you leave the how-to books aside and begin talking to real mothers of real newborns. Here is a sampling of stories from women who tried and tried but just could *not* get breastfeeding to work.

"I Tried and Tried . . ."

Mothers Talk About Trying to Make Breast-feeding Work

I went through hell trying to breastfeed. I had lots of support, my son latched on fine as far as anyone could tell, but he simply didn't gain weight on my milk alone. I never was able to bring my milk supply up, but I did manage to continue, with supplements [of formula] for about five months. . . . The myth that every woman can breastfeed, if only she wants to enough or has enough support or whatever, is just that, a myth.

—Nancy

I was one of those nutso dedicated moms who tried every single thing to get my daughter to nurse. I used the SNS supplementer, I used eyedroppers, I used spoons. I pumped for months and months. She just wasn't able to nurse successfully. Because she was a twin and her brother was a champion nurser (he doubled his birthweight in four weeks), I knew what I was doing was right. I used two certified lactation consultants, one from the Nursing Mothers' Council, the other from my pediatrician's office. . . . When I gave up, and gave Virginia a combination of pumped breastmilk and formula, she started gaining weight and was much happier. . . . Every time I read one of these guilt-trip inducing messages that cite unreliable statistics about how every woman can nurse, but they just don't try hard enough, I want to scream. Most women on this [e-mail] forum do want to nurse. They are dedicated and devoted parents. Telling them they are failures without knowing the specifics about their situations is irresponsible and unkind.

—Margaret, responding to an on-line message
writer's assertion that 98 percent of all women can
nurse successfully

I tried to nurse all six of my children. I had the first at nineteen. I just didn't know how, and I had no help from anyone. I had my second when I was much better prepared, at twenty-six. I tried for three weeks, despite having contracted thrush. I was in pain, and the baby was in pain. I stopped because I could see it hurt her mouth to nurse. With my third, it was a case of mutual exhaustion. She was nursing round the clock, but apparently not getting much milk, and neither of us was getting any sleep. With my fourth, it was a repeat of the same pattern as with my third. With my fifth, I had a postpartum infection. I was kept in the hospital, and the baby wasn't allowed to stay with me. With my new baby [this mother had given birth just six weeks before the interview] I had painful, cracked nipples, and each nursing session was excruciating. With all but the first, I had lactation consultants each time, but their advice always came too late, or wasn't good enough. Their suggestions to ease the pain didn't work. But all five of my older ones did great on the bottle, and my new one seems to be doing fine, too.

—*Laura*

Your notice [in *Washington Parent* magazine seeking out bottlefeeding moms] really hit a nerve with me. I had such a time trying to breastfeed. I'd really been looking forward to nursing. I didn't anticipate any problems. . . . From the start my baby nursed every hour and a half, all day, all night, never sleeping more than ten minutes at a time. Every night, nursing was a living nightmare. She gained so little weight, and she was miserable at the breast. I thought, "Why isn't this working?" The pediatrician said I had to supplement with formula. When I gave her a bottle, she was satisfied. She drank the whole four-ounce bottle and went right to sleep. But I kept trying to breastfeed. I read books . . . All the books talked about solving problems, but I wasn't having a problem *getting* her to nurse. Finally, after two months I said, this is ridiculous. She

> can't be happy if I keep trying to make her breastfeed.
> Still, I felt such guilt when I put the bottle in her
> mouth. But then you see that baby smile . . . you know
> it's gonna be okay.
>
> —*Tina*

Breastfeeding: Everyone *Can't* Do It

The breastfeeding literature acknowledges—indeed, is even
largely focused on—the difficulties that may arise early on:
problems of latch-on; stimulation of sufficient milk supply;
engorgement; painfully cracked or bleeding nipples; inverted or flat nipples; babies with poorly developed sucking reflexes; cleft lip or cleft palate syndrome; premature or
sick babies who must remain in intensive care; mastitis;
thrush; plugged milk ducts; mothers' exhaustion from babies who demand marathon nursing sessions—to name
only a few that appear frequently in the most popular
breastfeeding self-help books.

I reviewed over twenty guides and found that *all* of them
stress that a properly educated and sufficiently committed
breastfeeder can overcome these and any other problems,
given proper guidance, patience, and perseverance. Some
of the books blithely tell the new mother not to worry
whether her newborn is getting enough nutrition in the
early days of life, because "There's no danger that the baby
will starve in the meantime, since newborns have little need
for nourishment during the first few days of life."[3] *The
Womanly Art of Breastfeeding* reassuringly puts it: "If you
feed your baby in the way that is naturally intended for the
human infant, his weight gain will be what is natural for
your particular child." The advice is echoed in *Breastfeeding Your Baby*, put out by The Nursing Mothers' Council
of the Boston Association for Childbirth Education: "Some

breastfed babies gain slowly no matter how long they nurse."[4] If a mother will just follow what La Leche League calls the "golden rule of breastfeeding" ("The more the baby nurses, the more milk there will be"), she can be assured that she will end up with "an abundant milk supply and a contented baby."[5]

None of the materials named above includes a list of the warning signs of dehydration that can occur within a few days of birth if the baby is not taking in sufficient fluid. Both the La Leche League book and the Boston Nursing Mothers' Council's guide make mention of the number of wet diapers that a well-nourished baby will produce (that is, five to six really soaked ones per day), but neither book details any of the other indications that the baby's health may be in jeopardy (such as depression of the soft spots on the baby's head, or weak or listless crying). Nor do these books contain any hint of the possibly life-threatening consequences if the evidence of necessary fluid intake is *not* present—and they don't alert the mother to the need for *immediate* assessment by a pediatrician if dehydration is suspected.

The consequences for such ignorance can be truly tragic. In a front page article in the *Wall Street Journal* on July 22, 1994, reporter Kevin Helliker told the story of new mother Pam Floyd, who followed the advice of breastfeeding books and experts to keep trying to nurse her newborn, despite initial difficulties. By the end of his first week of life her son Chaz had taken in so little liquid that he suffered irreversible brain damage. The newspaper article went on to document other instances of infants hospitalized because their mothers did not recognize the signs of inadequate milk production, including two cases that resulted in death. Strikingly similar reports also appeared in *Time* magazine on August 22, 1994, in *U.S. News and World Report* on December 5, 1994, and on the television news magazine *Primetime Live*, August 4, 1994.[6] Among the sixty-four mothers I interviewed were two whose babies had to be rushed to emergency rooms due to breastfeeding-related dehydration (see "Julie's Story"). Both of their babies were fortunate to be diagnosed and put on formula in time to prevent any permanent harm.

Julie's Story

A Near Tragedy with a Happy Ending

I tried valiantly in the hospital. I never had any let-down. I was too tired. [Julie had been hospitalized a number of times during her pregnancy for severe vomiting.] My husband and I were both out of a job, and feeling a lot of stress. I had too little support. I was released from the hospital [after her daughter's birth] too early. For three days I had no sleep, but I kept trying [to nurse]. From the birth on Saturday at 5:30 P.M., then overnight, then Sunday and Monday, we didn't see many wet or dirty diapers. I called the lactation consultant, who said, "Give it a week."

By Tuesday I didn't see *any* wet diapers, so I called the lactation consultant back. She said, "Don't worry about it—she's getting more than you think." I told her that when I squeezed my breasts, nothing came out. She said, "Oh, the baby can get it out far better than you can."

On Wednesday the baby became listless, sleeping all day, looking weak. I thought, "She's a newborn, it must be normal". . . but still no wet diapers.

I called the pediatrician. He said, "She needs a bottle. You must get fluid into her right now."

I called the lactation consultant back (she was the director of lactation at the hospital where I gave birth), who got annoyed at the pediatrician for "jumping the gun." The lactation consultant said, "If you will only relax, your milk will come in. Go upstairs, take long baths, massage your breasts, use ice packs, and if that doesn't work, come in tomorrow and we'll lend you a breastpump."

I'm practically going nuts, and she says, *relax*! She told me if I gave even one bottle, it would cause "nipple confusion" and the baby wouldn't breastfeed. She really discouraged me from following the pediatrician's advice. She said, "Don't worry. Nothing will happen overnight."

I tried all the things the lactation consultant said. By then the baby was crying so weakly. I said, I just can't do this [go on trying to breastfeed her]. I can't wait until morning. I felt the situation was critical. I called the pediatrician back.

He said, "You've *got* to give her a bottle. If she's too weak to take a bottle, she'll have to be kept in the hospital."

Well, I tried to rouse her to bottlefeed her, but she was too weak to move. I undressed her and got no reaction. The pediatrician had told me not to bring her to the hospital where she was born, one hour away, but to the nearest emergency room. He was afraid she'd die. His advice saved her life. At the hospital they got her to take a bottle, and she guzzled it down. She drank as if she was starving—and she was!

I called the lactation consultant back, and she said, "All is not lost." She was *displeased* that the baby had been given a bottle! Yet if I'd done what she said, I *know* my baby would have died! Still, a week later, I felt guilty that I'd given up the breast. I tried to go back to it but couldn't. . . . I felt a tremendous sense of relief that the baby was okay, but at the same time, guilt. All those studies about allergies, infections, IQ, and so on . . .

On August 2, 1994, leaders of La Leche League International issued its response to the *Wall Street Journal* article, which, in effect, blamed the mothers' "mismanagement" of the nursing situation or attributed the problem to the lack of guidance from trained La Leche League Leaders. The organization's press release states: "What is sometimes perceived as insufficient milk supply is in reality a result of breastfeeding mismanagement or a baby's inability to suckle properly. LLLI Leaders are carefully trained to be alert to these conditions, to offer practical management information, to encourage mothers to stay in contact with their healthcare providers, and to support a mother's decision to use appropriate supplements upon the advice of her physician."[7]

In many interviews and on-line discussions with women who had attempted with great determination to breastfeed I discovered that the majority (55 percent) had done what La Leche League recommended and had contacted a trained leader or certified lactation consultant for advice. But "management" by lactation experts isn't always the panacea that breastfeeding advocates might like it to be.

Of the women I interviewed who had received help from a trained La Leche League Leader or a certified lactation consultant, only 29 percent found the expert's guidance useful. Far more typical were the comments and stories such as those found in "Mothers Talk About Breastfeeding Advisors." These stories are representative of the experiences of the bulk of my respondents who found that trained intervention did nothing to make a bad situation better (and in many cases, by overloading the parents with rules and instructions, made matters worse).

Mothers Talk About Breastfeeding Advisors

Interview question: Did you seek or receive any expert help with your breastfeeding difficulties, such as from La Leche League or a certified lactation consultant? How helpful did you find the expert's advice?

I prepared for breastfeeding by going to La Leche League meetings. I found that bottlefeeding mothers were portrayed there as career-driven, too concerned about their dry cleaning to breastfeed. It was like brainwashing: If you don't nurse, you're just not trying hard enough, you're not a good mother. I read the La Leche League book [*The Womanly Art of Breastfeeding*] cover to cover, and nowhere did it say there are some cases where women can't nurse. But from day one in the hospital I had trouble. The baby wasn't latching on. I felt like I was working at nursing 24 hours a day. I called La Leche League and they said, it's normal. My nipples were bleeding and infected. The baby was losing, not gaining weight. She was hungry all the time. In retrospect, I feel it was selfish of me not to have put her on a bottle earlier. Finally, at six weeks I got mastitis on both sides. I was howling in pain while I was nursing. My family doctor said, "Put the baby on the bottle. I promise you it won't affect her SAT scores. You are a wonderful mother." Instantly, her colic disappeared. The baby made the switch and became cuddly and happy. We bonded *better* because of the bottle.

—*Elizabeth*

Here's a mother who tried La Leche League twice, with very different results:

With my first baby I called La Leche League several times, but they gave no concrete advice beyond "Nurse more, and nurse more often." I was so tired and miserable that at the time it was like telling someone with a broken leg to "walk it off." . . . With my second baby, I went to four La Leche League meetings and saw a lactation consultant. [This time around] La Leche League got me through many tearful, desperate nights, just being there on the phone. At meetings they showed me techniques, proper positioning, etc., to decrease soreness and heal my poor, raw nipples. I could never have adjusted and been successful without them.

—*Carla*

La Leche League is really too militant. They tell you, "Everyone can nurse. You can do it, you can do it." I was militant myself, before I went to bottles. I found out [with my second child] I was just a low producer of milk.

—*Sheila, mother of five, of whom only the first was easily and exclusively breastfed*

I saw a lactation consultant in the hospital, but it was very rushed. Nurses came in to help with latch-on, but never stayed there more than a couple of minutes. When the baby still hadn't latched on by the time of my discharge, thirty-six hours later, the lactation consultant gave us a rental pump and said go home and feed her your milk in bottles. . . . La Leche League was not helpful. They lectured me when my baby was only five days old. They said I shouldn't have given her pumped milk in bottles. I should have been forcing her to breastfeed. They said I should "take control of my child" and asked, "When she's older, are you going to let her drink and drive?". . . One La Leche League person was on an aggressive campaign to get me to feed the expressed milk through a dropper. We tried that, but within twenty-four hours the baby stopped passing urine and became extremely lethargic. I tried to feed her but she had no interest. I couldn't wake her. I called the La Leche League person and told her this, and she got very alarmed and said feed her a bottle.

—*Cathy*

Sixty-seven percent of my respondents initially intended to breastfeed. They accepted unquestioningly, as I had, the claims made by breastfeeding advocates for the superiority of breastmilk over formula. They did not give up when beset by *minor* difficulties. In nearly all cases, the mothers tried, for weeks, even for months, before deciding to satisfy baby's needs in a different way. Upon switching to the bottle, most reported feeling relieved and happy for the baby—though, for a whopping 70 percent, relief was mixed with feelings of guilt, of having "failed" their babies in some basic way; a few added that years later the memory of that time is still painful. For mothers' own words about their struggles with guilt, read on.

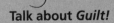

Talk about *Guilt!*

Mothers Talk about Losing the Battle of the Breast

I felt awful about it. I cried and cried beforehand and felt a twinge of guilt with every bottle I gave her.

Some friends made it worse—a few of them said I didn't try hard enough [though this interviewee had suffered three weeks of painful, bleeding nipples, and the baby wasn't getting enough milk]. I look back on it now [five years later] and still feel guilty. I know it's not rational—my daughter is fine—still, I feel I gave her less than the best.

—Nicole

During the time I was still giving my baby pumped-out breastmilk in a bottle, my husband and I had dinner with another couple, who also had a new baby. During the meal the wife and I discussed the feeding problems we were having. The woman's husband said, "I have to hand it to you—you put up more of a fight than Lynn did." I saw tears coming to Lynn's eyes. When I mentioned the incident later, Lynn said, "You know, I don't think anything in my life has ever bothered me as much as not being able to feed my baby." I knew exactly how she felt.

—Donna

Society is always telling women what to do with their bodies in one way or another. Society dictates how your breasts should look to please a man, then what to do with your breasts once you have a baby. In the first instance your breasts are supposed to be perfect sex objects, and after that, they are supposed to be perfect feeding instruments, and any variation engenders criticism. It's no wonder that women who breastfeed feel pressured, and women who don't breastfeed feel pressured.

—Lisa, a clinical social worker, who breastfed her first child but bottlefed her second, telling why she felt uncomfortable about both feeding methods.

> My baby would latch on, and it wasn't painful, but my milk never seemed to come in. It made me feel as if I was the only woman in the whole world who wasn't producing milk. . . . My mind read the pregnancy books, but my body didn't.
>
> —*Ellen*

Tell Me Your Story

Mothers turn to bottlefeeding for a host of reasons. The list here includes those I heard from 278 women in my pool of respondents, but obviously I could not get in touch with every woman who has ever used a bottle. If the reason *you* are bottlefeeding your baby is not on this list, please write and tell me about it, so that I can add it to a future edition of this book. Send letters to Peggy Robin, 3409 29th Street, N.W., Washington, D.C. 20008.

38 Reasons for the Bottle

1. **Latch-on troubles.**   The baby is unable to make an effective connection to the mother's nipple for sucking.

2. **Pain.**   The mother suffers from cracked, sore, bleeding nipples with each nursing.

3. **Nipple confusion.**   The newborn, having been given bottles or pacifiers, has learned the sucking motions that work with an artificial nipple but has trouble drawing milk from the irregular-shaped, slower-flowing human nipple. Thus when the baby is put to the mother's breast, it appears confused or rejects the breast altogether.

4. **Postpartum exhaustion.**   Following a long, hard labor or C-section, the mother is simply too worn out to attempt to nurse. The baby is initially given bottles, resulting in nipple confusion.

5. Breast infections. The mother suffers from mastitis (a bacterial infection), thrush (a fungal infection), or plugged milk ducts. Such infections may occur at any time, and in some women, recur frequently. If not treated in time, a breast infection may result in an abscess, which may need to be surgically removed.

6. Overly enlarged breasts. A woman who was unusually large-breasted before pregnancy may find herself made uncomfortable by the size and weight of her milk-filled breasts. The woman who while nursing needs to wear a J-, K-, or even an L-cup bra may be troubled by constant back and shoulder pain caused by her change in size, often compounded by the emotional discomfort resulting from becoming the object of stares and rude remarks from leering men.

7. Insufficient milk production. An estimated five percent of nursing mothers are unable to produce enough milk to meet their babies' nutritional needs. Because of the controversy surrounding this reason, it is the subject of further discussion in this chapter, beginning on page 74.

8. Excessive milk production. Just as there are mothers who report problems in producing enough milk, there are those who report troubles caused by overproduction. The milk "lets down" in such rapid gushes that the baby can't swallow easily and gags, or swallows the wrong way, or ends up biting down on the mother's nipple to shut off the flow; the mother's clothing is constantly soaked and stained from leakage, and neither one enjoys the nursing sessions.

9. Adopted baby. Virtually all of the 25,000 infants adopted annually in America are bottlefed.

10. Workplace problems. The mother's work schedule does not leave her sufficient free time to express milk for her baby, or she has no place to sit comfortably and use her breast pump in a private and hygienic way, or she finds the social environment discouraging or even outwardly hostile to the practice while on the job. (Because of the importance of this issue in the lives of new mothers, I have devoted chapter 5 entirely to the discussion of how employment often impedes the new mother's free choice of feeding style.)

11. The mother is not the primary caregiver. The person in charge of most of the feedings may be the father, grandparent, aunt, nanny, au pair, daycare provider, or another adult who cannot breastfeed. The caregiver may not be willing to deal with the task of properly storing and thawing the mother's frozen expressed milk, or the mother herself may be unwilling or unable to use a breastpump efficiently, and so the caregiver must use formula.

12. The mother must travel without her baby. Emergencies may arise to disrupt the nursing relationship. For instance, the woman who must travel across the country or abroad to tend to a dying parent or arrange a funeral may well decide it's best to leave the baby at home, especially if the destination is to an area with uncertain sanitation, known hazards, or poor accommodations.

13. Compromised milk quality. The mother is taking a medication that taints her breastmilk, or she has come into contact with some environmental toxin, such as lead, irradiated water, or certain chemicals used in farming or manufacturing (the cattle growth hormone PBB, for example, or the herbicide dioxin); she suffers from an illness such as anemia, Crohn's disease, or colitis that leaves her incapable of producing a nutritionally complete milk; or she is infected with a virus, such as HIV, cytomegalovirus, or a hepatitis strain, that has been proven able to infect a nursing infant.

14. Dangerous habits. If the mother smokes, drinks alcohol prior to nursing, or uses marijuana or cocaine or other mood-altering drugs, most medical experts advise against nursing. Smoking as few as ten cigarettes a day has been shown to reduce the fat content per ounce of breast-milk by an average 20 percent and to reduce its caloric value by an average 10 percent.[8] The woman who drinks alcohol is warned to wait at least one hour per ounce of alcohol consumed before nursing to be certain of providing her baby with unaffected breastmilk. If the mother is uncertain of her ability to forswear a dangerous habit, the safest course is for her to rely on formula from the outset, avoiding any risk to her baby by a lapse on her part.

15. Low birth weight. The newborn is too tiny and underdeveloped to latch onto the breast and nurse. Premature babies under 3.5 pounds will generally be tube-fed, while those weighing between 3.5 and 5.5 pounds will, in many hospitals, be fed a specially enriched formula from a bottle using a specially designed "preemie" nipple.

16. Failure to thrive. This is a medical term applied to newborns who have lost more than ten percent of their birth weight within the first two weeks of life, or used to describe babies who fail to gain weight adequately during their first year of life. Abbreviated as FTT, the syndrome's cause is poorly understood by pediatricians, but the treatment nearly always includes use of formula as a supplement or as a complete infant diet.

17. Baby's mouth or tongue defect. Most problematic is the cleft lip or palate that makes it difficult to impossible for the baby to suck effectively. Surgical correction of the defect is seldom performed before the baby is several months old, by which time it is usually too late for the mother to initiate breastfeeding. Another common defect is the short frenulum, in which tongue movement is constrained by the band of tissue that connects the tongue to the floor of the mouth. A short frenulum may also be corrected surgically; alternatively, the baby may be trained in special sucking techniques to make breastfeeding possible. However, the problem often goes unrecognized, or the lactation consultant tries without success to teach the nursing baby the new sucking patterns.

18. Severe newborn jaundice. When a newborn baby's liver is not working efficiently to cleanse the blood of bilirubin, the baby is said to be jaundiced. In mild to moderate cases, all that needs to be done to alleviate the problem is to expose the baby to sunlight a few hours each day. In severe cases it is necessary to keep the baby in the neonatal nursery for phototherapy (exposure to bright lights), which, as a side effect, may cause dehydration unless the baby receives extra fluids. Because few new mothers are able to pump out the extra milk needed to meet the jaundiced baby's needs, other liquids (formula, sugar-water, or just plain water) are generally given in bottles. The babies then run the risk of nipple confusion—that is, only learning bottle-sucking and not how to latch onto a natural nipple for breastfeeding.

19. Vomiting or severe diarrhea in infancy. Because dehydration can occur rapidly in an infant and cause permanent and devastating damage (such as mental retardation or loss of limbs), pediatricians often treat instances of diarrhea or vomiting in infants aggressively, requiring the mother to suspend breastfeeding so that the baby can receive intravenous rehydration fluids or be bottlefed with an over-the-counter electrolyte solution such as Pedialyte or Ricelyte. Once breastfeeding is interrupted, even for a few days, it may be difficult to reestablish.

20. The need to measure infant food intake. In certain circumstances—for example, following a diagnosis of failure to thrive or before the baby may receive a precise dose of a medication—a pediatrician will declare bottlefeeding to be medically essential so that the baby's food intake can be ascertained. Without the bottle, the only way to check food intake is to weigh the baby several times a day on a hospital scale that is calibrated to the gram—and even then mistakes can easily creep in (since babies seldom lie still on the scale). By using the bottle to measure food intake at home, the parents avoid exposing the baby to other sick children in the hospital, as well as the difficulties involved in transporting a new baby in the car several times a day.

21. Severely allergic baby. When a baby appears to suffer gastric distress after every nursing, has constant nasal congestion but no other signs of an upper respiratory infection, or is troubled by frequent hives or eczema, the diagnosis may be allergy to something (or more likely, many things) in the mother's diet. To continue breastfeeding the mother may need to follow a course of trial-and-error elimination of suspected allergens such as dairy products, wheat, berries, corn and corn syrups, nuts, citrus fruits, and fish. Rather than spend several weeks or months experimenting with her diet, she may instead simply opt to put the baby on a hypoallergenic soy-based formula, made with predigested proteins and easily broken-down fats for maximum digestibility by even the most sensitive babies.

22. The baby must be hospitalized. A seriously ill baby, attached to tubes or a respirator, can seldom be breastfed. Even if intubation is not necessary for feeding, the neonatal intensive care unit (NICU) may enforce rules that restrict contact with the baby and effectively prohibit the establishment of the nursing relationship.

23. The mother must be hospitalized. Hospital rules may bar a mother from keeping her baby with her when the baby is not the patient. Even when permitted free access to her baby, a mother hospitalized for a serious illness or in need of critical care after an accident may be in no condition to maintain the nursing relationship.

24. The mother has breast cancer. There is no question but that the woman receiving radiation or chemotherapy should *not* breastfeed. Of course the woman who has had a double mastectomy cannot do so, and the woman with a single mastectomy or a lumpectomy in which there

was significant tissue loss will in all likelihood have difficulty producing sufficient milk to do so.

25. The mother has had cosmetic breast surgery. Breast
reduction surgery typically removes enough of the milk
glands to impair breastfeeding ability. Breast augmentation
surgery, intended to enhance a woman's bustline, may interfere with breastfeeding as well, the milk ducts having
been damaged or removed during the insertion of silicone
or saline implants—an outcome that few plastic surgeons
adequately advise their patients to expect.

26. Fertility problems. The mother who has had trouble conceiving in the past may not want to do anything that
would compromise her fertility in the future. Since breastfeeding usually suppresses ovulation, the subfertile woman
may be advised by her fertility specialist to breastfeed only
for a short time or to avoid the practice altogether.

27. The baby is extremely irritable during feedings.
Some babies, mothers report, just seem miserable at the
breast. The fussy baby will latch on all right, but will break
off sucking after a minute, or even a few seconds, then cry
and refuse to resume. Nothing seems to soothe the baby
except a bottle, which the baby will easily and happily
empty. In such cases a mother may decide to wean for the
sake of her baby's emotional as well as physical well-being.

28. The baby is often too sleepy to nurse. This is the
opposite of the problem of the too-fussy baby, cited above.
To establish sufficient milk supply, a new mother usually
must nurse for at least 20 minutes every 2 to 3 hours.
However, some newborns just will not wake up to nurse
on schedule, despite the use of the recommended wake-up
tricks such as tickling the feet, removing clothing, or
touching the skin with a wet washcloth. When the long-
sleeping baby finally does wake up, it may well be so hungry and impatient to eat that it can't latch on properly. So
begins a problematic cycle of oversleeping, followed by
frustrated attempts at nursing, followed by the baby's cry-

ing itself back into an exhausted sleep, a pattern that may be broken only by weaning to the easy-flowing formula bottle.

29. Marathon nurser. Some babies want to nurse every two hours around the clock, for forty-five to ninety minutes at a time. Mothers of such babies get little sleep and can barely find time to take a shower, go to the bathroom, or sit down and eat a normal meal. Mothers of marathon nursers who decide to wean do so because (as one mother put it), "That was the only way I knew to get my life back!"

30. Bad breastfeeding advice in the hospital. Many mothers who wanted to nurse reported that they were unable to get started because of wrong or inadequate advice they received while in the hospital. Some babies were simply put on bottles right away and the mothers were never given a chance to learn to breastfeed. Others reported being given contradictory advice by different nurses or being handed the baby but never being shown by anyone what to do.

31. The mother has twins, triplets, or more. There *are* a few mothers who have managed to breastfeed twins exclusively, but such cases are rare, and with more than twins, it is all but impossible.

32. The mother is a single parent. Without a partner to help share the many burdens of parenthood, everything about infant care is harder to manage. As bottlefeeding is faster and easier to learn than breastfeeding, it's the choice of the majority of single mothers, for whom time is at a premium.

33. Postpartum depression. Up to 20 percent of all women who give birth report some symptoms of postpartum depression (general misery, weepiness, feeling overwhelmed, isolated, or unconnected emotionally to the baby).[9] A frequent symptom of postpartum depression is tension that interferes with the "let-down" of milk. Often therapists urge that the mother be relieved of many, or even all, of the infant-care chores until her symptoms ease, a course of action that will almost certainly require weaning the baby to formula.

34. The mother finds breastfeeding too confining. She may discover that she can only "let down" her milk in limited circumstances—for example, while sitting in one position, in one room, only when she has a special nursing pillow on her lap, or has her feet elevated by a special nursing stool. Nursing becomes impossible or uncomfortable in other circumstances, and the mother ends up feeling trapped and miserable until the baby is weaned.

35. Lack of familiarity with breastfeeding. Less than 10 percent of the bottlefeeding women that I interviewed had been breastfed by their own mothers or had a sibling who was breastfed. Some had even given birth without ever having seen the act of breastfeeding performed. Many new mothers decide, quite logically, that they don't want to complicate the already stressful first days after childbirth by trying to master a new skill. They consider that by bottlefeeding from day one, they need not worry about possible harm to the baby from inadequate feedings, breast infections, or any other problem, and they avoid the often traumatic process of weaning at a later date.

36. The mother wants to treat both children equally. When a mother has an older child whom she did not breastfeed, for whatever reason, she may be unwilling to do so with the second. Some mothers worry that the older child, seeing the new baby at the mother's breast, will feel less loved for not having received the same treatment.

37. Interference with the couple's sex life. Loss of libido and pain during intercourse are two commonly experienced but little discussed side effects of lactation. Nursing mothers produce the hormone prolactin in abundance, which in turn depresses the production of estrogen, the chief female sex hormone. When a couple has a strong, secure relationship, a temporary dampening of their sex life may not become an issue for them; but for the couple whose relationship has been frayed by the stresses, both financial and emotional, of caring for a new and totally dependent member of the family, the loss of sexual compatibility could have serious consequences. If bottlefeeding helps the highly stressed couple to find their way back to a pleasurable intimacy, avoiding discord and possibly even divorce, the benefit to the baby is incalculable.

38. Mother's inhibitions about breastfeeding. Many women have been raised to believe that in polite society bodily functions are not to be mentioned, much less demonstrated in public. Even with the use of coverings such as blankets or specially designed nursing clothing, the inhibited woman may still feel exposed and ashamed, leading her to feel tense and troubled as each feeding time approaches. The mother who does not want to exude such negative emotions each time her baby is hungry may conclude that she would be giving her baby a better quality of mothering by choosing to bottlefeed instead.

Mothers Tell Why They Chose the Bottle

My baby just never learned to latch on. So I pumped round the clock every two hours for two and a half months. It was very hard. Eventually I stopped pumping. The pediatrician said six weeks of breastmilk gives a baby the bulk of the benefits. Doing all that pumping, it was too hard for me to function, with everything else I had to do.

—*Cathy*

When Caitlin was born I immediately made my first attempt at breastfeeding but found out that with inverted nipples, latch-on would be difficult. My confidence wasn't bolstered when the nurse shrieked, "Oh my God, you have inverted nipples!" I went home and was still having problems, not to mention feeling very inadequate. La Leche League came to my house to show me the correct way to breastfeed . . . I continued to try for a couple of weeks, then gave up. . . . Now twelve years later I am happy to report that my child has grown up happy and well adjusted.

—*Sarah*

I had sore nipples, not just cracked and bleeding, but with mini-craters. Scabs formed but came off with every nursing. I was going through a 200-tablet bottle of Tylenol a week. At the doctor's suggestion I switched to the bottle at three weeks. The baby seemed happy not to have me crying each time. I couldn't have gone on like that!

—*Nicole*

My daughter didn't know how to suck. I tried for two months to teach her, working with three different lactation consultants (yes, certified ones), and two doctors. She was a jawer. She would just chew on the nipple and get no milk. Her chewing caused scar tissue to build up on my breasts. The nipples would turn deathly white after nursing sessions—it's called vasospasm, and it's very painful. Sometimes I would lie in bed, moaning and tossing from pain for the hour between feedings. Some days I couldn't hold my baby because I hurt so badly. . . This went on for more than two months. The doctors told me I should consider bottlefeeding. One day, when the pain had abated a bit, I went to pick up my baby and hold her. My baby, my precious child, got a look of confusion and started to cry—she was so unused to my holding her. I realized then that my daughter needed her mother more than she needed mother's milk. That day I gave up . . . She drinks from bottles now and will be starting solids any day. Her weight is fine. And she gets held by her mommy a lot.

—*Maria*

By the time I got home from the hospital, we had the problem of nipple confusion. Because Emily had been given several bottles in the hospital [as ordered by the doctor to prevent dehydration due to the baby's inability to latch on], she still hadn't learned to latch on properly. I used a nipple shield to try to make it easier for her and me. For five weeks I attempted to breastfeed Emily at the start of each feeding. When that was unsuccessful, I would use the pump and feed her breastmilk from a bottle. It was obvious after a while that she preferred the bottle.

—*Brenda*

The nurses offered some help with the breastfeeding, but after 24 hours of labor, including three and a half hours of pushing, I was so tired I barely knew what day it was. Later, I couldn't remember anything they told me . . .

—*Kate*

After about ten days of successful though uncomfortable breastfeeding, I developed mastitis with a 104° fever. Antibiotics cleared it up quickly, but the nipple was severely cracked. I was only able to nurse on one side. When I developed mastitis on that side, too, they [the doctors] were unable to control the fever. My husband had to leave work—I was too weak to take care of the baby. After that, I decided to switch to the bottle.

—*Susan*

I breastfed my first child for four and a half months and had mastitis *eight* times. The first time I was really sick, with a 103° fever. With the second child, despite knowing almost everything about breastfeeding, having a lactation consultant, etc., I again got mastitis at about six weeks. When I had a second bout of mastitis, I vowed to quit. I decided to bottlefeed my third child from birth. Judging by some people's reactions, you'd think I was going to beat my child or something. My OB, however, didn't question my decision to bottlefeed, given my history of infection.

—*Rita*

I was always large-busted, a 36D. When pregnant I became a K-cup and I'm 5'2"! By the time of the birth, when my milk came in, I was a 38L. I also had very large nipples. The baby just couldn't latch on. My nipples were bleeding and infected. I wasn't making enough milk. I've since learned it's pretty common for large-busted women to have trouble producing milk.

—*Elizabeth*

I've gone through a lot of "what ifs," because we never did determine why I couldn't produce enough milk. I tried everything, too. As for frequent nursing, I'd feed Allen every time he squeaked. The midwife even suggested cutting back the frequency to no more than every two hours to see if that helped, but it didn't. I tried the SNS supplementer [a bottle with tubing that is taped to the nipples allowing the baby to receive formula by sucking on the woman's breasts], so that he would stimulate me while he got his formula, but I didn't get anywhere with that, either.

—*Nora*

I had a problem with low milk supply with my second daughter. At two weeks she had lost more than 13 percent of her birthweight. I used the SNS nurser. I found the hardest part was keeping the feeding tube clean, as it seemed no sooner did I get the baby fed and the tube cleaned, I had to feed her again. After about four weeks I broke down and gave her a bottle. Even with the SNS I did not see an appreciable increase in my milk supply. (I had supply problems with my first child as well.)

—*Linda*

Everything I read assured me that a mother's milk supply always increases to meet the baby's need. The hospital staff told me this, too. It is frustrating to find myself in a category that apparently doesn't exist!

—*Monica*

We brought our adopted daughter home at two days old. She was bottlefed in the hospital. When I was pregnant [this respondent had had three miscarriages], I always figured I would breastfeed. . . . So many things in life don't work out as you plan. Adoptive parents are spared the guilty feelings because they don't have any choice.

—*Alice*

I worked all through my pregnancy and went back to work at one month. I'm a public defender, and it would be completely impossible for me to say, in the middle of a jury trial, "Judge, excuse me, I have to go nurse my baby now."

—Barbara

I started working full-time six weeks after giving birth. My mother, sister, and grandmother provided childcare. They were supportive of my decision to bottlefeed. I know breastfeeding is time-consuming, and this way I can have some time for all the other things that need to be taken care of.

—Kelly, a single mom

With my second child my mother was dying and I had to travel back and forth without the baby. I know I couldn't have taken care of both her and the baby.

—Joyce

I started off breastfeeding and did it for two months without problem, but then I had a severe allergic reaction to an antibiotic. It affected my central nervous system. My doctor put me on a drug and said I couldn't breastfeed any longer. I was sad, because I'd breastfed my first child for over three years and enjoyed it. But breastfeeding didn't help *his* allergies a bit. He reacted to everything in my breastmilk: dairy, citrus, wheat . . . . I had to take it all out of my diet. I put my second child on a soy formula, I-soyalac, without corn solids, and she's been fine.

—Isabel

I had to stop nursing. I had a blood pressure check and it was through the roof. My doctor warned me that my pressure was high enough to worry about "stroking out" and leaving my children without a mother. He said I could still nurse, but that the medication would make Chloe sleepy, and I am not going to let that happen.

—*Maureen*

My pediatrician wanted me to breastfeed (my kids are in their teens now) but I have a serious calcium shortage and must take medication for it. My own doctor advised against breastfeeding because of the difficulties I was having at the time getting my blood levels to normal. When the pediatrician heard this, he immediately backed off.

—*Carol*

LaTosha was extremely premature and weighed only one and a half pounds at birth. She was a "crack" baby, whose biological mother was too addicted to care for her. LaTosha was kept in the hospital for six months, until she came to live with us. [This interviewee was in the process of adopting LaTosha; she also has two teenage sons, both of whom she had bottlefed as babies.] Even if her birthmother had been able to breastfeed, LaTosha would have been too small and weak for it. The hospital used a special formula, and it worked wonders. By the time we got her she weighed ten pounds. Now [just a few months later] she's already fifteen pounds, well within the normal limits for her age. We're told with therapy she has every prospect of developing into a perfectly healthy girl. I know that without formula she would never have survived.

—*Nancy*

I nursed my older child for six months without any problem, but I had to stop with my younger child when he was two months old. The doctor said my breastmilk wasn't providing him enough nutrition.

Though my son latched on and appeared to nurse well, he simply wasn't gaining weight fast enough, and even lost weight between one visit and the next. I could see the doctor was right. He suggested that I try pumping and nursing, and I did that for a while, but then I found that my whole life was just nursing and pumping. It wasn't putting me in a good frame of mind. I think using bottles really improved my relationship with my son.

—Lydia

The lactation consultant was patient and sympathetic to my extreme exhaustion. She said the shape of Jon's hard palate was making it difficult for him to suck properly. Getting him to breastfeed was going to be such a long, hard task, that she said she was not sure I was physically up to it.

—Kate

Within five days of her birth my baby got jaundice. I had to take her back to the hospital and she stayed for three days on an IV, under lights [phototherapy]. The hospital said that jaundice can be passed to the baby through mother's milk, so they fed her sugar water and formula. They told me to save my milk, but I just couldn't pump out enough. I finally realized we were all too miserable. The hospital wanted me to keep on trying . . . my husband, my doctor wanted me to keep at it . . . everybody but my baby.

—Joyce

Mother's question posted on a medical forum: Is there any time that a baby should not *have breastmilk?*

Pediatrician's on-line answer: If I feel that a vomiting infant is in danger of dehydrating, I would hospi-

talize the infant and attempt rehydration intravenous-
ly. The clear liquids, e.g. Pedialyte, are thought to be
better tolerated than even breastmilk.

*This exchange about bottlefeeding to measure food
intake in a hospitalized infant took place on a medical
forum on-line.*

Lactation consultant's comment:	Unless the mom is having problems [with nursing], it seems silly to lose the benefits of breastfeeding to measure formula intake. Why doesn't the pediatrician just ask the mom to give the baby the breast more often to keep fluids up? Or why not just weigh the baby before and after feedings?
Pediatrician's answer:	Test weighing isn't all that accurate unless done for every feeding over a 24-hour period or on an extremely accurate, electronic scale (which I doubt most hospital nurseries own). Test weighing is also more stressful for the mother.

When my daughter was a year old I finally took her
to an allergist. The result: sensitivities to everything I
had been eating: eggs, dairy, peanuts, corn, legumes.
Her pediatrician was shocked. I guess there are differing opinions on what travels through breastmilk. My
own non-medical opinion is that her condition improved as soon as I altered my diet.

—Hope

*Eileen posted a message describing having weaned
her four-week-old baby just prior to her hospitalization
for gall bladder surgery. Alexandra posted a reply that*

*she, too, had had gall bladder surgery but had kept on
nursing, adding that Eileen's doctor had been wrong to
urge her to stop nursing. Here is Eileen's response:*

Alexandra, I admire you for breastfeeding when
many other women would have given up; however, I
don't feel I received bad advice from my doctor. The
advice I received was exactly what I needed. After an
extremely long labor resulting in a C-section, compounded by gall bladder disease, breastfeeding would
have been a strain I could not have handled, either
physically or emotionally. I really don't feel I missed
anything. I have a healthy daughter—which is more
important than how I fed her! That's the goal everyone was working for from the beginning.

During the third month of my second pregnancy my
doctor discovered breast cancer. I underwent an immediate mastectomy, followed by aggressive chemotherapy, both during the pregnancy and afterwards. My
situation was so unusual. Nobody knew anyone who
had all the answers [about breastfeeding in her situa-
tion]. I called La Leche League and the contact there
said, "Don't do it. The chemotherapy will affect the
milk in your remaining breast."

—*Erica*

I had a breast reduction done when I was nineteen. I
had both physical and emotional difficulties from having large breasts. But I wasn't properly informed about
the risk—I'd been led to believe I could still breastfeed.
I tried for eight weeks, but my supply dwindled, and I
kept having to supplement more and more. The most I
could get out by pumping was twelve ounces a day. It
was exhausting and depressing, so I finally gave it up.

—*Kristin*

I deliberately limited my breastfeeding of Kevin to just three months, in the hope that I would be able to conceive again quickly. I'm 38 and I'd really like to have a second before I'm 40. It's been a few months since I weaned him, and I still haven't got my periods back.

—Leslie

My son *hated* being put to breast for each attempt at feeding. By the end of the first couple of weeks, I felt like I would be torturing him if I were to try anymore. Interestingly enough, because my husband became so active in feeding and caring for the baby early on, it allowed a special bond to develop between my son and his dad.

—Donna

I just could never seem to satiate her. One night I had her with me from 1 A.M. till 4 A.M., and she never stopped crying.

—Mary Lou

My second child had problems nursing from the first. I don't know whether it was because I was on the epidural so long (my first child was the result of a completely unmedicated labor, while my second had to be induced), but he just seemed to sleep all day. Then, when he was awake, he'd be extremely fussy and wouldn't latch on. I was frustrated, because I had nursed successfully before, and thought I knew what I was doing. Eventually, I called in a lactation consultant, but by the time I saw her, my son had already lost too much weight, and the pediatrician put him on formula. I suppose I could have tried harder to get him back on my breast, but frankly, I was relieved, because it was so much less stressful to bottlefeed.

—Maggie

I had an *awful* hospital experience. I had a C-section after a two-day induction of labor, which failed. I was not given my son to attempt a feeding until the next morning. Someone had already given him a bottle by then, because they had accidentally marked "bottle-feeding" on his chart. My son, who was nine days early and weighed only 5 pounds, 14 ounces at birth, was a little "tongue-tied" and had a very small mouth. He did not latch on while I attempted feeding. I then developed "complications" [which, after several days of invasive testing, turned out to be nothing more than malfunctioning hospital equipment]. Anyway, I was unable to get my son to nurse, and getting nourishment into him by any means became more crucial than the breast-vs.-bottle debate. Although I continued to try to get my son to latch on [for three months!], he preferred to take breastmilk from the bottle.

—Donna

I had no instruction from anyone about breastfeeding. On the fifth day [after birth] I took the baby in to see the nurse practitioner. The baby had lost weight, and had signs of dehydration, but fortunately, no brain damage. The nurse gave her formula, but encouraged me to keep breastfeeding. On the seventh or eighth day I was still trying. I needed a lactation consultant, but that was not covered in my insurance plan. The pediatric nurse's advice consisted of shoving my nipple in the baby's mouth. I had La Leche League on the phone, but they just said "Keep at it," with no suggestion of how to get additional help.

—Annette

We knew all about bottlefeeding from our first baby [adopted at six weeks], so when our son was born, we decided to stick with what we knew. That way our biological son and our adopted daughter would be treated equally.

—Heidi

When I had the twins, I called La Leche League for help. They said, "You can do it. Lie in bed all day and nurse and you'll have enough milk." But when you have an older one, you just can't do that. There's too much stress. I couldn't get any let-down. So I'd nurse one and bottlefeed the other, switching back and forth. I could never breastfeed both at the same time, anyway. When you have two babies in your arms, you don't have a free hand to put the nipple in the baby's mouth.

—Sheila

I got pregnant for the first time before I started college. I was still planning to go to college part time after the birth, and knew I couldn't do that and nurse. My mother, who was wonderful, looked after my baby. After college I got married, I had my second, and breastfed him until problems with my milk supply forced me to stop. From someone who's done both, I'd say that there are certain advantages to bottles. I definitely disagree that breastfeeding makes for better bonding, or that breastfed babies are better. I challenge anyone to look at my two children and say which is the breastfed and which is the bottlefed one!

—Larissa

I really only felt comfortable nursing in my own home, on my overstuffed couch, with my special pillow. In public I was happier with bottles. Plus, I happen to have mega-sized breasts that gushed all over the place, and I felt I had to be equipped with beach towels to mop up the mess. Megan was famous for popping her mouth off my nipple to look around, during which a geyser of milk would be shooting out (yikes!).

—*Sally*

We bottlefed our daughter. My only prior experience with nursing was through a cousin, who nursed her four sons until they were three, at least. She was not discreet, and as the boys became older, they seemed uninterested, but she made sure she kept nursing a part of their lives. The boys were allowed to pull her shirt up and yell for "ninny" at any time. I remember one family gathering where the youngest ran across the yard yelling, "Mommy . . . ninny!" By the time he got there she had her shirt unbuttoned. To me, it wasn't a nurturing activity going on there. Although I'm not against nursing toddlers, I was put off by the way she went about it. It was extremely embarrassing to my father. So when I was pregnant, that was the only image I had of breastfeeding. Everyone else in my family had bottlefed. It's very hard to get past feelings such as those.

—*Irene*

I exclusively breastfed our first son, and while I don't regret it, I have to say it contributed to our marital stress at the time. I wasn't getting enough sleep, because I was nursing all night. I'm the sort of person who really needs a full eight hours, and for nine months I hardly had more than three hours at a time. So I was cranky a lot. My husband was at work all day, and when he came home, he didn't seem to appreciate how hard it was for me to be alone with the baby all day. Also, whenever we had sex (which was rare, since I was hardly ever up to it), it was uncomfortable for me. I tried all the recommended lubricants, but they didn't do much. After I weaned Alex, my relationship with my husband got much better. With our second, we did things differently. I started supplementing with formula early on, and I was able to get more rest. My husband could give a bottle in the middle of the night, and the baby slept longer. It was much better for our marriage.

—Charlotte

I'm just not comfortable with the idea of breastfeeding. This may sound silly, but I just can't help thinking of my breasts as being sexual. The idea of a baby manipulating them seems almost . . . incestuous. As a nurse, I know breastfeeding is the most natural process . . . but I also know a lot of mothers who had to give it up because of problems.

—Kelly

Are the Reasons Valid?

The National Center for Health Statistics reports that 54 percent of all new mothers in the U.S. start out breastfeeding their babies. Breastfeeding drops off to 40 percent by six weeks, and by the fifth or six month, is down to a mere 20 percent. These figures suggest that even for those who are able to breastfeed easily from the start, there must be real difficulties that keep a high percentage of mothers from sticking with it longer.

However, when an individual mother, in recognition of whatever problems have arisen in her own unique situation, turns to the bottle as a solution, she will often find herself the object of criticism. During the three month period from October through December, 1994, that I followed breastfeeding messages on four different electronic forums, I counted 58 messages that expressly criticized the bottlefeeding choice. Twenty-two of the messages went farther than simply getting across an anti-bottle opinion but used terms of abuse for bottlefeeders (including "selfish jerk" and "shithead") or made extreme comparisons, such as between formula and poison or between bottlefeeding and child abuse (in e-mail jargon, such personal attacks are known as "flames").

Typical perhaps of what bottlefeeding mothers are hearing over the nation's electronic airwaves was this scolding response to a message posted by a mother who had switched to the bottle while hospitalized for gall bladder surgery just one month after childbirth: "Medical problems, etc., do not preclude breastfeeding, FYI. I had my gall bladder out when my baby was six months old, yet she basically only had breast milk until she was seven months old."

The bottlefeeding mother replied by filling in some additional details of her condition, including the fact the she had become extremely malnourished and debilitated due to the intensity of her disease, but neglecting to point out that her own surgery had occurred while her baby was a few weeks old, whereas the breastfeeding writer's surgery had occurred when her baby was already half a year old and breastfeeding was well established.

Another example came from a woman with very large breasts, not yet pregnant, but contemplating having a baby some time in the future. When she speculated on-line that she might bottlefeed to spare herself increased discomfort from further enlargement of her double-F-cup-sized breasts, a horde of breastfeeding zealots jumped all over her for worrying about her own comfort. Here's one reply, posted by one of breastfeeding's rare male militants: "The primary consideration in breastfeeding, in my humble opinion, should be the well-being of the infant. There are many studies that others are vastly more qualified to cite that show breastfeeding to be vastly preferable to formula. [The writer then devotes most the next paragraph to a list of claims for the superiority of breastmilk] . . . In any case it would seem to me that cup size should be one of the last considerations." (Of course, cup size was *not* her real concern; it was the back and shoulder pain that she experienced due to her large breasts—something the male writer had not seemed to comprehend.)

No matter how strong a mother's reason, there is always someone ready to second-guess her, though they may at the same time deny that that's what they're doing—as in this case of on-line criticism of a bottlefeeder by her breastfeeding in-law: "My sister-in-law had a baby in June. My other sister-in-law and I both encouraged her to nurse, which she did for about six weeks, but she complained of being 'tied down' and eventually stopped. Some women don't like having to be there constantly for their babies. It's sad. Nothing against it—it's their decision—but it's too bad for their child."

In this next example, a certified lactation consultant is quick to characterize a wide variety of bottlefeeding reasons as "flimsy": "We [lactation consultants] are all understanding of mothers who try very hard and cannot breastfeed . . . but we are frustrated that so many mothers still choose to formula feed for the flimsiest of reasons: for the convenience of being able to leave the baby with others for extended time periods, or out of embarrassment and discomfort with the idea of breastfeeding; or because the grandmother or father of the child wants to see the intake and participate in the feeding."

It would be heartening to conclude that the e-mail networks have somehow become clearinghouses for intolerant minds, and that the public at large is more understanding. Not so, according to the mothers in my interviews. From friends, family, and acquaintances, too—and, of course, from nearly all the breastfeeding guides I collected—the message comes through loud and clear: Your reasons are not good enough. You should have worked harder to try to overcome whatever problem you encountered.

If the reason revolved around the baby's sucking problems, you should have sought expert help, and stuck with the recommended measures, for as long as it took to get the problem solved.

For mothers who find nursing painful, the message is, endure silently, and put your own feeling aside—you matter less than the milk you produce. As a woman and a mother, you are meant by nature to sacrifice yourself for your children's sake. (Because this view of women appears so often in breastfeeding literature or in comments made to bottlefeeding mothers, the subject is discussed in greater detail in chapter 3.)

In circumstances of mother-child separation, the mother is urged to change her plans, to take baby with her wherever she must travel, or to rearrange her worklife to avoid leaving the baby. If that is not possible, she is urged to use a breastpump to store milk for her baby's use while she's away—though such advice assumes that every woman will be able to produce sufficient milk through pumping, or will be able to pump without pain. (The anti-separation rhetoric in many of the breastfeeding books I found in the bookstores today is so marked, and has such serious implications for working mothers, that I give the issue closer examination in chapter 3.)

When a mother's reasons for bottlefeeding are based on concerns for the quality of her milk, opponents of bottlefeeding have a trickier time of it. No one would argue that it's right to give a baby dangerous food. Rather than advocate formula for babies whose mothers, for example, are infected with transmissible viruses, La Leche League's guide, *The Womanly Art of Breastfeeding*, is curiously silent on the problem. Though it has been known for many years that HIV, the AIDS virus, can be transmitted through breastmilk, in the 35th anniversary edition of *The Womanly Art* (1991) there is no mention of this danger. Nor does the book address the need for hepatitis, herpes, and cytomegalovirus infected mothers to avoid breastfeeding.

With regard to the milk of smokers, the book does bring up the problem, only to downplay the harm: "Some mothers smoke and breastfeed with no problem. In general, if a mother smokes less than a pack (twenty cigarettes) a day, the amount of nicotine in her milk is not usually enough to cause any problem for the baby."[10] No medical study is cited to back up this assertion; I had no trouble finding a recent study showing just the opposite, that as few as ten cigarettes a day had a significant adverse effect on the quality of the smoker's milk.[11]

When it comes to medications, *The Womanly Art's* approach is even more cavalier: "Few drugs have been *proven* harmful to the nursing infant [my emphasis added]," the book assures the reader, but if the drug you need is not approved for use during lactation, the book suggests that "it may be possible to alter or postpone treatment until the baby is older."[12] Such advice conveys a subtle but very real implication that the mother should assign breastfeeding a higher priority than her own medical needs.

When use of formula comes about following a pediatrician's recommendation, due to a diagnosis of newborn jaundice, low birth weight, failure to thrive, or any other condition that might be improved by rapid weight gain, the anti-bottlefeeding argument may include a blast at the entire medical profession. As authors Karen Pryor and Gale Pryor charge in their guide *Nursing Your Baby,* "physicians graduate with a feeling that breastfeeding is not very interesting, complicated, or important . . ." and "Furthermore, they live and work in climate of opinion that downgrades breastfeeding to just one of many suitable options, in a hospital system that frustrates normal lactation, and in an absolute blizzard of propaganda from the manufacturers of synthetic milk formulas for babies."[13] The mother who accedes to a doctor's treatment plan by adding formula to the baby's diet or stopping breastfeeding altogether may escape censure for bottlefeeding, but will still be portrayed as the unthinking, passive recipient of pressure from the medical establishment intent on "medicalizing" infant feeding.

Recently, there has been new evidence that early intervention in the assessment and treatment of neonatal feeding problems does save lives. As the *Washington Post* reported on July 4, 1995, "neonatologists in Washington, Cincinnati, Providence, San Francisco, and other cities say they are treating newborns who have suffered permanent brain damage because they did not receive prompt treatment for jaundice, breastfeeding dehydration, or undetected bacterial infections. The director of the neonatal intensive care unit at Washington's Children's National Medical Center says that, in the past two years alone, she has treated four babies for kernicterus, a rare and preventable complication of jaundice that many doctors say they had not seen in 25 years."[14] Yet the woman who is home one or two days from the hospital and begins to notice that her baby is looking yellowish may look up jaundice in a breastfeeding guide or read La Leche League's pamphlet on the subject and get the message that there's no cause for alarm, and that she should go on breastfeeding as usual.[15] She may not seek a doctor's advice, or if she does, and is told to bring the baby back for phototherapy and supplement the baby's diet with extra fluids from a bottle, the breastfeeding literature that she has on hand may leave her reluctant to follow her doctor's advice.[16]

Even adoptive mothers are not wholly exempted from the pressure to nurse. La Leche League's *Womanly Art* tells adoptive mothers that they too can feed their babies from their breasts. There are two devices on the market, one called Lact-aid, the other the Medela Supplemental Nursing System (SNS), that adoptive mothers can buy to attempt to induce lactation without childbirth. Both devices require the mother to tape tubing to her nipples, which connects to a formula bottle that she wears around her neck. The adopted baby sucks from her nipple, receiving formula, and at the same time stimulating her own glands to begin milk production. In a few cases, a woman will build up a satisfactory milk supply after weeks or months of using the device, and can cease the use of formula. However, La Leche League's pamphlet, "Nursing Your Adopted Baby," includes this caution against expecting too much in the way of milk supply: "It is now known that the emphasis in adoptive nursing must be primarily on the nurturant aspects of mother's milk. The production of milk, if it happens, is a pleasant side effect of a happy nursing relationship. An induced supply may build very slowly or plateau very frequently. This often results in a baby who is well over six months old before the supply reaches a significant number of ounces per day."[17]

Mothers who used the SNS reported that it was time-consuming, and cumbersome, and that the lengthy set-up and cleaning time took away from their enjoyment of their babies. Some adoptive parents also find the promotion of adoptive nursing a troubling concept, containing the implication that the mothering is not "real" until the baby is nourished from the mother's body.

The mothers who come in for the sharpest rebukes are those who have made a judgment about the impact of breastfeeding on their quality of life and have chosen the bottle, not because nursing presents them with insuperable physical difficulties, but because of its emotional ramifications in their lives. In some cases the husband was upset at the idea of his wife exposing her breasts to nurse, or the woman herself felt too inhibited to take out her breast to feed her baby. Breastfeeding may be abandoned because the woman finds herself feeling too tied down or depressed while doing it, or because her baby seems miserable and unsatisfied while nursing. When one mother posted a message on an e-mail forum saying that she had ceased nursing because it had not turned out to be the happy, soothing experience she had imagined it would be, she was told her attitude was "disgusting" by one breastfeeding militant, and her reason dismissed as "trivial" by another.

One of the most commonly cited reasons for bottlefeeding is the inability of the mother to produce enough milk for the baby's needs. Women who have struggled with this problem may be interested in the research done by Dr. Marianne Neifert, director of the lactation program of Presbyterian-St. Luke's Medical Center in Denver; who has concluded that in most cases the cause is anatomical; the woman simply lacks sufficient glandular tissue for exclusive reliance on breastfeeding.[18] Most lactation consultants who have written on-line on this issue have hotly contesting such a conclusion, insisting instead that virtually all of the women who are low milk producers can build up sufficient levels if they would only follow three recommended steps. These are:

- Cease all other activities besides nursing. The mother should get into bed with the baby for between two to seven days, nursing every two hours around the clock.
- Use a breastpump when not offering the breast to keep stimulating more production.
- Use a supplemental nursing system, such as the Medela SNS or Lact-Aid, to allow the baby to receive formula, if necessary, while still stimulating the mother's glands to increase production.

Both the breastpump and the supplemental nurser require the mother to spend time before and after each nursing in set-up, cleaning, and sterilization of parts. Many low-milk-producing mothers conclude it's better for the baby to get the immediate benefits of formula than to force themselves to keep nursing under these difficult conditions. I also interviewed several women who followed each one of the recommendations and *still* were not producing enough milk for the baby's healthy development.

Why is it so hard for breastfeeding advocates to believe that there really are women with low milk production? Why should milk be different from any other bodily fluid? There are diabetics for whom the pancreas will not produce enough insulin; there are hemophiliacs whose blood doesn't produce sufficient clotting factor; there are those whose eyes don't produce enough tears, and women whose ovaries don't produce enough estrogen and whose wombs don't contain enough progesterone. For every other body part that manufactures something, we know there can be a hitch. Do breastfeeding advocates think the breast is the one body part that will always work perfectly? And if her breasts *don't* work perfectly to produce milk, isn't it better for the mother to have a substitute on hand, rather than go on trying to get her body to go on producing something it seems ill-equipped to do?

The widespread rejection by breastfeeding experts of low milk production as a justification for bottlefeeding lends credence to what one bottlefeeding mother concluded: "It doesn't really matter *what* reasons you give. There are some breastfeeding fanatics who will always tell you you're wrong. In the end, you just have to have confidence in your own knowledge of yourself and your child, and trust your own inner voice."

CHAPTER 2

The Overselling of the Breast

"Breastmilk is best for babies." These words are so widely accepted as true that even the makers of formula repeat them, right on every can. Just as we have looked critically at the widespread belief that every woman can breastfeed, it is time to take a closer look at the related view that every woman *should* breastfeed, because breastmilk is always better for babies than formula.

First, let us consider whose breastmilk. Not all mothers, as we have seen, are capable of producing a wholesome milk in sufficient supply. There are mothers with nutritional deficiencies whose milk is too low in calcium or fat or other essential ingredients. There are mothers whose milk has been exposed to toxic chemicals, transmissible viruses, or harmful medications. There are mothers who, no matter what steps they take to increase their output, still cannot seem to make enough milk to meet their babies' needs. Second, let us consider which babies. There are babies who can't latch on and suck effectively, jaundiced babies who need more overall volume of fluid than the mother can usually produce for a newborn, and low birthweight babies who need extra nutrients to reach a safe weight as rapidly as possible.

Taking these mothers and babies into account, the old dictum must have a few qualifications added to it, as follows: "Breast is best when the woman is producing unadulterated milk in sufficient quantity for an infant who is capable of latching on and sucking in a manner mutually satisfying to both baby and mother." For all others, formula seems to be an exceptionally good alternative.

Who am I to question this conviction that so many other mothers hold as indisputable? First (lest any reader be suspicious of my legitimacy), let me say who I am not: I am not in the pay of Ross Laboratories, the Nestle conglomerate, or any other producers of formula, nor am I in any way involved in its sale or distribution. I am not a man writing under a female pseudonym, nor am I the pawn of some male conspiracy. I am a writer and a mother of two, who, at the start of bottlefeeding my second child, needed to know if all those terrible things I heard about formula, and all those miraculous claims I heard about breastmilk, could possibly be true.

I began my own investigation, talking to other mothers and learning from their experiences. My method is admittedly not scientific but anecdotal; you the reader will form your own judgments about bottlefeeding based on your own experiences and by listening to what my respondents had to say. I make no pretense of having assembled a medically valid study.

I have collected all recent mass media reports on medical studies of children given breastmilk versus formula, but not being a scientist, I won't be discussing any particular study's data and methodology; what does interest me is how we mothers *react* to those studies—that is, how we come to believe this or that is indisputable, when it is based on something we may have heard on TV or read in the newspaper, or been told secondhand by another mother. I always asked my interviewees to talk about what they *believed* to be true about formula or breastmilk, based on the coverage of the subject in the mass media.

Everybody cites some sort of study to back up her own views. At times I've felt tempted to break into a modified version of that old refrain from Porgy and Bess: "Studies, studies, all God's chill'n got studies."

I may not be a medical expert, but in college I did learn a few things about studies. Most important is that a retrospective study is by and large worthless. A retrospective study is one that starts with a given population—let us say a thousand obese men—and then looks into their pasts to identify the common element that may be responsible for their present condition. Now suppose it turned out that 91 percent of the obese men had been bottlefed as babies. The implication is, of course, that bottlefeeding in infancy strongly predisposes a boy to obesity later in life.

The misleading nature of the retrospective approach becomes clear, however, when you start with two groups of babies, a breastfed group and a bottlefed group, and work forward. The researchers will need to follow both groups throughout their lives to record how many go on to become obese adults.

To reproduce meaningful results a study must be more than just forward-looking rather than retrospective. The study must be set up so that the effects of all significant factors (called variables) other than the one under research (breastmilk versus formula) can be controlled. The problem is that the scope of any study undertaken of a population from infancy to adulthood is so great that the number of variables is unmanageable. Researchers could never be certain whether any individual man's weight gain was due to use of formula or to any of hundreds of other factors in his upbringing, such as parental eating habits, household income level, sleep patterns, amount of exercise, or due to predetermined factors such as genetic makeup (to name just five examples).

Even those studies that seek to control for the most significant variables in the children's lives are suspect, because of differences in the lives of the mothers of breastfed versus bottlefed children that skew a study's findings from the outset. I found, for example, that mothers who were able to breastfeed easily and happily were, generally speaking, women who were in good overall health, who had enjoyed healthy pregnancies. Their deliveries were less likely to be complicated by drugs or surgery. Among my interviewees, those women who were satisfied breastfeeders were usually more health-conscious in other ways, too, and had generally taken good care of themselves, being careful to eat right, get sufficient exercise, and avoid tobacco and alcohol while pregnant. Given these predispositions, it follows naturally that their babies were more likely to be born in good health; this good start may be the foundation for better health throughout life.

So the next time you hear about a study showing breastmilk *causes* this or *prevents* that, consider it with a healthy dose of skepticism. If studies don't necessarily have the answers, who does? The new mother herself, relying on her own common sense and knowledge of her baby . . . and if she's too inexperienced and unsure of herself to go by these alone, then she may rely on the advice of medical experts who are familiar with *her individual situation, her child, her needs.* An inexperienced new mother should never go by what she's told by someone she's never met (who may be advising her over the telephone or posting messages on a computer forum) or what she reads in a book (including this one!).

I don't mean to dissuade any reader of this book from breastfeeding when her own inclinations tell her she can, and her doctor finds no medical reason for her not to try.

It is my intention to reassure the formula-using woman that she is not consigning her child to a lifetime of ear infections, allergies, lower IQ, or behavioral problems— despite what she may have heard on TV or from her next door neighbor, who read about a study in some magazine. It is also my intention to reassure the mother whose baby *does* happen to suffer from colic, or asthma, or diarrhea, that it is far from proven (or even provable) that formula causes any of these ills. Remember that breastfed babies get sick sometimes, too. *There is nothing to feel guilty about.*

Judging from what some of my interviewees were told by friends and advisors about breastfeeding as well as from what I noted in breastfeeding discussions that took place on-line, there are many in the breastfeeding movement making excessive claims for the benefits of breastmilk. I have compiled the following list of claims made based on these sources, as well as breastfeeding guides, magazines, newsletters, and other media reports.

What Breastfeeding Advocates Claim

Breastfed babies . . .

- will be protected against diseases such as chickenpox, measles, mumps, rubella, etc., because the mother's immunities are passed on to the baby in her breastmilk.
- will be far less likely than formula-fed babies to suffer from colds, flus, ear infections, and intestinal illnesses. When they *do* get such illnesses, the duration and severity of the illness will be less than that experienced by bottlefed babies.
- will be far less likely to have allergies.
- are less likely to have diarrhea.
- are more likely to have good self-esteem later in life.
- tend to have higher IQs.
- are less likely to have tantrums or become problem kids at school.

- are far less likely to have asthma.
- are less likely to fall victim to SIDS (sudden infant death syndrome).
- are less likely to become diabetic.
- are less likely to suffer from various geriatric disabilities, such as osteoporosis.

And they say that mothers who breastfeed their babies . . .

- will "bond" better with their babies because of the influence of certain hormones released during lactation that foster "love and attachment."
- are less likely to develop breast cancer later in life.
- can count on the contraceptive effect of lactation instead of using artificial birth control.
- will save money.
- will find breastfeeding far more convenient than bottlefeeding.

Breastfeeding Mothers Talk About Why They Believe "Breast Is Best"

All quotes were taken from messages publicly posted on e-mail forums.

Recent studies have shown that breastfed babies are smarter, have increased immunities, and that mom's milk responds to each illness, giving the baby 24 hours to help fight it off.

—Kara, who breastfed her son 2½ years

There is a significant IQ difference between children who had been fed human milk and those who had

not. We *know* that there is a connection between diabetes and cow's milk. We *know* the long- and short-
term costs of otitis media [ear infections] and that
there are some lymphomas connected with the lack of
human milk.

—*Pauline*

There are many health benefits. . . . fewer speech
problems resulting from better jaw and muscle development, fewer ear infections, intestinal problems . . . a
more secure child, fewer temper tantrums, etc.

—*Leila*

It has also been shown that with the extra holding
that breastfed babies usually experience over bottlefed
babies, along with the likelihood of having fewer caregivers in the early months, such babies tend to develop
a greater trust, which grows into a heightened self-
esteem and ability to love and be loved. . . . There is
now a suggestion from research that breastfeeding
also has health benefits for the mother, and the fact
that she has breastfed her babies can protect her in
later life from ovarian cancer, breast cancer, and osteoporosis.

—*Gwen*

There's a study that's been done repeatedly that
proves that if you breastfeed for a certain length of
time, your child will gain IQ points. It's been shown
that children [who were breastfed] have fewer problems at school, and they are something like ten times
less likely to go to prison [as adults] than children who
were bottlefed.

—*Danielle*

It isn't possible in a book of this sort to analyze in depth each of the commonly believed claims for breastmilk to determine which are based on flawed studies, which are partly true, which are wholly myth. Discussion here must be limited, intended merely to stimulate your own further investigations. For each of the items that follow, let me just suggest some questions to start you looking skeptically at the claims.

Questioning the Claims

Immunities   This is without doubt the most widely believed of the claims I noted for breastmilk. Most mothers I talked to believed that breastfeeding somehow magically protects babies from virtually all diseases prior to their being vaccinated. But what about the mother who never had chicken pox or rubella, or never was vaccinated herself? What if her own immune system has been compromised by poor nutrition, chronic illness, or some environmental contaminant? Breastfeeding advocates imply that the benefit to the breastfed baby's immune system is lifelong, leading at least a few breastfeeding mothers to conclude that an early vaccination schedule is unimportant. (Some on the fringes of the breastfeeding movement are opposed to vaccination altogether; more on this in chapter 3.) Babies brought up in areas where vaccination levels are near 100 percent are at low risk for exposure to disease, so the bottlefeeding mother need not fear that her as-yet-unvaccinated infant is at a greater risk of these diseases than if she had breastfed.

Colds, flus, infections, and gastrointestinal illnesses   No study can adequately control for all the factors that contribute to susceptibility to colds. My own survey of mothers of both breastfed and bottlefed children has led me to the following statistical interpretation (though I won't pretend that my polling "proves" anything): that all small children, no matter how they are fed, who are kept at home and out of playgroups, who have no older siblings in school or daycare centers, will have few or no colds, flus, or ear infections. But put a child, whether breast- or bottlefed, in close contact with groups of children every day, or even just a few times a week, even if they're all breastfed, and that child *will* get sick!

Parents who work as teachers or in enclosed settings with a fair amount of hand contact are more likely to pass on germs that lead to frequent illnesses in their small children (even if they themselves seldom come down with anything). With bottlefeeding parents who answered "yes" to my question about frequent illnesses, I made a point to find out what kind of work they did, and how much contact their babies had with other children. In all cases, the frequently ill child was exposed to multiple sources of germs. Mothers who had breastfed one child but bottlefed another reinforced this view of risk of infection; the subsequent child (whether it was breastfed or not) reported more colds during infancy, due to an older sibling who brought germs home from school.

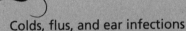

Colds, flus, and ear infections

Thinking back on the breastfed babies you've known, how did your bottlefed baby's overall health seem by comparison?

In our case, Hilary was not sick until well after her first birthday, and has had two colds in her entire life (knock on wood!). We've had no trips to the doctor aside from regular check-ups . . . On the other hand, I know mothers who breastfeed and their children are in the doctor's office at least once a month. These are just my experiences and I certainly don't mean to make a general assumption.

—*Eileen*

My second child, the breastfed one, had more colds and ear infections than my bottlefed one—but then there was an older child bringing home germs.

—*Jill*

My first baby [the bottlefed one] had *many* more ear infections and colds than my second one [the breastfed one—but that could have been because my first baby was in daycare. For my second one I stayed at home.

—*Carla*

There were also these two notes on an e-mail forum on children's health issues:

I thought they said that breastfed infants are usually better off than formula-fed infants in fending off colds. My baby is almost four months old, exclusively breastfed . . . . So far she has had one ear infection and two colds, one that gave her congestion and a slight cough and the other a runny nose and congestion. I am a bit surprised that she's been sick so much at this tender age. I'm still on maternity leave, so she's not in a daycare situation.

—*Janine*

My first son [exclusively breastfed] seemed to get a lot of colds, and they would linger into long-term runny noses that drove me up the wall. Later, he developed croup, triggered by colds and allergies, which eventually became asthma . . . .

—*Lori*

Allergies *Mothers Talk* stories in chapter 1 told how some breastfed babies reacted to substances received through their mothers' milk. Bottlefeeding mothers do not have to worry about baby's possible allergies to anything in her diet. I did come across one study that concluded that breastfeeding did *not* reduce the incidence of allergic eczema outbreaks before the age of one.[1]

Diarrhea A report in the *New York Times* confirmed that diarrhea is more prevalent among bottlefed infants but explained that this was due to the presence of lactic acid-producing bacteria in mother's milk. When formula was prepared with the addition of a powdered form of the same bacteria (available at drugstores over-the-counter under the brand name Lactinex™), the bottlefed babies had similarly low rates of diarrhea as the breastfed infants.[2]

Self-esteem Self-esteem is a psychological component of the personality, which, like most elements of a person's character, cannot easily be ascribed to any fixed source or even combination of sources. Certainly, having stable, loving parents who encourage their children's best efforts is important to the development of self-esteem. So is the outside environment; that is, children who live in neighborhoods and attend schools where expectations and achievement levels are high will be more likely to think of them-

---

Allergies

I've nursed my daughter now for two years, and am in no rush to stop. . . . She's got a severe dairy allergy and even small amounts of milk proteins in my diet will affect her.

—*Lena*

selves as smart, as having a good future, as worthy of love and respect, etc., compared to children who live in neighborhoods and attend schools where expectations and achievement levels are low. Among the poorest and least educated segment of our society, only about 9 percent of mothers nurse their babies.[3] Among middle- and upper-income women the percentage who nurse, at least initially, is estimated at 75 percent.[4] So if researchers have found a high degree of correlation between being breastfed and having high self-esteem, it is may be attributable to the fact that high self-esteem children were probably brought up in higher income, better-educated households than their poorer, bottlefed counterparts.

IQs The same explanation for a finding of better self-esteem in breastfed children would apply to a finding of higher IQ. Higher IQs are more likely to be found among the better educated and higher income families. Of course, whether IQ itself is a measure of anything beyond the ability to do well on an IQ test is a topic of heated debate among social scientists. Another possible explanation is that breastfeeding mothers are more likely to stay at home with their children during the preschool years,[5] and thus may be providing their children with a more stimulating and individually tailored learning environment than children who are left at an early age with poorly educated sitters or at crowded daycare centers.

Tantrums or behavioral problems If one accepts the claim that breastfed children are less likely to have tantrums or behavioral problems (and I am not saying you should), then parental income levels may again serve to explain the variation. Lower income children, who are more likely to be bottlefed, are apt to be dismissed as problem kids when they misbehave, while their higher income counterparts are more likely to have parents take them in for a professional evaluation, resulting in the diagnosis of a specific, treatable disorder (such as dyslexia, attention deficit disorder, or a hearing or visual impairment).

Asthma   This disease is on the rise in the industrialized world, and has been rising throughout the 1980s when breastfeeding rates were rising to their peak of 62 percent overall in 1982.[6] Doctors have identified parental smoking as the number one factor contributing to the rise, and though smoking has declined in the population at large, it has in fact gone up among teenage girls, too many of whom are also mothers of young children (and the majority of teen mothers are bottlefeeders). Other environmental factors accounting for the rise in asthma include air pollution, certain chemical additives in foods, lawn care products (herbicides and pesticides), and poor air circulation in overly insulated homes and schools. To these facts I add my own anecdotal experience: the three children I have known with asthma severe enough to require hospitalization were all breastfed for more than nine months, one of them beyond age two.

SIDS   The central problem of SIDS is that its cause is unknown. SIDS is a catch-all term used in cases involving an infant before its first birthday whose death cannot be ascribed to any other cause. Certain similarities have been identified among SIDS victims: the mothers were more likely to be smokers; the babies were more often put to sleep on their stomachs than on their sides or backs; they are more likely to be low birthweight babies or failure-to-thrive babies; the parents are more likely to be low income or poorly educated. Which if any of these is truly a significant risk factor for SIDS? An honest pediatrician would admit that we simply do not know.

Diabetes   The discovery of a component of cow's milk said to have a tendency to disturb pancreatic function (the production of insulin) in children with an inborn sensitivity to it has led some people to conclude that breastfed babies are less likely to develop diabetes.[7] To become diabetic, one must have an inherited predisposition to it resulting from what geneticists are now able to identify as a diabetic cluster of genes. If it is true that cow's milk can contribute to the development of the condition, then the formula-feeding mother who knows of a family history of diabetes can choose a soy-based formula to reduce her baby's degree of risk.[8]

Geriatric disabilities   Though it may seem impossible for any valid study to be designed to account properly for all the influences on a person's health from infancy to old age, there are researchers who claim to have shown a causal connection between breastfeeding and certain geriatric problems—for example, osteoporosis. The only trouble is that different teams of researchers have reached opposite conclusions. On the one hand, La Leche League cites a study claiming that "breastfeeding provides maternal protection against osteoporosis and hip fractures later in life,"[9] while another study, reported in *Science* News, found that "women who nurse their infants for six months or more lose a significant amount of the mineral calcium from their bones," and concluded that "women who bottlefed their infants for less than a month showed no such [bone density] loss."[10] The study was controlled for differences in age, diet, and level of physical activity; however, "most of the women in the extended lactation group [that is, those who had nursed for six months or more] had consumed large amounts of dietary or supplemental calcium." In other words, it didn't help to eat right or take calcium pills; long-term nursing still left women with significantly reduced bone densities.

Bonding   Much is made in the breastfeeding literature of the release of the hormone oxytocin during nursing. Often called the "love hormone" in breastfeeding books, oxytocin is supposed to have an almost magical effect on the mother, relaxing her, and flooding her with feelings of joy and attachment to her child. This notion presupposes that the female biological parent (the only one who can nurse) is able to love her child in a way that no father and no adoptive mother can match because of this hormonal release. This assumption insults the parenting abilities of fathers, adoptive mothers, and other women who can't nurse, and implies that the love of children is an inherently female trait. Flowing out of this hormonally based understanding of love comes the idea that the woman who works outside the home instead of staying with the baby must somehow be denying her own female nature, and at the same time, shortchanging her child. (In chapter 3 I discuss in greater detail what I see as the strong anti-working mother theme that runs through much of the breastfeeding literature.)

The idea that bonding is correlated to breastfeeding overlooks history: if it were true, mothers in the pre-industrial age who breastfed would have been better, more loving mothers than the (largely bottlefeeding) mothers of our own era. How then to account for high rates of infant abandonment, virtually universal use of corporal punishment (even on the very young), and other hardly child-friendly but commonplace practices of the pre-modern, pre-bottlefeeding era?[11]

Speaking for myself, I am no less deeply "bonded" to my bottlefed daughter than to my breastfed one, nor did the way I nourished each have anything to do with my love and attachment to them both. Were the mothers of the 1950s, that great bottlefed baby boom bulge, less loving, less attached to their children than the mothers of the past?

Of the mothers I interviewed who had both bottlefed and breastfed children, not one said she felt a greater attachment to the breastfed baby; if anything, the mother who realized she would not be able to feed her baby at her breast made an extra effort to cuddle and hold her baby, during feedings and at other times, too. My respondents also mentioned the ability of the father of the bottlefed

Bonding

I feel more "bonded" to my third child, who was bottlefed from day one. I think I could not become emotionally bonded to my first two quite as quickly, because they represented an emotional drain to me [due to constant pain, exhaustion and milk supply problems with the first two babies].

—Pam

Bonding does not occur only at feeding times—it's a lifelong process. It is physically impossible to do *everything* right as a parent. You do the best you can, better in some areas than in others, and you let your children know they are loved. Pressure on mothers to breast-feed only leads to guilt and anxiety, and that can be far worse for the baby than a bottle. . . . I doubted my abilities as a mother [for not being able to breastfeed, but] as I watched my son grow, I realized that the feeding method did not matter. He is healthy, very happy, and in our opinion, the most wonderful baby. We have bonded. Being rested and healthy has allowed me to bond with him more than breastfeed-ing ever could have done.

—Kate

baby to develop a deep feeling of connectedness to his child through the act of feeding.

Breast cancer   The study that appears to substantiate the claim that breastfeeding protects against breast cancer con-cluded that the protection was greatest for the woman who began breastfeeding while in her teens and continued for at least six months. The study found *no* evidence that breast-feeding reduces the risk of the disease occurring after menopause, though it noted that pre-menopausal breast cancer is relatively rare.[11] For women who began nursing in their twenties or later, or women who nursed less than six months, the reduction of pre-menopausal breast cancer risk was characterized as "small."

Most women will find the social disadvantages of teen-age motherhood and long-term nursing to outweigh by far the reduction in the already minor risk of pre-menopausal breast cancer. Far more significant than breastfeeding history appear to be such factors as history of breast cancer among maternal relatives, age of first childbearing, smoking, percentage of fat in the woman's diet, and exposure to environmental carcinogens. Because over 75 percent of breast cancers appear in post-menopausal women, and quite often among those with no strong identifiable predisposition to the disease, the prudent woman is best advised not to rely on breastfeeding as protection, but is urged to practice monthly self-examinations for lumps, and if over age 50, have a mammogram once a year.

If a woman assumes that breastfeeding will keep her at low risk for breast cancer throughout her life and on that basis decides to forgo self-examination and mammograms,

Breast cancer

I've found that nursing makes breast self-examination more difficult. Lactating breasts are firmer and have more lumps and bumps than non-lactating breasts. Mammograms are also pretty useless on lactating breasts—they're too dense.

—Amy's answer to an on-line survey about the advantages and disadvantages of breastfeeding

she will, in fact, greatly *increase* her risk of dying from the disease.

Contraceptive effects   There is no doubt that lactation acts in many women to suppress ovulation and prevent conception. But that by no means guarantees any *individual* woman freedom from worry about unwanted pregnancy. Because a woman will ovulate about two weeks prior to the resumption of her period, the absence of menses cannot be taken as assurance against conception. Only the woman who has been trained to recognize the signs of returning fertility* can feel confident about reliance on breastfeeding for its contraceptive effect.

The contraceptive effect is unlikely to persist much beyond nine months in any event; as the baby relies more upon solid food and less upon breastmilk as its nutritional mainstay, the mother's lactation hormones decline and her fertility is likely to return.[12] There are, of course, cases of

---

Contraceptive effects

You *can* ovulate while you're nursing. Each woman is different. I must have ovulated about five and a half months after my oldest was born, because I got pregnant while I was still nursing, before my periods started again.

—Elaine

Personally, I have become pregnant three times while nursing.

—Libby

---

*These include: keeping and correctly interpreting a basal body temperature chart and examining her cervical mucus daily to detect the clear, copious mucus that is ideal for the transport of sperm.

women who breastfed exclusively and yet became pregnant again within just a few months of birth.

Costs   There are women who will find the cost of formula burdensome and would certainly save money if they were able to breastfeed exclusively for an extended time. But for those women who need to rent a hospital quality breast-pump, and buy nursing bras in hard-to-find sizes, and supplement their own diets with minerals and extra calories, and especially for those women who need the services of a certified lactation consultant to be able to continue, breast-feeding will not result in significant savings. For the woman who needs to gives up her job to maintain the nursing relationship, breastfeeding can even be the more costly choice.

Because of widely available sources of savings on formula (coupons, price clubs, hospital giveaways—see Resource Guide), the cost of buying formula can be substantially decreased. Low-income women can qualify for federal subsidies for their formula purchases through the Women, Infants, and Children (WIC) program. However, the program is periodically in danger of elimination due to attacks by breastfeeding lobbyists who charge that the subsidies undercut breastfeeding progress among the poor to the

Cost

I breastfed my first child successfully, but I was a stay-at-home mom then. This time we really need the income, so I need to be able to leave my daughter with someone. I was leaving her with bottles of expressed milk for a while, but I was starting to feel like my breasts were constantly out. For me to have enough time to enjoy my job and my family, it makes sense to use formula.

—Jean

profit of the big formula companies. As of this writing, the WIC program is scheduled for the budget-cutter's axe.

Convenience   If breastfeeding were truly more convenient, why don't most women who start off breastfeeding continue the practice beyond the first three months? In fact fewer than half (43 percent)[13] of new mothers keep it up longer than that. The many inconveniences, and the recognition that the baby has already absorbed the main health benefits from breastmilk, are the reasons cited by most mothers for the switch to formula. Breastfeeding *does* tie the mother down, does dictate that she spend most of her day with her child (and often, most of the night) or spend a significant portion of her day using a breastpump. For the mother with few competing obligations in her life, the in-

Convenience

There are a lot of good reasons to breastfeed, but I'm tired of hearing how convenient it is, how the milk is always there, how hard it is to sterilize bottles and carry the stuff around, etc. I've done both, and I can tell you, for me bottlefeeding was definitely easier! My doctor said that these days with safe tap water, there's no need to sterilize each time—just clean the bottles in the dishwasher. It's no trouble at all to carry an empty bottle in the diaper bag. Just add some powdered formula and find a water fountain. Prepared bottles can be kept cool in one of those little thermal totes. When I was breastfeeding my first child, if I was stuck in the check-out line at the grocery store and my child was screaming from hunger, I couldn't do anything. With my second child, I whip out a bottle, and voila!

—*Hannah*

convenience may well be outweighed by the rewards. For the mother whose work environment is not conducive to breastfeeding, the inconvenience can rise to the level of impossibility.

I often heard the word freedom used by mothers who have weaned. Some women may find the preparation and storage of formula inconvenient, but from the stories my respondents have told me, I'd say bottlefeeding wins the convenience round with points to spare. Imagine that you are standing in an hour-and-a-half-long line to renew your driver's license (I have chosen this example because I was in this situation myself when my bottlefed daughter was just a month old). Now ask yourself which baby would be more likely to be content while waiting with mommy in a dingy, benchless, municipal hallway: the one with the bottle, or the one whose milk supply is stuck inside her mother's unavailable breasts?

The "Worldwide Average"

One "fact" was repeated frequently by breastfeeding advocates on-line: that the worldwide average age of weaning is 4.2 years (sometimes cited as 4.3 or 4.5 years). In the three-month period between October and December, 1994, I collected sixteen messages from e-mail writers on four different networks citing this average. Why such emphasis on this number? Breastfeeding advocates use it to assure themselves that there is nothing unusual or questionable about keeping a child on the breast past infancy, or even past toddlerhood. If nursing mothers from all around the world keep up the practice long term, these women conclude that there must be much value in it for both mother and child. That late weaning is the norm mainly in the unindustrialized and tribal parts of the globe underscores for them the naturalness of the practice—that is, where women's lives are "unpolluted" by mainly male-invented technologies, women appear to have little trouble with breastfeeding,

Mothers Talk About the Worldwide Average Age of Weaning

As reported on various e-mail bulletin boards:

Many 21-month-old children nurse. It is usually a healthy dependency. The worldwide average age for weaning is 4.2 years.

—*Leila*

The average worldwide age for weaning is 4.2 years, and our previous surgeon general [C. Everett Koop] commented, "Lucky is the child who is nursed until he is at least two." There is research to show that nursing toddlers still gain health benefits, as well as the obvious emotional benefits. They are supposed to have fewer tantrums, and that's a good enough reason for me.

—*Lois*

Worldwide, the mean age for termination of nursing is something like 4.5 years. That's much longer than what we see here in the USA, so there's lots of pressure to quit early, but we believe that our daughter should nurse until she just stops more or less by herself.

—*Rachel*

Well, this isn't going to be hard data, because I can't find the original article, but . . . the article reported that children in the Punjab region of India nursed until age 9 and that children in parts of China nursed until age 7. Another source reported that children in Malaysia often nurse until age 8.

—*Daisy*

and they enjoy it enough to keep at it for more than four years per child.

What's the Truth?

Is there in fact a whit of truth to these claims? This question was posed over the Internet on a forum called Misc.kids, and answered by a graduate student named Laura Marple, who unearthed from a medical library two studies, each finding a much lower, much more believable average to exist in the unindustrialized world.

The first study is part of a 1985 report by the Population Division of the Department of International Economic and Social Affairs of the United Nations Secretariat:

Worldwide Average Age for Weaning

Area/Duration	3 months	6 months	12 months	18 months	24 months
Africa	94%	90%	79%	53%	24%
South/Central America	71	56	37	19	5
Asia and Oceania	85	77	63	48	28

And from a 1981 study titled "Breastfeeding in the Developing World: Current Patterns and Implications for Future Trends" included in "Reports of the World Fertility Survey" by Mary Mederios Kent:

Median Months of Breastfeeding:

Less than 10 months:	Colombia, Dominican Republic, Guyana, Jamaica, Malaysia, Costa Rica, Panama
10 to 20 months:	Kenya, Jordan, Pakistan, Rep. of Korea, Mexico, Peru, Philippines, Sri Lanka, Thailand
21 or more months:	Bangladesh, Indonesia, Nepal

Africa, Bangladesh, and Indonesia are the areas in which breastfeeding is most likely to continue past the first birthday, and it is in those parts of the world that infant death rates are highest. It would be a misreading of statistics to infer that breastfeeding in itself poses any risk for infants in these extremely poor parts of the world; yet it seems evident that these children are not being saved either just because they're getting lots of breastmilk; there is no substitute for vaccination, good sanitation, adequate housing, and maternal nutrition, when it comes to safeguarding children's health.

The Demonization of Formula

Breastfeeding militants like to praise the wonders of breastmilk—that is to be expected. But beyond that, they also point out the dangers (in their view) to which "innocent victims" (babies) are exposed to when fed formula. Following is just a sampling of the worst of the anti-formula remarks I found on various e-mail forums.

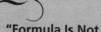

"Formula Is Not Evil, But. . ."

Breastfeeding Militants Talk about Formula

I think people react . . . in defense of formula because they don't want to admit to themselves that feeding a child formula is detrimental to the health of that child. There is no reason to formula-feed a child, unless there are extreme circumstances involved. Why don't doctors take a more honest approach and say, "Your child will not be as healthy if you decide to formula feed." That is the truth, so why not tell the truth?

—*Dave*

Giving one bottle of formula a day, or [one bottle] a night, *can* cause harm, especially if there are cow's milk sensitivities, or if there is a supply problem. If there wasn't a supply problem, one bottle a day can create one.

—Rosemary

In twenty, fifty, one hundred years, someday we will begin to understand the damage we have done and are doing to our children by considering formula "safe and nutritionally sound."

—Chris

Infant formula has been well proven to be of detriment to infant health. Let us use the *Lancet* article about the brain development of preemies as a starting point. . . . The conclusion was that breastmilk promotes proper brain development—optimum development. You can look at it that way, or that formula causes subtle brain damage. Then there are the well-known auto-immune diseases, Crohn's disease, and colitis. The link between formula in infancy and the predisposition to these diseases has been proven as well. Juvenile-onset diabetes is another disease that is proven to be associated with cow's milk. . . . You might think that breastfeeding prevents auto-immune diseases; I wonder if formula isn't a causative factor.

—Anita, who a few days later posted the message
below, as well:

Formula is not evil, but the companies who sell it are not acting in the best interests of their customers by their marketing practices. In many ways some of us feel they are more reprehensible than the tobacco companies, foisting their products on tiny babies who cannot make a choice.

The Anti-formula Movement

The anti-formula mindset is part of a total ideology of parenting (described in more detail in chapter 3) that refuses to acknowledge any data assembled on the safe use of formula, even though an entire generation of formula-fed babies has grown up to be the healthiest, longest-lived Americans thus far. To those whose belief in breastfeeding is an article of faith, no evidence can be admitted that appears to contradict their fundamental judgment that using formula is wrong.

Wherever there has existed a movement in possession of a basic "truth" about life, there has been the urge of those in the movement to organize and proselytize, so that their views and practices will become widely accepted. The breastfeeding movement's leaders have been vigorous and effective activists for their point of view. They have not restricted themselves to the worldwide task (itself an enormous undertaking) of educating parents to the advantages of breastfeeding; another priority has been to restrict governments and private industry in the distribution of formula, and to eliminate, or at the very least, restrict, advertising for the product.

The anti-formula movement has established itself in three different arenas, whose short-cut identifying labels are:

1. the Nestle boycott;
2. the WHO Code;
3. the American Academy of Pediatrics voluntary formula ad-ban.

The Nestle boycott　Throughout the sixties and seventies formula companies were worried. Nineteen sixty-four was the last great baby-boom year; after that came the "baby bust," and where would new consumers of formula be found? The answer seemed to be in the largely unexplored markets of the underdeveloped world, where contraception was all but unknown. In these years billboards showing chubby-cheeked babies drinking from bottles began showing up where no advertisements had gone before: along rutted jungle roads, rising above tin-roofed shantytowns, and outside makeshift clinics and overcrowded maternity wards in the burgeoning capitals of many Third World countries. Sales representatives, often dressed in white coats or in nurses' uniforms, were sent to hospitals to dispense free samples of formula to new mothers.

Among the poorest countries of the world breastfeeding rates dropped and formula use went from nearly zero to a noticeable percentage—but as usage rates rose, so did infant death and disease caused by improper preparation. Babies who were well fed from sterilized bottles in the hospitals all too often would be taken home to tin shacks or mud huts without a clean supply of water. When the mothers used water from their neighborhood pump or well to mix the formula, they contaminated the bottles with bacteria that may be tolerated by the adult's mature immune system but can be deadly to the infant's system.

If the infant did not succumb to bacterial diarrhea, it might be equally at risk of malnutrition. Formula is expensive, and once the mother's free supply ran out, she might be tempted to try to make her purchases of formula last longer by over-diluting them with water. An infant continually fed a thinner formula will not be getting sufficient nutrients, and will be left vulnerable to any number of nutrition-related diseases, such as rickets, anemia, and kwashiorkor. Moreover, the infant will not have the benefit of any of the mother's antibodies through breastmilk—antibodies that would have helped ward off the ill effects of the bacteria and viruses normally present in countries without safe drinking water. Should the mother realize that her baby is suffering through lack of breastfeeding, it would be too late for her to attempt to build up her own milk supply; once the baby has gotten used to the easy flow of liquid from an artificial nipple, it usually can't or won't adapt to the different sucking motions needed to draw milk from its mother's nipples; and in any case, her milk supply would most likely have dried up already.

Problems of formula misuse became so prevalent in Third World countries that by 1976 the World Health Organization (WHO) had taken to grouping together all formula-related illnesses under the term "baby-bottle disease" and estimated that deaths from such illnesses exceeded one million a year.[14] Something needed to be done.

In 1977 an organization called the Infant Feeding Action Coalition (INFACT) was formed to respond to the infant mortality crisis in the Third World. INFACT quickly set on a strategy, announcing a boycott against the largest manufacturer of formula in the world, the Swiss-based Nestle Company, which controlled up to 50 percent of the global formula market. Activists lobbied quickly and effectively through ties to consumer groups, church groups, and political organizations to spread the word that no one should purchase any Nestle products, until Nestle agreed to change its infant formula marketing tactics. Just a year later, students were successfully persuading their school cafeterias not to stock Nestle chocolate milk, and leafletters could be found outside grocery stores from coast to coast handing out flyers showing a skull and crossbones made of baby-bottles over the legend: "Nestle Kills Babies."

Seven years of a worldwide boycott are estimated to have cost the Nestle company a billion dollars in sales. Not only did the organization succeed in forcing Nestle to change its marketing practices in the Third World, but INFACT can also claim a large share of the credit for helping the medical profession in affluent countries to support rather than discourage breastfeeding, leading to a substantial leap in breastfeeding rates in Europe and America. As breastfeeding became more popular among well-educated

women and medical professionals, it became easier still for
activists to raise money and intensify and expand the campaign against formula.

The WHO Code   After half a decade of pressing their
case, INFACT and other anti-formula lobbyists won their
greatest victory in the promulgation by the World Health
Organization of a comprehensive set of regulations for the
marketing of formula in all countries signatory to the
agreement. Formally known as the Code of Marketing
Breastfeeding Substitutes, the WHO Code, as it is more
commonly called, requires adherence to ten restrictions, the
most important of which are:

- no advertising to the general public of any formula
  products;
- all formula products must carry a statement in support of breastfeeding as the preferred choice in infant
  nutrition;
- no formula giveaways to new mothers;
- no formula giveaways to healthcare professionals.

Most American hospitals still supply formula gift-bas-
kets to new mothers because the United States refused to
sign the WHO Code. Nor has this country signed any of
the revisions to the WHO Code adopted in subsequent
years. In May of 1994 WHO came out with an even
tighter set of regulations known as the Baby Friendly Hospital Initiative, that directs all maternity hospitals and birth
centers in signatory nations to encourage breastfeeding
within an hour of each baby's birth and to further restrict
the free distribution of formula to new mothers. Again, the
United States refused to sign, and while hundreds of hospitals around the world have been designated Baby Friendly
by WHO, as of the start of 1995, not a single hospital in
the United States has been so labeled.

Breastfeeding activists in this country generally lay the blame for this situation on the uncentralized and largely for-profit healthcare system that often leaves hospitals dependent on gifts from corporate sponsors. Look in the maternity wing of almost any new hospital and you may see a plaque thanking a formula company for its generosity. You will almost certainly see the major formula makers' names on any listing of corporate givers. If American hospital administrators fought hard to keep the U.S. from signing the WHO Code, breastfeeding activists charge, it was due to an understanding of what was the *quid* that was owed *pro quo*.

The failure to get the U.S. to adhere to the WHO Code was a setback for breastfeeding advocates; but that is not to say that the U.S. remained immune to other aspects of the anti-formula movement. Most of the rules of the WHO Code are being observed, not through the mechanism of government regulation, but as a result of a voluntary agreement between the American Academy of Pediatrics (AAP) and two of the major formula manufacturers. However, the ad-ban has not had the intended pro-breastfeeding effect that its supporters had supposed would result.

The AAP voluntary formula ad-ban   According to officials of the AAP, the organization historically has supported breastfeeding.[15] Once the WHO Code was set forth, the AAP endorsed the principles on which it was based, and in 1982 adopted its own position opposed to formula advertising aimed at the general public. However, it did not object to advertising aimed at medical professionals. Two of the largest domestic manufacturers of formula, Abbott Laboratories and Bristol-Myers (which, together, control 80 percent of the U.S. market), apparently concluded that it would be better for their companies' public image to abide by the AAP rules. Following the agreement, all advertising on television or in general interest magazines or newspapers for the two largest brands, Similac and Enfamil, was ended; the two formula giants also put pro-breastfeeding statements on every can of formula they turned out. In addition, the formula-makers contributed more than 8.3 million dollars to the AAP, including $1.3 million designated for the construction of its new head-quarters building in Elk Grove, Illinois. Indirect support for the AAP amounted to millions more in the form of paid advertising in AAP journals and other publications.

In return, the AAP discouraged its member doctors and hospitals from allowing giveaways to patients of other brands—or so it was alleged in an anti-trust lawsuit filed against the AAP, Abbott Laboratories, and Bristol-Myers by the maker of a competing formula, Carnation (Nestle's U.S. subsidiary), which was not a party to the ad-ban agreement.

In its court filings Carnation has argued that the ad-ban has worked in restraint of trade, by inhibiting the free choice of consumers. In addition, consumers were harmed by the higher prices of the brands promoted through doc-tors' office and hospital giveaways, while the price of brands produced by Carnation and other manufacturers who broke the ad-ban was on average 15 to 25 percent less.

In a planned counterattack against Carnation, the AAP hoped to show that by advertising to the general public, Carnation was undermining the purpose of the AAP's agreement, which was to promote breastfeeding. However, the study that the AAP commissioned to establish proof of the link between advertising and the woman's decision to breastfeed reached quite a different conclusion, that there exists "no hard evidence to support the claim that direct marketing will reduce breastfeeding."[16]

In its defense the AAP has responded that there is simply not enough formula advertising for an accurate assessment of its impact on consumer choices. The AAP has also denied ordering member physicians to discourage patients from purchasing any particular brands, but has simply reit-erated its support of the voluntary ad-ban.

While the AAP and its adversary formula makers continue to wrangle over the advertising issue, and while INFACT and other breastfeeding advocacy groups issue renewed calls for a boycott of all Nestle products, and while WHO steps up the pressure on hospitals around the world to further stigmatize bottlefeeding, what are we, the bottlefeeding parents of America, doing in response? Answer: *nothing*. There is no independent organization of parents and consumers that is speaking up for our interest in these struggles—yet we may well end up with our access to information severely restricted, with our choice of products dictated more by the judgment of some medical bureaucrats at WHO headquarters in Geneva than by our babies' own needs and preferences, and our pocketbooks hit by the loss of discounts and promotional gifts.

Some of the women I interviewed expressed concern over the kind of marketplace the anti-formula movement will ultimately bring us. A few were even insulted by what they described as the patronizing implication of the anti-formula campaign: that if women are allowed to see ads for formula themselves, they will be so seduced by the pictures of beautiful women and rosy-cheeked children that they will be unable to make the choice that best serves their babies' interests.

I asked each of the women I interviewed three questions:

1. Before you began bottlefeeding, had you paid special attention to formula advertising?

2. Did you receive any free samples of formula, either during your hospital stay for labor and delivery, or afterwards, through your pediatrician's office?

3. What role, if any, did advertising and/or free formula play in your decision to bottlefeed?

Virtually all of my respondents had received a few free samples, and not a single one reported being moved to bottlefeed, just by having on hand a free can or two. Yet when mothers, in tears at two in the morning, after listening to the baby scream in hunger for over an hour, finally decided to try a little formula, most were grateful that they didn't have to go out and buy that first trial mixture.

Advertising was noticed only after the baby was set on the formula course. At that point the parents were chiefly concerned with price, baby's reaction to the taste, and baby's ability to digest the formula without stomach upset. No one took the advertisers claims' completely at face value. Most consulted with their doctors about the choice, but only those with colicky or highly allergic babies reported being told by a doctor to purchase a particular brand.

One response I heard more than a few times about the impact of the anti-formula movement was an expression of annoyance over the fact that each can of formula now carries the guilt-reinforcing dictum: breastmilk is best. It is *not* best if the woman can't produce milk without agony to her nipples; it is *not* best if she can't produce enough for her baby's healthy growth; it is *not* best if she's in poor health herself and on a potentially toxic medication. As one angry respondent put it, "If the formula makers can't put all these qualifications on the can, they shouldn't put on any advice at all."

Bottlefeeding Mothers Talk About the Anti-Formula Movement

I don't think it's been fair. They portray bottlefeeding mothers as uneducated or selfish—as women who don't know the benefits of breastfeeding, or who just want to run back to their jobs.

—Shirley

The media has become so pro-nursing that you're made to feel you're not doing your best by your child if you bottlefeed. Then, if the media doesn't get you, your friends get you. With every [childhood] illness it's another opening of the door for comments from others.

—Ella

It's insulting that the formula cans all say "breast is best" and put it in their ads. Pressure to breastfeed is everywhere. There's a bit of self-righteousness in it [the anti-formula movement]. Some of that may be necessary to combat [the way breastfeeding was discouraged in] the past. In the hospital where I delivered there was a huge poster with eleven reasons to breastfeed. Bottlefeeding was very discouraged. With twins, I expected there'd be pressure on me to use bottles, but it was just the opposite. I had a C-section—I hadn't slept well in months because of the complications of a multiple pregnancy—still, they'd wake me and bring me both babies to breastfeed at once.

—Faith, who ended up breastfeeding one twin and bottlefeeding the other

And summing it all up . . .

I breastfed my second child, and I can say from experience that many of the claims about breastfeeding made by the La Leche League folks and other breastfeeding advocates on this [e-mail] forum are inaccurate, or at least not true for everyone's experience. I did not find it easier to nurse a baby than to carry around supplies for bottles. I did not bond more easily with the child I nursed than with the child I didn't nurse (if anything, it was the opposite). I don't think the health of the children was significantly affected either way by nursing. If anything, the breastfed child was sick more often in the first year (partly because big sister was bringing germies home).

—*Eva's conclusions on a parenting forum*

More Than a Simple Feeding Choice

For most women who choose to breastfeed, the decision is one calling for the exercise of personal choice, medical judgment, and due consideration of breastfeeding's impact on the woman's family and future. For most health professionals who promote breastfeeding, the question is how best to lead the new mother into making the choice that is, in their view, most beneficial to both infant and mother.

However, for a small but intensely driven segment of the pro-breastfeeding movement, the question goes far beyond the personal or even the medical considerations that the more mainstream breastfeeding advocates point out. For these ardent few, breastfeeding is the central tenet of an entire lifestyle adhered to with almost cult-like totality. The most dedicated adherents are interested not only in persuading every mother-to-be to practice nursing exclusively, but wish to see *all* parents shape their whole lives according to certain principles and practices that, like breastfeeding itself, are touted as best for the child's health, development, and self-esteem.

Who are the gurus of this cult-like minority within the breastfeeding movement? What practices and principles (above and beyond breastfeeding) do they support? I intend to answer these questions, but first, let me defend my perhaps shocking characterization of a segment of the breastfeeding movement as a cult.

When we hear the word, most of us think of people who share an out-of-the-mainstream *religious* faith that governs the conduct of their lives. But a cult could be any group of people who share the same basic views about how life is to be lived. The nine numbered paragraphs that follow list some hallmarks of a cult.*

The Breastfeeding Movement and Nine Characteristics of a Cult

1. Cults have charismatic leaders whose writings are treated as Truth. On the e-mail breastfeeding forums I followed, the most frequently cited revered name was Dr. William Sears, author of many books on baby care, parenting, and breastfeeding (some co-authored by his wife, Martha Sears, R.N.). The indisputable "bible", however, is La Leche League's *The Womanly Art of Breastfeeding*—the book calls itself the bible in the foreword to the third edition.[1] Two other experts whose writings are often urged upon new mothers are Tine Thevenin (a La Leche League Leader and author of the influential work *The Family Bed*, as well as the lesser-known *Mothering and Fathering: Gender Differences in Parenting*), and Norma Jane Bum-

---

*I am indebted to Larry Kahaner, a private investigator who is expert on cults and the author of a book (*Cults That Kill*, Warner Books, 1989), for his help in compiling this listing of cult characteristics.

garner, author of *Mothering Your Nursing Toddler*, the guide for those nursing children over a year old.[2] Nursing a child past infancy, sharing one's bed with nursing babies and older children, and maintaining sex-segregated roles in parenting are all key tenets of the breastfeeding cultists, as advocated by these authors.

2. *Cults promulgate a code of behavior for adherents that covers all aspects of life.* In addition to breastfeeding, cultists share a good many other beliefs about childbearing, childrearing, marriage, sexuality, work—all the primal questions of life.

A philosophy of life

In New Beginnings *(September/October 1994), in her article "Breastfeeding in Italy," writer Barbara Bricoli describes how she and her husband have altered their lives under the influence of breastfeeding leaders' views:*

We began to devour every book we could get our hands on and began to attend La Leche League meetings. I couldn't get enough. We read *The Continuum Concept,* and it changed our whole parenting style. We were now firm believers in marsupial parenting. We read *The Family Bed* and wondered how families did it any other way. We read *The Womanly Art of Breastfeeding,* and everything written by Dr. William Sears, including *Nighttime Parenting* and *The Baby Book.* We were convinced of the importance of natural child spacing and the need for Eva to wean when she was ready. . . . My pre-pregnancy plans were to return to my career and put Eva in daycare—after all, couldn't anyone care for a child? Wrong again! Despite our efforts, Eva refused to take a bottle with expressed milk (and forget pacifiers)—she was trying to tell me that she needed her mother and nothing else. I left my career and became an at-home mother. . . . I am very content and so grateful to our daughter. We are even considering home schooling. . . . Eva and I now attend La Leche League's toddler meetings and have met wonderful mothers who share the same philosophies.

Here's a dialog that took place on-line between two mothers who dropped out of their La Leche League chapters because, though they nursed their babies, they did not buy into the total cult philosophy:

Polly: People [at the meetings] who supplemented with formula, who wanted to wean before two years of age, and did not let the children sleep in the bed with them were made to feel at best irresponsible, and at worst, dupes of society.

Dawn: I had a similar experience in Massachusetts, where my first child, now 8, was born. The women in the La Leche League group wanted to have as many children as possible. There was one woman who was still nursing both her 3-year-old and her 6-year-old, who talked about how to get her husband to agree to have another. They also group-slept . . . I wondered where she planned to conceive this child!

3. *Cults base their teachings on Faith, God, or Nature— something eternal and sacred.* Most breastfeeding cultists cite the naturalness of breastfeeding as proof of the universal correctness of the practice, and some underscore the point with religious reasoning (for example, that God gave women breasts for the purpose of feeding their babies). In writings by breastfeeding cultists it is common to find words like "holy," "sacred," "sacrifice," and other words that one expects to see in a religious context, used in connection with the act of breastfeeding or the state of a nursing mother.

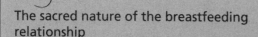

The sacred nature of the breastfeeding relationship

The experience of pregnancy . . . is so holy and omnipotent that I was constantly surprised at the lack of respect accorded to me during my state of grace. And then came the discovery that the being who emerged took part of me with her, so that any separation produced the dull, throbbing ache that an amputee feels in his or her phantom limb. This kind of love is not the flowery, pink affection that we women are accused of favoring; it is love so ineffable and deep that it manifests itself as our devotion to fulfilling every need of that self before any of our own. I remember nursing while sitting on the toilet; days in which I ate nothing before my husband returned from work because preparing food required two hands and my infant daughter always required a minimum of one; waking nine times a night to nurse and soothe her back into another uselessly frustrating nap; surrounding an armchair with enough magazines and snacks to fill the two hours she might sleep if I kept her nestled against me, because she refused to nap for longer than twenty minutes out of my embrace; sleeping sitting up in the rocker by her crib when she was sick, her hot body stretched across my stomach, so as not to disturb my husband with attending to her cries throughout the night.

The preceding paragraph was excerpted from a letter to Harper's magazine (September 3, 1993). The writer considers pregnancy to be a "state of grace," and employs the rhetoric of sacrifice that one associates with religious duties. The letter expresses several other sentiments typical of the breastfeeding cult: the assumption that women's love of children cannot be understood by men, the opposition to even the briefest of separations between mother and infant, and a sleeping arrangement that pairs mother and baby, placing the father in the outsider's role.

The comparison of breastfeeding to religion was made explicit in *The Compleat Mother* (Summer, 1994) when it put forth its "Ten Commandments of Lactation."

   I. Thou shalt not watch the clock.
  II. Thou shalt not judge milk by its appearance.
 III. Thou shalt not use any bottles.
  IV. Thou shalt not overwork thyself.
   V. Thou shalt not compare the baby to one being fed artificially.
  VI. Thou shalt nurse frequently.
 VII. Thou shalt nurse in different positions.
VIII. Thou shalt practice discreet nursing.
  IX. Thou shalt enjoy babying the baby.
   X. Thou shalt associate with others who are supportive of breastfeeding.

4. Cults reject any evidence that is not in line with core beliefs. For breastfeeding cultists this means that any study contradicting the superiority of breastmilk or denying the dangers of formula must be wrong. The clearest case of this characteristic at work was seen in the reaction of some breastfeeding militants to the article in the *Wall Street Journal* of July 22, 1994, about babies who starved to death or suffered brain damage due to their mothers' failure to give formula when their breastmilk production proved inadequate. The e-mail networks were humming with cultists doubting the truth of the reporting. (The quote that follows is quite representative.)

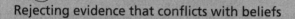

Rejecting evidence that conflicts with beliefs

Did anyone happen to see the front page article of the *Wall Street Journal* on Friday [July 22, 1994]? The title of the article was "Dying for Milk," subtitled, "Some Mothers, Trying in Vain to Breastfeed, Starve Their Infants." I was pretty outraged after reading it. . . . It makes me very suspicious that some formula company sensationalized one mother's nightmare for their own profit by somehow getting the *Journal* to run the story on their front page. Simply put, it's a scare tactic to discourage breastfeeding, and it's aimed at fathers who are likely to be less informed about breastfeeding in general.

—*Mary Beth*

5. Conspiracy is used to account for persistence of "wrong" beliefs among general public. If breastfeeding is bliss, why then do the great majority (80 percent) of American women stop doing it by the time their babies reach six months? A worldwide conspiracy must exist among formula producers to hook women into buying their product, to numb their minds with seductive ad images, and deceive them into thinking that breastfeeding is difficult to do, cow-like, and uncomfortable.

Here's how authors Karen and Gale Pryor, in their breastfeeding guide *Nursing Your Baby*, account for the prevalence of formula-feeding in America:

> The manufacturers present themselves as helpful friends to the physician, supplying not only free milk and bottles to hospitals, but free tape measures, parent information pamphlets, M.D. educational seminars, pencils, notepads, all-expense-paid trips to medical conferences, and so on. No one in these companies does any of this without the well-founded expectation that it will add to the bottom line. . . .
> Doctors are just as susceptible as the rest of us to Madison Avenue techniques. Individual practitioners usually don't have time to review new research personally and must rely on outside sources. This leaves them wide open to propaganda. . . .
> The drug companies that manufacture synthetic milks also fund much of the research on infant feeding. Unsurprisingly, a lot of this research is in areas where it is possible to minimize or denigrate the advantages of human milk. . . .
> One particularly insidious promotional practice, which also utilizes the medical environment's aura of approval to influence mothers, is the free "baby kit," containing pamphlets on infant care, baby clothes, and small toys, given to mothers as they leave the hospital. In addition, the kit contains a product sample, which may amount to as much as five days' supply of synthetic milk (enough, once it has been put into the baby, to make lactation hard to re-establish). Research shows that mothers, in a moment of insecurity, are likely to use the samples, and that use of the samples is directly related to early cessation of breastfeeding. The mother is now a customer. . . . (pp. 196–197)

It's not enough that formula companies seduce and hook vulnerable new mothers or harried obstetricians with their irresistible gifts; the Pryors charge some even more nefarious schemes.

> Sometimes the propaganda is truly ingenious. The *Journal of Human Lactation* reports on breastfeeding advice pamphlets, published by milk manufacturers and distributed free to mothers, that purport to teach breastfeeding, but stress dif-

ficulties and drawbacks, and treat hospital-generated problems such as engorgement as the expected norm, and pamphlets with bland and more or less accurate texts, but with illustrations in which breastfeeding mothers look unhappy and impoverished, and bottlefeeding mothers look radiant and upscale. Other illustrations show mothers holding babies in positions guaranteed to cause sore nipples (positions that the new mother is likely to emulate, consciously or not). Free educational videos have been created with the same kinds of hidden agendas: an emphasis on the difficulties of breastfeeding, and visuals that, if used as examples, might well bring about such difficulties. (p. 199)

6. *Cults view the world in black and white, moral and immoral, with no ambiguities.* Formula feeding, to the breastfeeding cultist, is not just a matter of personal choice, nor is it a medical matter: It is a moral question, and one that has only one right answer. Giving a child formula is akin to child abuse; it is a matter of concern to all of society, something that we all should be working to prevent. There is no room for compromise when it comes to "innocent babies."

Black and white

After one parenting forum participant complained about some of the anti-bottlefeeding messages posted on-line, she got this response:

I don't think it's enough just to say "let's agree to disagree" on an issue like this. It's not just a matter of opinion. There is a lot of misinformation and ignorance that can be cleared up on a [computer network] bulletin board like this. . . . The new information we are getting all the time makes it very clear that there are physiological and emotional benefits to breast-feeding that bottlefeeding cannot match. These are facts, not just opinions. They are founded on scientific research. Don't you think it's worth hearing about?

—Janet

. . . and one of the bottlefeeding mothers I inter-viewed said this:

The husband of one of my cousins told us that breastfeeding is the only way, and anyone who doesn't breastfeed is wrong. He said he'd never allow his wife to bottlefeed. He said it does great harm to the baby.

—Jane

7. *Once they have joined the cult, members must attend many meetings, and have close relationships only with others who share the same beliefs.* The militant breastfeeder tries hard not to miss a meeting of La Leche League, the Nursing Mothers' Council, or whatever group of like-minded women she has joined. A common complaint I have found posted on e-mail forums by breastfeeding absolutists is their estrangement from a sister or sister-in-law who chose the bottle. The desire to associate only with those who share the faith of breastfeeding is also evidenced by number 10 of the Ten Commandments of Lactation (see page 116): "Thou shalt associate with others who are supportive of breastfeeding."

8. *Cults prefer adherents to assume a child-like, unquestioning, unintellectual role.* This characteristic was evident in the way many breastfeeding militants signed their e-mail messages: seldom with their names alone; more often as (for example) Billy's Mommy, or using childish pseudo-

nyms, such as Pooh-Bear, or Bootsy. Breastfeeding guides make much of not thinking too much, not watching the clock, just relaxing and letting one's instincts take over, being natural and simple[3]—the implication being that a woman who holds a high-powered job, with many responsibilities, will be too stressed to nurse well.

9. *Cult adherents idealize the past, or hold a vision of some utopian future.* Again and again in breastfeeding books, journals, and e-mail correspondence, breastfeeding absolutists hearken back to a perfect past when no bottles and no formula marred the planet. All children were healthy, un-neurotic, unpolluted, living in tribal paradise. If it's natural or ancient, it must be for the best (no mention of female genital mutilation, infant sacrifice, intertribal slaughter, or any other of the endless catalog of human depravity practiced by these breastfeeding paragons of old). The idea seems to be that if all babies from now on could be assured of getting breastmilk for two years, that would mean an end to war, greed, disease, and suffering.

Life was better in the past

I always remind myself, when questioning something, how things most likely were handled a century or two or five ago. I strongly believe in the wisdom of nature over science, and it is interesting to know that in the U.S. at the turn of the century many babies were breastfed exclusively for one year before the introduction of solids.

—*Amelia*

Lifestyle of the Breastfeeding Cultist

To learn about the practices and views that are the gospel of the breastfeeding cult, I looked for as many points of contact with practitioners as I could find. To this end, I:

- subscribed to La Leche League's bimonthly magazine *New Beginnings*;
- read messages and letters publicly posted on parenting, medical, and holistic health forums on four different computer networks: the Internet, Prodigy, Compuserve, and America On-line;
- read magazines, journals, and newsletters devoted to breastfeeding and related issues, including: *The Compleat Mother: The Magazine of Pregnancy, Birth and Breastfeeding; Parenting from the Heart*, a newsletter enclosed with the Motherwear catalog of fashions for the nursing mother; *WomanWise*,[4] the quarterly of the Concord [N.H.] Feminist Health Care Center, and *The Nurturing Parent*,[5] self-described as "an international newsletter to encourage healthy parent-child relationships through attachment-continuum parenting"; and *Mothering* magazine;[6]
- noted what books, pamphlets, and products were featured in catalogs put out by breastfeeding/baby-supply companies, such as Motherwear, The Natural Baby, and Ecobaby;[7]
- conducted interviews in person or by telephone with nursing mothers who held absolutist views.

As my research was focused on bottlefeeding mothers, I interviewed only a small number of militant breastfeeders—about a dozen women. A few women contacted me directly, incensed by my author's query seeking out bottlefeeding women, having correctly surmised that my book would be supportive of bottlefeeding mothers. Other militants were mothers I happened to meet on trips to the playground or through participation in my daughters' preschool functions. If I could get the woman to accept that my purpose was not irremediably sinful, I would then ask her if I could interview her about her views at some later date. A few of the women I met in this manner said yes. Here's how such contact would typically get under way:

Other Mother:	"What do you do?"
Me:	"I'm a writer."
Other Mother:	"What do you write?"
Me:	"I'm working on a book called *Bottle feeding Without Guilt.*"
Other Mother, revealing herself to be a breastfeeding militant:	"Are you serious? Bottlefeeding women *should* feel guilty! Bottlefeeding is so much worse for babies than breastfeeding!"—and so on and so forth.

Within the space of a few months of collecting breastfeeding cult literature, I had accumulated 19 file folders' worth of material, each file stuffed full of letters, article excerpts, and e-mail printouts in support of one or more of the 19 themes I have identified as key elements of the breastfeeding cult lifestyle. These themes are:

1. Breastfeeding should continue until a child is at least two years old. With an unswerving faith in the oft-cited "fact" that the "world-wide average age of weaning is 4.2 years," the breastfeeding cultist ideally would like to see most children nursed that long—although later weaning is also fine. The most dedicated breastfeeding cult adherents nurse their older children occasionally until even seven years old and love to find citations of breastfeeding mothers

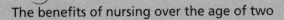

The benefits of nursing over the age of two

The bonus of nursing an older child is they can tell you how tasty your milk is and how much they like to nurse. It's gratifying to be so appreciated by a healthy, lively, bright, gorgeous little person.

—letter in The Compleat Mother *(Summer 1994)*

Irene, a bottlefeeding mother, told this story on-line of an encounter with a long-term nurser:

My friend got married last summer. Her sister was still nursing her four year old son—but that's not what amazes me. She nursed him right at the wedding! Though she did it off to the side of the reception hall, I still think that at four, a kid is old enough to understand that now is not the time for such things. Nobody else seemed to notice or be fazed by it, but I was kind of floored.

Here's an on-line advocate who's all for toddler nursing, but thinks you do have to wean sometime:

I'm entertaining the thought of [still] nursing my son [now eighteen months] if he wants to, after the next one is born in February [in four months' time]. So I think toddler breastfeeding is healthy and should be more accepted. My husband knew a lady that nursed her *eight-year-old boy*! I do think *that* is weird.

—Danielle

from other countries who continue to offer the breast to that age or older.

2. *Breastmilk must be the exclusive form of nutrition until at least six months of age.* Introduction of solid food

Solid foods should be delayed

My pediatrician suggested I start introducing solids at six months, but I waited until nine months.

—*Hope, who nursed her child for 2³/₄ years*

should be delayed until that age, at a bare minimum, and introducing solids as late as one year is often cited as something mothers have accomplished, to the supposed benefit of the child's health.

3. Breastfeeding represents a woman's highest, most sublime and creative function in life. Any difficulties and strains that breastfeeding may cause are holy sacrifices, and being self-sacrificing and nurturing is the quintessence of femininity. Nothing a woman might devote herself to—be it a career, an artistic creation, an athletic accomplishment—will be as meaningful as her role as giver and sustainer of life to her children. Flowing from this tenet come some anti-working mother sentiments, indicated by the emphasis in the La Leche League catalog on books that promote staying at home with a nursing infant or child.[8]

Anti-working mother

La Leche League's "Breastfeeding Rights Packet" (Publication No. 78, Revised July, 1986, p. 24) quotes from childcare expert Dr. Rene Spitz, professor of psychology at the University of Colorado Medical Center:

Working mothers who return to their jobs shortly after the birth of a baby are endangering the future lives of their children. . . . The biggest cause of school dropouts and failure in adulthood is the lack of a normal infant-mother relationship in the first year of life. . . . The growing trend for more mothers to seek outside employment increases the risk that more children from middle class and poor families will not be able to make the grade in school. . . . Recent studies at the University of Colorado and elsewhere have revealed how the lack of mothering can turn normal babies into idiots. . . . By the end of a year, the child either learns to learn, or he blocks his mind to the learning process.

Fulfillment of a woman's nature

As The Womanly Art of Breastfeeding *puts it:*

Successful lactation is an expression of a woman's femininity and she doesn't need to count how often she feeds the baby any more than she counts how often she kisses the baby. (p. 73)

This sentence contains two troubling implications: 1) the idea that the bottlefeeding mother must be somehow less "feminine" than a breastfeeding mother; and 2) that the breastfeeding mother doesn't need to concern herself with how much milk her baby is getting, because quantification is alien to feminine nature, which is based more on maternal instinct, intuition, and emotion than on "objective" reasoning—implying that measurement, infant growth charts, and other scientific approaches are strictly masculine concerns.

Karen and Gale Pryor in their book Nursing Your Baby, *state on the first page their belief that a mother, by the act of breastfeeding, is fulfilling her creative urges, as much as the woman who writes a poem or engages in any other creative act:*

> Nursing a baby is an art; a domestic art, perhaps, but one that like cooking or gardening brings the woman the release and satisfaction that only creative work can give. The author Anne Morrow Lindbergh wrote, "When I cannot write a poem, I bake biscuits and feel just as pleased." Nursing gives the same sort of satisfaction and joy. (pp. 3–4)

Such an attitude invites putdowns of women's artistry. Throughout history, literary critics (most of them men) have dismissed the work of the woman writer by saying she should better have confined her creative efforts to the baking of biscuits and the raising of children.

4. *That women can give birth and produce milk is what makes them not only different biologically from men, but different in thinking, in their moral nature, in all other important ways.* Much breastfeeding cult literature asserts that men are all but superfluous in parenting, useful mainly as a means to gain income to support the family. Because they lack the ability to produce milk and the "nurturing hormones" that go with it, they can never truly understand what goes on between a mother and baby, and they are also somewhat deficient in moral awareness (which can explain why so many men fail to support, or even actively discourage their wives' prolonged nursing) and in most respects are less in touch with Nature or things spiritual.

Properly, men are meant to stand in awe of the earth-goddess woman who gives them children and nourishes those children from her body. And if they don't, get rid of them! The anti-male undercurrent (that men should be providers and are good for little more) comes to the surface in this example from a breastfeeding militant who was a regular on an e-mail forum; she signed all her messages with the tag-line, "Men—can't live with them, can't kill them."

Here's what *The Womanly Art of Breastfeeding* had to say about the differences in men and women when it comes to parenting abilities:

> Mothers and fathers both nurture their children, but they do not provide the same kind of nurturing. Understanding and respecting these differences is an important part of parenting.

At a La Leche League conference in San Francisco, a Colorado father, Tom Kerwin, spoke to this issue:

> There are psychological and emotional differences between men and women which are more than simply accidents, and which are not the result of discrimination or cultural emphasis. I suggest that we make better husbands and fathers if we learn something about these differences—if we appreciate the beautiful mystery of them and know better what to expect of our wives and ourselves. On the other hand, I think our wives make better wives and mothers if they help us to learn the difference and to look for the clues, since we men are nowhere near as observant of these things.

Page 22 of La Leche League's "Breastfeeding Rights Packet" quotes this conclusion by Humberto Nagera, Professor of Psychology at the University of Montana (excerpted from *Child and Family*, Vol. 14, No. 2):

> This reaction [of traumatic distress when a child is separated from its mother] of young children is so well known in the field of mental health that we have coined the term separation anxiety to describe it. The term refers to the biological unity that exists between the mother and her infant, a unity that, if disturbed, leads in some cases to very unwelcome results in the development of the child. It must be clear in this case we are not referring only to permanent separations but to transitory ones as well, separations that may last just a few hours at a time.

After several more paragraphs in support of the notion that the biological mother is irreplaceable, Dr. Nagera has this to say about fathers and other relations:

> Fathers, grandparents, older siblings, and others become part of the toddler's enlarging world. Yet it should be clearly realized that these other relations take place only under the shadow of the relationship to the mother. The two-year-old child can spend much time playing with grandparents and others away from the mother (if these people can appeal to the toddler's interest), secure in the knowledge that the mother is around in the house, though not necessarily in sight. To assume that this behavior suggests the toddler's independence from his mother is quite mistaken. (p. 24)

The view of the male's proper role as that of an occasional helper, who needs to be encouraged to feel competent, is expressed in this condescending passage titled "Dads Can Help," excerpted in *The Womanly Art of Breastfeeding*:

> He can step in to provide you with a welcome respite when he is home, and your older one will thrive on the extra attention. Dads are often masters at keeping toddler minds and hands busy when mother needs some time alone with the baby, or when she decides to take advantage of baby's nap for a relaxing bath or some much needed rest. Father and toddler will both enjoy some toddler-size roughhousing, and who but daddy can add such excitement to stories by putting in all of those low, rumbling noises? . . . Let your husband know how much he is needed and appreciated, encourage him to spend some extra time with your toddler or preschooler, and be prepared to watch the two of them become the best of friends. (pp. 214–215)

Notice that La Leche League doesn't advocate that the father take care of *both* toddler and infant while the mother is resting. Maybe dad can handle a kid for an hour or two on a weekend, but he's certainly not up to dealing with more than one, is he? And the result when he does spend time with his child? Not the "unity" or lifelong, intense "bonding" that the mother gets when *she* spends time with her children; according to *The Womanly Art of Breastfeeding*, all he can hope for is to be the child's "best friend."

5. *When the child is allowed to eat solids, the food must not be processed or tainted by additives of any kind.* The La Leche League catalog features these books about feeding the family: *Whole Foods for the Whole Family; Mother's in the Kitchen; The Natural Baby Food Cookbook; Healthy Snacks for Healthy Kids; Sugar-Free Toddlers;* and *The Good Breakfast Book: 450 Whole Food/Vegetarian Recipes.* Now look at what's in the Motherwear catalog: *The Vegetarian Lunchbasket; Cooking for Consciousness; Whole Food Recipes for the Vegetarian Kitchen;* and *Vegetarian Baby.* The people who put together these catalogs clearly don't expect the concerned breastfeeding mother to feed her baby any old Gerber's from a jar. She'll buy only organic fruits and vegetables and grind her own baby food from scratch (being a stay-at-home mother, she'll have the time for this sort of thing). Cultist journals refer approvingly to the practice of an ultra-strict form of vegetarianism called veganism, which involves forgoing not just beef, poultry, and fish (all of which could easily be contaminated by industrial farming methods) but abhorring equally all mass-produced dairy products (cow's milk, cheese, yogurt, ice cream, and eggs). These products are said to exacerbate allergies, or to be full of growth hormones, irradiation, or other pollutants.

6. *Birth should be a joyous, completely natural, non-medical event.* It should be attended by midwives, occur at home, and without, of course, any drugs.[9] A cesarean section represents failure and disappointment, the mother having been deprived of a sublime experience. If, for some reason (for example, that the mother has fallen under the sway of some insensitive male medical "experts" who have persuaded her that she has a life-threatening condition) a

Medical intervention in childbirth

This mother is still angry that her first child was delivered by C-section:

I was a home VBAC mom at age 43. Our first child, Adam, was born by C-section in 1986 ("fetal distress"— bah, humbug. I was not well informed enough to refuse medical intervention). . . . [After her first child was diagnosed with autism, the mother brought him in for an evaluation]. The professionals who evaluated Adam were impressed that he was doing as well as he was and credited my style of mothering (although they seemed taken aback that Adam was still nursing, shared our bed, etc.)

—*letter to* The Compleat Mother *(Summer 1994)*

woman does end up having a C-section, then the next time around, she must do everything within her power to prevent that situation from recurring, and try for a vaginal delivery (called VBAC, for Vaginal Birth After Cesarean).

7. *Pure cotton is better for skin than any manufactured fiber.* No disposable diaper should ever touch the baby's delicate bottom. All clothing, whether for the baby or for anyone else in the family, should be of natural fibers only. Catalogs of nursing fashions and baby products bear this out.[10]

8. *The whole family should share the same bed.* The practice of co-sleeping (as one of its advocates, Dr. William Sears, has dubbed it) may be continued as long as the children find it desirable, but certainly should be kept up while a child is still waking at night to nurse. Two books with

Cloth diapers

Disposable diapers can kill? Read what one source of breastfeeding and baby supplies, The Natural Baby Catalog, has to say about disposable diapers:

It's not clear just what caused the higher incidence of rashes among babies using disposable diapers. . . . It may be due to allergic reactions to chemicals used in disposable diapers. Or it may simply be the lack of air circulation, and higher temperature inside the disposable diaper. More serious health problems from the use of disposable diapers have been reported to the U.S. Consumer Product Safety Commission. These include injuries due to foreign objects in the diaper material, chemical burns, and even death from suffocation on the tabs or lining of the disposable diapers. (Spring, 1995, p. 2)

the status of cult gospel endorse this nighttime arrangement: *Nighttime Parenting* by Dr. William Sears, and *The Family Bed* by Tine Thevenin. When I see a message online by anyone urging others to read either or both of these two books, I know I'm hearing from a hard-core member of the breastfeeding cult, and can predict what advice will be contained in any future messages from the same address (nurse your children for three or four years, use only cloth diapers, eat a vegetarian diet, and you know the rest).

Tine Thevenin, in her highly influential book *The Family Bed*, says this:

An interesting and revealing study, "Sleep/Wake Patterns of Breastfed Infants in the First Two Years of Life" (Elias et. al., 1986) reports among their findings that breastfed babies who sleep with their mothers awaken more frequently to nurse than their counterparts who do not sleep with their mothers.

The co-sleeping mothers, following maternal care practices common in non-western cultures, did not, however, consider night waking a problem. It was also found that bottlefed babies who slept by themselves slept longer hours during the night. This may seem tremendously appealing to the modern working mother. However, given the natural phenomenon of frequent nursing, touching, and the continual bonding that takes place in a co-family sleeping arrangement, one may well question the long-term effect that long, separated hours during the first few years of life may have on a child. (p. 84)

Here's Thevenin's answer to those who say they would like their babies to learn to sleep through the night early on: "The problem is not the baby's waking up, but our getting upset about it and feeling tired because of it." (p. 86)

9. The baby should be physically apart from the mother only rarely. When small enough, the baby can be "worn" all day in a sling or front carrier.[11] Constant skin contact with the mother is necessary for bonding, which in turn is necessary to foster emotional well-being, security, and the capacity to love. The baby is not portrayed as an independent personality but as an extension of mother, part of the "nursing dyad" or "nursing couple." The baby is commonly referred to as "the nursling," emphasizing its dependence on its mother for the necessities of life. This constant physical togetherness is described in the many books of Dr. William Sears and Martha Sears, who tout parenting practices which they have dubbed attachment parenting (or continuum parenting). You can tell that a mother is under Sears' influence if she doesn't own a stroller, wouldn't dream of leaving her two-year-old "nursling" with a sitter or grandparent overnight, or if you see her carrying her three-year-old everywhere on her hip or in a backpack, though the child has no physical problems to prevent walking.

10. The mother of small children is not to be regarded as a sexual being. Cuddling with her baby or her whole family in bed should be sufficient to meet her need for

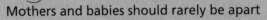

Mothers and babies should rarely be apart

On one parenting forum a father expressed his annoyance at the no-separation pressure brought to bear on his breastfeeding wife:

My wife called La Leche League. Boy, do they get under my skin! I'm all for breastfeeding. In my opinion, it's pretty obvious how beneficial and natural breastfeeding is, but the people at La Leche League are so fanatical. You know what they told my wife? They said if we go on vacation [just the two of us], that our children will think we are dead. Then when we get back, they won't trust us anymore. The gall—as if nobody ever left their children for a weekend. . . . I would have liked it so much if La Leche League were there to provide valuable information regarding breastfeeding. Instead, they are just another fundamentalist group, pushing their cause at all costs.

warmth and intimacy. She sacrifices her own comfort and even her own health to do so much daily for her family, that it's understandable that her sex drive has dropped. She may be experiencing loss of libido or vaginal dryness caused by the estrogen-suppressant effects of prolactin (a nursing hormone), but she is expected to regard her baby's need for breastmilk as paramount, and her own sex life as dispensable. To accommodate ease of nursing, she wears only shapeless nursing jumpers with hidden slits or baggy sweaters that can be easily lifted by her child. She wears no perfume or makeup. Her most important emotional and physical relationship is not with her sexual partner and father of her children but with the nursing child, who in much of the breastfeeding literature is described in terms more commonly reserved for a sexual lover (the baby and mother are a couple and weaning is called a divorce).

Nursing Mothers Don't Need Sex

Authors Karen and Gale Pryor (in their book Nursing Your Baby*) make the assumption that the breastfeeding woman won't feel much desire for sex, but much like the prim marriage manuals of Victorian times, they advise that the woman "be generous" when it comes to meeting her man's carnal needs:*

The closeness of a mother and her nursing baby, while it brings joy to the father, sometimes partially eclipses the mother's need for other close relationships, including sex. That may be due in part to the temporary abeyance of the menstrual cycle, with its mood swings and peaks of desire, and its high levels of estrogen. The nursing mother may feel compliant about sexual relations without actually being eager. Perhaps, too, nursing a baby provides some of the fringe benefits of sex, such as closeness with another person and a feeling of being admired and wanted; so a mother may turn less often to her husband for the balm of touching and physical closeness. A mother who notices a reduced need for lovemaking in herself during lactation should take thought to be generous and affectionate to her lover; he needs to be touched and to feel wanted, too. (pp. 296–297)

Sex and nursing

For some breastfeeding mothers the act of nursing appears to give the sort of physical and emotional

> *satisfaction one more typically associates with sexual climax. Here is how one such mother (in an article posted on-line) described her joy at the end of her son's "nursing strike":*
>
> Joey latched on and happily nursed until he drifted off to sleep. . . . Overwhelming feelings of happiness much like I'd felt the day of Joey's birth filled me. Adrenaline pumped through my system, as excitement, joy, and satisfaction swept over me. I was soaring. My baby was still my baby. He still wanted me. We were whole again.
>
> —Janice
>
> *In an article in* Mothering *magazine (Spring 1995, p. 88) writer Marion Wink plays up the lover-like parallel of the nursing relationship:*
>
> I'm in love with the little guy, head over heels, what can I do. He can get my bra off faster than anyone I ever met, no hands at all, just a hungry look.

11. *All artificial nipples are bad.* If a baby is exclusively and frequently nursed, that baby will not need to engage in any non-breast sucking, whether a thumb or an artificial object. The pacifier is especially vilified because it is so much like a bottle nipple. It induces the baby to suck in an unnatural tongue-and-mouth configuration, and may teach the child incorrect suck patterns for nursing. Cult mothers are full of pride that their children "did not have to resort" to sucking on anything other than a mother's breast, just as they are proud that nothing has entered their babies' tummies other than breastmilk before the six-month mark.

No artificial nipples

I scoffed at the bottles I received as gifts [when pregnant and told myself], "These are going back where they came from. My baby's lips will never feel a fake nipple, and he will get all the benefits of breast-feeding I never had."

—Mariel

One of the most reliably absolutist of all the breast-feeding advocates on the e-mail forums was Marla, who had this to say about artificial nipples:

By the way, the sight of a kid over a year with a pacifier or bottle *does* kind of revolt me.

12. *Breastfeeding advocates have a moral duty to spread their beliefs.* Too many mothers are harming their children's health by bottlefeeding; breastfeeding cultists in possession of this "truth," must play the often thankless role of "lactation police" and attempt to enforce Nature's law. Many of my respondents were motivated to talk to me after having had a run-in with a breastfeeding cultist who had taken on this attitude, their comments full of anger and frustration at being made to feel like criminals.

The desire to accost bottlefeeders is the real dividing mark between the normal breastfeeding mother who simply loves nursing and wants to do it for a long time, and the cultist, who is intolerant of those who have chosen a different path. Convinced that her actions can help to protect "innocent babies" from harm, the evangelizing cultist will not be restrained by appeals to common courtesy or compassion.

Proselytizing

My husband ran into a casual acquaintance—male—on his way to work. He asked my husband, "Is your wife nursing?" My husband answered, "No, she's been having some problems." The next thing I knew, the wife of this acquaintance called me up and did a hard sell, telling me to call La Leche league. I was noncommittal. But then she called back *again* to pressure me some more. And this wasn't even someone I knew, just a wife of someone my husband knew!

—Judith

13. *Against artificial methods of birth control.* Since having children is a blissful, holy experience, one should have as many as possible. The only method to be used for child-spacing is the natural pause in a woman's fertility that tends to occur when a woman is nursing a baby full-time.[12] It's not necessary to comb through the writings of breastfeeding's chief advocates to find citations for this belief; one need only look at the number of children per family of the leaders of the breastfeeding movement: Dr. William Sears and Martha Sears, eight children; the seven founders of La Leche League, as follows: Mary Ann Cahill, ten children; Edwina Froelich, three; Mary Ann Kerwin, nine; Viola Lennon, ten; Marian Tompson, seven; Betty Wagner, seven; Mary White, eleven!

If you're wondering what was the matter with Edwina Froelich, the answer is that she married in her late thirties, and had all the children she could during her remaining fertile years. Though she couldn't manage a great number, at least she was able to have homebirths and breastfeed them long term, and, as her biographical note in *The Womanly*

> **Birth control**
>
> It is not only the presence of children, whether in the parental bed or not, which results in the foregoing of impulsive sexual relations. Many parents choose not to subject themselves to the known and unknown physical danger or moral responsibilities of artificial contraception. When they wish to limit the size of their family or postpone pregnancy, they use the highly effective method of natural family planning. (*The Family Bed* by Tine Thevenin, p. 113)

Art of *Breastfeeding* informs us, gave up a flourishing career as a businesswoman for full-time motherhood. Her write-up is careful to add: "Early in her mothering, Edwina found it quite a struggle to give up the organized approach to life that had served her so well in the business world. It was only after she relaxed and accepted the unscheduled needs of her baby that she was able to truly enjoy motherhood."[13]—a truly classic description of the breastfeeding cult's view of what's wrong with working women.

14. *Anti-abortion.* When it comes to a woman's body, the world is full of people who are convinced that they have God's own instruction for what a woman should do, whether with her breasts or with her womb. It is consistent with the views of many breastfeeding cultists who regard both pregnancy and childbirth as sacred states, that abortion is anathema, and that once the beginnings of a human baby have formed within the womb, that new life—a "baby" (not an embryo or a fetus)—should be considered as a full human being, whose needs take precedence over the pregnant woman's needs. The best examples of the anti-abortion stance of militant breastfeeders came from stories by two respondents who had attended La Leche

Abortion

The breastfeeding/anti-abortion camp is filled with vocal militants who believe their way is the only way, and they know what the right decision is for everyone. They proceed to list all the reasons why you are a terrible person for believing what you do. Pro-choice and pro-formula people generally respect the woman's right to do what she feels is morally acceptable for herself. They don't bad-mouth other women's decisions.

—Jane, on her run-ins with anti-abortion activists in the breastfeeding movement

League meetings, one in the midwest, outside of Chicago, the other in Northern Virginia. In both cases my respondents, who believe that abortion is a personal decision, were appalled to find that their local chapter was being used as an anti-abortion lobbying group. Women who attended were propagandized against abortion by the chapter leaders, who assumed that all breastfeeding mothers shared their views. Although La Leche League International takes no official position on abortion rights, it appears that some of its chapter leaders and members are using LLLI meetings to push their own agendas.

15. *Much of modern pediatrics is rejected as "unnatural."* Breastfeeding cultists prefer holistic healing methods and naturopathy.[14] Breastfeeding provides so many health benefits that it shouldn't be necessary to have baby checked, poked, prodded, and given various manufactured chemical compounds when sick. Most pediatricians are men and as such can't understand the baby the way a mother can—these sentiments show up in letters in breastfeeding cult journals written by mothers who were about to let a pediatrician try some standard treatment on the baby, until, at the last minute, the mother decided to trust her own mothering instincts and try out some ancient tribal cure, or some other more natural or holistic form of healing. These stories always end happily, with the baby fully recovered. (Some babies and certain illnesses don't respond to holistic cures, but in those cases, the mother would not send a letter to one of these journals.) A multitude of ads for homeopathic books or substances appeared in every breastfeeding publication I reviewed.

16. *Modern-day, capitalist society is "sick," whereas ancient, tribal, or agrarian societies are good.* These attitudes come through over the e-mail networks every time a breastfeeding advocate cites the way things are done in the Third World or in pre-modern times as examples of how things *ought* to be done. The attitude shows when militants attack formula companies, not only for manufacturing a harmful substance, but also for being profit-making enterprises. Using technology to do what could be accomplished naturally is "male thinking" and inherently alien to the "nurturing" female perspective. Only women are capable of appreciating how out-of-whack our modern, technological society has become, because only women experience the natural, cyclical rhythms of life that course through their bodies in the regular ebb and flow of hormones (unless they suppress those hormones by using artificial methods of birth control, by failing to breastfeed, by going on replacement estrogen therapy after menopause, or otherwise denying their "female natures").

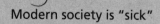

Modern society is "sick"

In the article "Sisters, Where Are You?" in The Compleat Mother *(Summer 1994), writer Theresa Rose yearns nostalgically for a simpler past in which women nursed together:*

What happened to the days when we lived with or near our supportive extended families? We can only guess what they must have been like: The monotony of their days was pleasantly broken by womanly companionship—talking, gossiping, singing, playing with children, and nursing. Necessary chores were done with a buddy. The constant responsibility for watching over the young was lessened by another woman or young girl who could keep an eye on the children while the mother bathed, read, or sat for a few minutes to gather her thoughts and quiet her mind. It is easy to look back at the women who lived 100 years ago as "those poor women," who had no microwave ovens, washing machines, frozen dinners, vacuum cleaners. But are they looking down on us with the same pity? . . . Today's mothers lack a necessity—companionship. . . .We nurturant mothers hold some similarities with our foremothers. Among them are exclusive breastfeeding, natural childbirth, and homebirth with midwives, natural diapers, organic food, unvaccinated, uncircumcised children, and homeschooling. But we "natural" mothers are rare. . . . [The author goes on to detail how childrearing practices have changed for the worse.] Formula has been proven inferior and harmful to babies. The cesarean rate is near 25 percent in America, medicated births are the norm, as are routine episiotomies. Cotton diapers are kinder to babies' skin, but plastic disposables are clogging our landfills after making babies' bottoms red, rashed, and sore. Pesticides are harmful, even carcinogenic. Vaccinations cripple, kill, and damage children. Routine circumcision is still frequently performed. No one can be a purist. I'm not suggesting that women should be barefoot and pregnant (although I'm both at the moment) or toss out her washing machine for an old-fashioned washboard. I'm just saying it would be wonderful to look out the kitchen window on any

> afternoon and see a neighborhood full of happily playing children and parents who shared my natural views on birth and parenting . . . .
>
> Only now are we beginning to grasp the extent to which the undermining of the maternal attachment process with its reciprocal bonding of infant to mother has contributed to the maternal and adult delinquency of a sick society. (*The Womanly Art of Breastfeeding,* La Leche League, p. xxi.)
>
> Bottles and formula, cribs and clocks, and night lights are inventions that have been tried on children over the past several short centuries. In the meantime, Mother's milk and Mother's arms have always been available, patiently waiting for the passing of man's foolhardy arrogance, which tried to convince us that his inventions were superior to nature. (*The Family Bed* by Tine Thevenin, p. 6)

17. Circumcision is a form of mutilation practiced on male babies which should be banned. Strong anti-circumcision rhetoric cropped up repeatedly in articles and letters in all the breastfeeding cult journals I collected.[15] A true cultist would never allow a son to be circumcised.

18. Vaccination is suspect—babies and children are probably better off without it. This is the belief of a radical fringe within the cult, but has enough support that I include it here. I found ads for nine different books or pamphlets opposing or questioning the need for vaccination in two different catalogs of natural baby products and breastfeeding supplies (Ecobaby and The Natural Baby).[16]

19. Homeschooling is the preferred method of educating children. Very few breastfeeding cultists actually put homeschooling into practice, but there is much admiration for those who do.[17] Anything that removes the child from the mainstream, industrialized culture is applauded. The homeschooled child can be breastfed until an advanced age without any fear of being discovered, will be assured lunches made from only organic, homegrown fruits and vegetables, does not need to present a certificate of vaccination, and will not become propagandized to accept the corporate, hustling, money-oriented concepts of success that teachers in public classrooms impart.

The Total Mindset

Some of the writings I found in my research perfectly exemplify the cult mind-set as a whole. The Compleat Mother *(Summer, 1994) is a veritable fountainhead of their views and practices. Here is a sampling of letters from that issue:*

I don't think [*The Compleat Mother* is] radical. What is radical is our society acting as if natural homebirth and breastfeeding are, and accepting early separation, circumcision, and vaccinations as normal. I sold out to hospital birth, circumcision, and vaccination, and now school, after ten years of homeschooling. I hope your presence helps others not to sell out—it hurts to go against what you know to be true.

• • •

My hubby has left and I am feeling stronger and more whole than ever. My daughter is almost four, still asks for her "nipple" at bedtime and during the night. Renew my subscription; my daughter and I need our *Mother.*

• • •

Our financial situation is precarious; I gave up a good income and career to stay at home with my two sons, ages four and ten months. It hasn't been easy, with opposition to my mothering methods—breastfeeding and the family bed. My husband even became distant and unsupportive, resenting the baby in our bed and the energy needed to care for two small children which he felt he needed more than they did. He resorted to another woman. I still hold fast to my heartfelt mothering and get love from the hugs and smiles of my happy and secure boys.

• • •

As I have cancer in the family, I want to protect myself as much as I can, which is a nice side benefit of breastfeeding. I don't want mammograms or estrogen when that "time" comes. I have a sister-in-law who let a doctor talk her out of breastfeeding two kids, has mammograms, and takes estrogen, as she has entered menopause. I feel like I am waiting to hear bad news.

• • •

I'm pleasantly surprised with *The Mother's* offerings. I am the mother of three homebirthed, homeschooled, cloth-diapered, nursed, vegetarian, nonvaccinated children.

CHAPTER 4

Bottlefeeding, Fast and Simple

Virtually all of the women I interviewed who had originally intended to breastfeed put a great deal of forethought and planning into their decision. They read books or articles while pregnant; they rubbed their nipples with washcloths daily to toughen them; they wore nipple shields for weeks on end to draw out flat or inverted nipples; they attended La Leche League meetings or Lamaze classes to learn techniques for breastfeeding success.

However, when breastfeeding did not work out, for whatever reason, and the new mother found herself giving the baby that first bottle, she was almost always on her own. There were no classes to take, no books to turn to, no magazine articles. Her doctor assumed no instruction was needed. The baby wouldn't need a lactation consultant (or that pricier subspecialty, the "suck therapist") to teach it to draw milk. The mother wouldn't need diagrams on correct positioning to help her get it right . . . right?

Not quite. Though it's true that bottlefeeding is easier to learn than breastfeeding, there are still some important issues involved, and new mothers still want and need information about how best to feed formula. First and most important: What sort of formula—milk-based or soy? Does it make a difference? What about preparation? Is ready-to-feed formula in cans better than liquid concentrate or the powdered form? (It's certainly more expensive.) Should bottles and nipples be boiled for sterilization before each use? If so, for how long, and will there come a time when the baby no longer needs to drink from a sterile bottle? What about feeding positions?

A pediatrician may give parents answers to these and other questions, but probably not at 3 A.M., when the family is in·crisis after five straight hours of the baby screaming and pushing away the breast. That's when the first hospital-supplied sample of formula is likely to be brought out.

Though the breastfeeding movement is against formula giveaways by pediatricians and hospitals, claiming that by the mere receipt of such packages mothers get the message that formula is the preferred choice of medical professionals, mothers themselves tell an opposite story.

All those I interviewed who were set on breastfeeding but received a gift-pack anyway stated that having the formula on hand had had no bearing on their decision to stop nursing. Many were grateful, once it became evident that the baby *needed* some other source of nutrition besides the mother's own milk, that they had a can or two on hand. Frantic parents did not have to run out to a grocery store in the middle of the night to round up supplies.

Did parents stay "hooked" on the brand of formula that they first received for free? Yes, if the baby appeared to accept it easily, and the pediatrician saw no reason to switch to another type. So in that limited way, hospital giveaways can be said to influence the new parents' choice.

If you plan from the outset to bottlefeed your baby, you have the luxury of time during your pregnancy (or while waiting for your adoptive baby) to consult a pediatrician about the pros and cons of different types and brands of formula, given your own set of circumstances (your budget, schedule, your kitchen and refrigerator space, and other factors). Unless your pediatrician identifies a specific *medical* reason* for using this or that formula, you are free to pick and choose among many varieties in today's market to find what works best for you and your baby.

Milk versus Soy Formulas

Parents I interviewed who chose soy formulas tended to feel strongly that it was best for babies' delicate digestive systems. Often they were directed towards soy by their pediatrician when the baby seemed gassy or upset following a feeding with a milk-based formula. If there is a history of milk allergy or lactose intolerance in either the mother's or father's family, soy might be the safest choice for the baby, even if there is no apparent discomfort with milk formula.

In some cases, babies who are capable of digesting cow's milk formula without problems may be directed by the pediatrician to soy formula during a bout of mild diarrhea.** My bottlefed daughter used to get mild diarrhea every time she cut a new tooth. Although she drank milk-based formula under normal circumstances, at the first sign of loose, too-frequent stools, we would switch her over to soy, and within a day or two, her diarrhea would be gone.

If soy seems better tolerated by some milk-sensitive babies and is better for all babies in times of mild diarrhea, then why shouldn't every parent prefer it? It does have a few disadvantages. It is somewhat harder to find in small

---

*For example, a strong family history of milk allergy, in which case you might be advised to use only a soy-based formula.

**In cases of moderate to severe diarrhea, pediatricians will usually tell parents to withhold all formulas and put the baby on Pedialyte™ or Ricelyte™, electrolyte replacement solutions designed to put back necessary body salts depleted by excessive bowel movements or vomiting.

convenience stores, and it tends to be a bit more expensive (about ten cents more per 32-ounce can, in my impromptu supermarket survey). Soy formula will leave your baby with stinky breath, and it must be said that there is hardly anything fouler-smelling than a soy-fed baby's poop. (One significant benefit of breastfeeding: the breastfed baby's poop is virtually without offensive odor; but among the formulas, all of which produce an offensive smell of waste, there is no question that soy makes for the most malodorous diapers.)

Another reason to use cow's milk formula (provided there is no medical reason to avoid it) is that by doing so your baby will become accustomed to the taste of dairy-based products. For most of us in the United States, cow's milk, cheeses, yogurts, and other foods made from or with milk will be our most important source of calcium throughout our lives. If, as most pediatricians recommend, you are intent on switching your formula-fed baby over to whole milk around the first birthday, you will probably have an easier time doing so from cow's milk formula than from soy.

Specialized Formulas

Lactose-free milk formula   Mead-Johnson, the maker of Enfamil milk-based and Prosobee soy-based formulas, sells a milk-based formula called Lactofree, from which all lactose (or milk sugar) has been removed. Many who are sensitive to milk-based products are not actually allergic to the proteins in milk; the stomach upset is caused by difficulty digesting the form of sugar found in milk. They do not need to avoid all milk products; they do fine with milk from which lactose has been removed. Adults can buy lactose-free milk in the supermarket (under the brand names Lact-Aid or Dairy-Ease), or they may buy enzyme drops to add to regular milk to neutralize its lactose content. Now

there is also an infant formula made without lactose. If lactose intolerance runs in your family or ethnic group (as it
does for a majority of Asian- and African-Americans), your
baby may not do well on a cow's-milk-based formula. You
may not have to switch all the way over to a soy-based formula; you might want to try Lactofree. Should you discover, after a week or two using Lactofree, that your child
still seems gassy or fussy after a bottle, then try switching
to soy, or perhaps try one of the hypoallergenic formulas.

Hypoallergenic formula   A trip to my local supermarket
turned up four brands formulated for babies with food
sensitivities. Nutramigen, by Mead-Johnson, announces on
its label that it is "recommended for infants with colic or
other allergy symptoms due to milk protein allergy." Its
main ingredients (after water), are corn syrup solids and
vegetable oils (palm, soy, coconut, and safflower oils). Alimentum, produced by Ross Laboratories (makers of Similac milk-based and Isomil soy-based formulas) bears a
label describing it as a "nutritionally complete formula for
infants and children with severe food allergies, sensitivity
to intact protein, protein maldigestion, or fat malabsorp-
tion." Its main ingredients after water are sugar (sucrose),
casein hydrolysate (a predigested milk protein), modified
tapioca starch, and various vegetable oils. Soyalac and I-
Soyalac, both made by Mt. Vernon Foods, Inc., are "completely free of animal products" for babies who may be
allergic to animal-derived proteins or fats—or for babies
whose parents, for their own reasons, adhere to a vegetarian diet. I-Soyalac will also suit the baby with a corn
allergy, as it is free of all corn syrups and starches; while
Soyalac contains corn products but no tropical oils—for
those whose family history of high cholesterol indicates a
need to avoid highly saturated fats.

   Two of the four hypoallergenic formulas were expensive:
Nutramigen and Alimentum (32-ounce cans) were both
priced a walloping 50 percent more than the same size cans

of Enfamil and Similac at the supermarkets I surveyed ($2.74 per can versus $1.84 per can—costing the family an extra three hundred dollars, on average, per year). I-Soyalac and Soyalac, on the other hand, were priced the same as easier-to-find, milk-based brands.

Should you try a hypoallergenic formula? Consider this: When a baby is consistently fussy after each feeding, the cause may be something other than an allergy to an ingredient in the formula. Some babies just tend to have "fussy hours" at regular intervals throughout the day, or it could be that their small, immature stomachs aren't used to the processes of digestion yet (this is one theory to account for colic). While one pediatrician may be quick to put the baby on a hypoallergenic formula, another may simply shrug and say, "Many babies spit up a lot and act colicky; wait a month or two, and see if things change." A few bottlefeeding parents I interviewed told of trying a week of this or that hypoallergenic formula and seeing dramatic improvement. As all formulas meet federally mandated nutritional standards when correctly prepared, I see no downside in trying out different brands for a week at a time, until you find one that seems to work for your baby.

Keep in mind, too, that a common cause of stomach upset in infants is over-feeding. Their tiny tummies can only digest so much formula at once. With breastmilk there is less danger of the baby getting too much at once, as the baby who keeps sucking on a breast will be getting only minute amounts. If you're getting a fussy, colicky reaction

How Much to Feed?

The general rule of thumb is this: Your baby needs 2 to $2\frac{1}{2}$ ounces per pound of body weight per day. That is to say, a ten-pound baby should be consuming between twenty and twenty-five ounces of formula per day.

from your baby after feedings, try offering less in each bottle (for a newborn, only a few ounces at a time) and offer the bottle more frequently to keep the daily caloric intake constant.

Diarrhea formula   Ross Laboratories makes Isomil-DF, specially formulated with soy fiber to help normalize the bowel movements of babies with mild diarrhea. *Always call your pediatrician first before attempting to treat diarrhea.* Improperly treated, diarrhea can become a life-threatening condition in an infant. Keeping a can of Isomil-DF as well as a bottle of Pedialyte on hand is a good precaution; in the event that your pediatrician directs you to use either one, you will be able to commence treatment immediately. Furthermore, Isomil-DF is not always easy to find in stores, and you don't want to waste any time shopping around for it, should the need become acute.

Premature infant formula   Ross Laboratories produces a brand called Neocare, which, according to its label, is specially formulated to meet the nutrition needs of premature infants. I compared the ingredients of Neocare to those of Similac and found that Neocare contains slightly greater vitamin, fat, and protein content per ounce, but significantly less linoleic acid (an essential fatty acid) than an ounce of regular formula. Parents of premature babies should consult their pediatricians to find out if the Neocare formulation offers any advantages in their case. The price of a tub of powdered Neocare was the same as that of a tub of Similac powder.

Toddler formula   The glory of our free market system is said to be the incentive it provides to solve problems by rewarding inventors with profits for innovations. Critics, however, claim that inventors of unnecessary products often use clever marketing campaigns to persuade consumers that a problem exists when it doesn't. Some view toddler formula as a prime example. Its manufacturers tout toddler formula as perfect for the child who is over a year old but not yet eating a well-balanced diet of table foods. The chief difference between toddler formulas and whole cow's milk is that toddler formula is iron-fortified, and has increased levels of vitamins C and E. Two brands of toddler formula are available at my neighborhood supermarket: Mead-Johnson's Next Step brand (as a powder, concentrate, or ready-to-feed liquid in cans, in milk-based or soy-based formulations); and Ross Laboratories' Toddler's Best brand (in single-serving disposable boxes with attached straws, in vanilla, chocolate, and berry flavors).

The chief disadvantage to toddler formula is the expense. I found the price per pint identical to that of most formulas (around $3.00 a quart)—but you can get whole milk for around 77 cents a quart, and you don't have to lug home those heavy cans. If you are concerned that your toddler is not getting enough iron and vitamins through solid foods, it's much cheaper to buy children's chewable iron-enriched vitamins (about $6.50 for 100 tablets) and offer one a day. Most kids love them. On the other hand, if your child balks at the switch to less rich-tasting whole

---

Can You Mix Your Own?

Out-of-date childcare books often include directions for parents to make up their own formulas from evaporated milk, water, and corn syrup such as Karo's. I can't think of any reason why parents these days might do this on a regular basis rather than buy commercially manufactured formula, which must meet stringent standards for nutritional quality and purity. However, if you find yourself snowed in for several days and have used up all your other supplies, get out your copy of Dr. Spock and follow his directions.

milk, toddler formula may work as a transitional drink, leading slowly to whole milk within a few weeks or months (see chapter 6 for other tips on getting your kids off the formula bottle).

Iron-fortified versus Low-Iron

The most important distinction between formula types, other than the milk/soy choice, is that some are iron-fortified while others are low-iron (1.8 milligrams iron per 100 calories of iron-fortified formula, 0.5 milligrams per 100 calories of low-iron formula). Babies at birth have about a four- to six-month iron reserve, though nearly all pediatric literature I read recommended using the iron-fortified variety from the start. Many parents I interviewed, however, preferred the low-iron variety, for one simple reason: their baby's comfort. Iron is hard to digest, often causing constipation (if you took iron-enriched prenatal vitamins, you may well have experienced this reaction yourself). Breastmilk is also very low in iron (0.3 milligrams per liter—though studies have shown the iron in breastmilk is more easily and completely absorbed than the iron in formula).

If the baby begins eating iron-rich, solid foods at four to six months, the parents need not worry about iron deficiency, and can safely use a low-iron formula. On the other hand, if the six-months or under infant appears to tolerate an iron-fortified formula just as well as a low-iron one, stick with the iron-fortified variety.

Pediatricians on the Internet's medical forum offer sharply differing opinions on whether iron-fortified formulas generally cause stomach upset or whether that is a myth. What I heard from formula-feeding parents (and know from experience) is that many babies on iron-fortified formula do become constipated and will appear to be straining when producing their bowel movements. If this describes your under-six-months-old baby on an iron-fortified formula, consider switching to a low-iron formula for a week and watch for improvement.

Are All Brands Alike?

As noted, hypoallergenic or diarrhea formulas are just two of the many choices you have for bottlefeeding your baby. Now suppose you are using an ordinary cow's-milk-based formula: Is there any real difference between Enfamil and Similac, or between Carnation and SMA? Nutritionally, the answer is an unequivocal no. Since 1980 the federal government has set stringent rules mandating the nutritional content of formulas. The percentages of vitamins, proteins, sugars, and fat must be the same from brand to brand, and even from variety to variety (that is to say, soy-based Prosobee is the nutritional equivalent of milk-based Similac).

Once you've decided on soy versus milk, shouldn't you go with whatever is cheapest? You may certainly do so without worry that you might be giving your baby an inferior product; however, just because all the brands must meet the same standards, that doesn't mean they will be alike in all ways. There can still be differences in the way the fats are absorbed, or how the proteins are broken down, and your baby will almost certainly discern differences in taste from brand to brand. If your baby appears happy with one brand, and it's not hard to find that brand in your local stores, stick with that.

I asked the sixty-four mothers I interviewed about their formula preferences, and milk-based formula won out over soy by a two to one margin. Similac With Iron was the number one choice, followed closely by Enfamil With Iron. Isomil Soy formula came in third, with all other choices receiving three or fewer votes. "Mothers Talk" stories tell some of the reasons moms had for choosing one formula over another.

Mothers Talk About Formula

The pediatrician told me if breastmilk is 100 on a scale of 100, the formulas today rate a 99.

—*Lorraine*

I'm tired of all this harping [on this e-mail bulletin board] about how difficult it is to mix/store/clean bottles. There are Playtex bottle liners—no cleaning involved. There are individual cans of formula (a little more expensive, but sometimes it's worth it). There is powder, which is *very* convenient—just find a water fountain. There are such things as coolers to keep things cold. We have one especially for bottles; it's 6 × 4 inches and holds four 8-ounce bottles. Excuse me for venting about this, but when I read messages from people saying how hard it is to bottlefeed [rather than breastfeed], I feel like they're just trying to give everyone who bottlefeeds a guilt trip.

—*Cassie*

I knew nothing about bottlefeeding. The hospital didn't give me any information on it—no one told me how to do it. I had no books on it. It's not as simple as you might think. I called the lactation consultant, who said, "If you *must* do it, at least use orthodontic nipples." I asked my doctor about formula. He said they're all the same, but if what you're using seems to work, don't switch.

—*Julie*

We tried Enfamil, but our daughter had horrible gas pains, so we switched to Isomil soy. The iron in the

Isomil made her constipated, and even on soy she had gas. We used lots of Mylicon [over-the-counter anti-gas drops for infants].

—Carla

During a time when I was unable to nurse I tried out many different formulas until I came upon one that my baby liked. It happened to be Isomil, a soy-based formula. Apparently, it is sweet, just like breastmilk.

—Angie

My mother, a pediatric nurse practitioner, says that a dishwasher set to "sani" temperature is fine for sterilizing bottles. She also advised me not to leave old, partially filled bottles out so long that they smell cheesy— then they're really hard to get clean.

—Jamie

My son had reflux [frequent spitting up]. For his first seven months the only formula that worked was Alimentum. Then he was on Nursoy, as was my daughter.

—Tiffany

I breastfed my son three months, but then had a problem getting him to adjust to infant formula. He had a lot of problems with gas. My pediatrician suggested SMA soy formula, and that did the trick.

—Claire

Feeding Positions

A breastfeeding guide will typically spend several pages, or even several chapters, discussing the pros and cons of the "cradle hold," the "football hold" or a number of other

Money-Saving Tip!

Buy in bulk. Warehouse-style supermarkets and price clubs offer a discount if you buy by the case. All formula has an expiration date, so check that you are getting formula in cans or tubs that won't expire for at least a year. That way, no matter how many cases you buy, you won't have to worry that it will go bad before you use it.

A Tip on Toting

One of the true conveniences of breastfeeding is that you don't have to run out and buy the product, nor do you have to lug home heavy cans from the supermarket. But here's a tip from some formula-feeding moms who found a simple way to make formula-buying less of a chore: Find a store that delivers! Nearly every city will have a pharmacy or specialized market that delivers, often for free with a minimum purchase, or perhaps at a nominal fee. If you buy in bulk, you may be able to get a discount large enough to offset any delivery fee.

positions for nursing. One of the advantages of bottlefeeding is that it matters far less how you hold your baby when you feed. Since you don't have to worry about improper latch-on or pain to your nipples from an incorrect position, you have many more choices. There are only three fixed rules to be observed:

1. *Do not* feed a baby who is lying flat. The head must be elevated so that the mouth is at least a little lower than the ears. This is to ensure that all the liquid goes down the baby's throat and none ends up flowing toward the nose and ear tubes, where milk bacteria could cause a serious infection.

2. Do not let the baby fall asleep while sucking. If the baby seems to be drifting off, remove the nipple from the baby's mouth and let the baby sleep. Allowing a baby to sleep with a nipple in its mouth will lead to nursing caries (also called "baby bottle mouth"—that is, decay of the incoming or already present baby teeth). Besides which, a baby who habitually drinks himself or herself to sleep will have a hard time learning to fall asleep any other way.*

3. Never prop the bottle in position. This is a basic safety rule. If the nipple should become dislodged, the baby could get the nipple stuck in its throat and choke. Some parents think, "I'm only leaving the room for a minute or two, and I don't want to interrupt my baby's feeding," and so they prop, but it only takes a few minutes for choking to cause permanent brain damage.

Other than these three rules, feel free to experiment to discover what position your baby likes best. Most babies like to be cuddled and held close to the mother's body, just as you would do if nursing. Many mothers I interviewed who had hoped to breastfeed made a point to give extra cuddling during bottlefeedings to compensate their babies for the lack of contact with the mother's nipple.

When the baby is old enough to sit with some support, many mothers find it convenient to use a baby seat or feeding chair that holds the baby in a semi-upright position. That way the mother can hold the bottle with one hand,

---

*This advice applies equally to nursing mothers, who may find it even harder to discourage the baby from nursing to sleep. One of the advantages of formula over breastmilk is that the feeder will find it easier to keep eating a waking activity. Warm breastmilk does have sleep-inducing qualities.

leaving her free to write, make phone calls, or feed herself, while tending to her baby.

Seat feeding gives bottlefeeding parents one particular advantage over breastfeeding mothers, and that is the ability to feed while in motion. Only bottlefeeding parents can satisfy a baby's hunger cry while in a moving car without compromising either the baby's or the mother's safety. Yes, it is possible for a breastfeeding mother, while a passenger in a car, to lean over the baby's car-seat, pull up her blouse and nurse—but the mother must remove her seat belt, putting her own life in jeopardy.

However, this advantage, in the minds of at least a few mothers, can end up being a disadvantage, in that baby can be given a bottle all too easily, in every situation to satisfy every little cry, resulting in overfeeding. Because a nursing mother must always stop what she is doing and take the time to open her shirt and position her baby (which may not be possible to accomplish each time the baby fusses), she may tend to become more discerning about the urgency of her baby's cry for food. Bottlefed babies are therefore more likely to end up regarding the bottle, not as the answer to true hunger, but simply as a comfort object, a prop more akin to a pacifier than a source of food. The baby who carries a bottle around all day and can't fall asleep except with a bottle at naptime or at night will be greatly at risk for nursing caries (dentists' term for decay of the primary teeth). To prevent this syndrome, many of my interviewees enforced rules such as "no bottles while walking around," or "no bottles in the stroller," as well as the basic safety rule, "no bottles in the crib."

Quite a few bottlefeeding mothers went even farther and would only give a bottle while the baby was held in the mother's lap, just as a breastfed baby would be fed. Some of these mothers had heard the charge, often made by breastfeeding militants, that bottlefed babies do not get enough physical contact with their mothers during feedings, nor do they receive their mother's full attention the way breastfed babies do, and they were intent on ensuring that such would not be the case with their babies. For that reason a few of the mothers I interviewed disapproved strongly of the use of feeding chairs.

On the other hand, those bottlefeeding mothers who do use feeding chairs say that their babies would squirm and fidget if forced to be held during every feeding; they don't think it's necessary for the baby to get constant attention during every feeding, and besides, there are plenty of breastfeeding mothers who talk on the phone or have a sandwich while nursing.

Mothers who favor feeding the baby in a chair usually will encourage the baby to learn to hold his or her own bottle at an early age, starting to teach this skill at perhaps two to three months, and the baby will be able to handle the bottle independently by four to six months. Ability to self-feed without doubt confers greater freedom on the parent; some bottlefeeding parents also claim it encourages an independent spirit in the baby. However, breastfeeding mothers hotly dispute the assertion; I noted some indignant e-mail messages on the subject from long-term breastfeeders, such as this one:

"I think of my three-year-old who is nursing . . . If there is a child more independent than my Harmony I would like to meet him/her!" And there was this, on the same forum: "I breastfed my son until he was two years old, and he is one of the most independent children I know."

Some bottlefeeding mothers make character judgments based on feeding style just as some breastfeeding mothers do; no matter where it's coming from, such criticisms are unwarranted.

Emergency Supplies

Let's say your area is occasionally hit by a tornado, hurricane, blizzard, earthquake, or flood, when you might not be able to get to a store. There is hardly a region on this planet that is not subject to some form of natural disaster, and parents of bottlefed babies, like all good scouts, should be prepared. Set aside, on a high shelf in the most protected storage area of your house (usually in the basement, except in places at risk for heavy flooding), a two-week supply of formula in cans. Use only ready-to-feed formulations, as your water supply could be knocked out or polluted by the disaster. The storage place should be protected from excessive heat or cold. A can opener and a few clean bottles and nipples should be sealed in a plastic bag and kept in the same safe spot. There is no need to stock up for the long haul: If there is an area-wide disaster of such proportions that no stores are left standing, the Red Cross will be opening shelters and will be sure to have formula on hand for infants whose parents are caught without supplies.

To Sterilize or Not

This question illustrates just how out-of-date is the bottle-feeding advice that most new mothers receive. The answer to the sterilization question, for most families in places that have safe water supplies, is a plain and simple no. Parents who turn to baby care experts such as Dr. Spock and Penelope Leach might read of a need for caution that is no longer necessary.

Dr. Spock's classic work *Baby and Child Care* devotes a number of pages to descriptions and comparisons of different sterilization methods for commercially prepared formula. Methods for sterilizing home-made formula are also detailed. In her best-selling guide *Your Baby and Child from Birth to Age Five*, Penelope Leach stresses the need for sterilization of all implements used in the making of formula, in all cases:

> To keep baby's milk as free from bacteria as possible:
> . . . use a sterile formula . . . .

Sterilize everything you use in measuring, mixing, or storing the made-up milk. That means measuring spoons, mixing jars, and the water in the food itself.

Sterilize bottles, nipples, and nipple covers. Provided that you put a sterile nipple cover over the sterilized nipple on your ready-filled bottle, that nipple will still be sterile and safe when you take the cover off to feed the baby. (1990 edition, p. 62)

Leach covers various methods of sterilization. Spock says that five minutes in a big kettle at a "hard boil" is sufficient time to kill bacteria, but Leach advises submerging everything in "fully boiling water for at least ten minutes." With advice such as this it is no wonder that breastfeeding mothers so often assume that bottlefeeding is tedious and time-consuming and that their way is more convenient.

Nearly all pediatricians are advising their patients differently these days about sterilization: It's unnecessary, they believe, except in a few special circumstances. Here's how the mass-circulation monthly, *Parenting* magazine, put it recently:

In most urban and suburban areas, hot tap water and detergent are all that's required for washing baby's bottles, nipples, and other utensils. (Always scrub bottles thoroughly to get rid of dried milk or juice, a breeding ground for bacteria). But in homes supplied with well water or nonchlorinated water, parents of babies younger than six months should take extra care: Be sure to boil all utensils for five to ten minutes before use. (*Parenting*, April 1994, pp. 117–118)

My own pediatrician told me the same, and I have found formula preparation to be quick and easy ever since. However, a sizable percentage (34 percent) of my interviewees sterilized all their equipment for a period of some months, even when they lived in cities or towns with safe, chlorinated water. Most kept up sterilization procedures for three to four months, with a few stopping at five to six months, and one reported having sterilized bottles for as long as the baby used them.

How do you know that the water in your area is safe enough? Do a little investigation. Your pediatrician might be a reliable source of information, but you can also send off a water sample to a laboratory for a complete analysis. In some areas you will have to pay a commercial lab for the service; but first call your local water utility company to find out if it will provide a free analysis for bacterial contaminants and protozoa. It may be helpful to explain that you have or are expecting a baby. Of course you will maintain the sterility of your equipment until you are assured such measures are not warranted.

All parents of infants (even breastfed ones) should have their water supply checked for presence of lead (since lead can pass to the baby's bloodstream through the mother's breastmilk). If it turns out you have lead in your water, do *not* use it for anything that will touch your baby's mouth. Use bottled water only, until you can have your lead problem eliminated, by means of filtration or replacement of all lead-soldered pipes with a safer type.

If your pediatrician does say to sterilize, ask for how many months the practice should be continued. At three to six months, depending on how your pediatrician views the risk, your baby's immune system should be developed enough to withstand most of the impurities that we adults routinely ingest without trouble.

If you have a dishwasher with a sani-rinse cycle (that uses an internal heating element to heat the water to a high temperature), ask your pediatrician if a sani-rinse wash will suffice instead of the usual boiling five minutes on a stove-top.

Using the sani-rinse cycle (if you have one) is a simple precaution to continue for as long as you will be washing bottles and nipples. That way, you may be assured that any bacteria that may be lurking in the crevices and crannies of your bottlefeeding equipment has been eliminated before it can do harm to your baby.

Always Sterilize on First Use

Bottles, nipples, rings, and tops should be sterilized ONCE before they are used. The simplest way to sterilize is to fill a pot with tap water, bring it to a vigorous boil, and drop in the items to be sterilized. Boil for five minutes. If the item floats, be sure it remains submerged in the pot so that all sides are in contact with boiling water for the full amount of time. Though you need not sterilize before each subsequent use (provided your area has a reliably clean water supply), there is one other hygiene precaution you should observe: Always wash your hands prior to preparing formula. (If you think this is an extra step, let me add that breastfeeding mothers are well advised to wash their hands before each breastfeeding, too. A good many cases of mastitis might be prevented if more mothers followed this simple safety step.)

Preparation Methods: Cans versus Powders

Following is a five-point comparison of the four most popular forms of formula: powdered, liquid concentrate, ready-to-feed in cans, and ready-to-feed in single serving "nursettes" (four- or six-ounce glass bottles).

Parents usually like to experiment with different types before settling on one that works best for them. Often, they prefer one form for a newborn but switch to another as the baby gets older. The most common pattern I found was an initial preference for ready-to-feed in cans (it's more expensive, but it's fast, and mistake-proof), then a switchover to the powdered form as the parents become more confident of their formula-making capabilities (powdered is significantly cheaper, and easier to take along on outings).

Formula Comparison

FACTORS TO CONSIDER	POWDERED (14-OUNCE TUBS)	LIQUID CONCEN-TRATE (13-OUNCE CANS)	READY-TO-FEED (32-OUNCE CANS)	NURSETTES (4- OR 6-OUNCE GLASS BOTTLES)
Cost per pint (avg. for 10 brands)	$1.17	$1.43	$1.70	$5.72
Ease of preparation	4 Steps Fill bottle with warm water to number of ounces desired. Add 1 scoop of powder for every 2 ounces of warm water in bottle. Stir well to break up clumps. Attach nipple/ring and serve.	3 Steps Fill bottle with water to half of number of ounces desired. Add 1 ounce of concentrate for each ounce of water. Attach nipple/ring and serve.	2 Steps Pour into bottle, attach nipple/ring and serve.	1 Step Attach nipple/ring and serve.
Portability	Highly portable. Measured, unmixed powder can be kept in small container or plastic baggie, along with empty bottle, and combined with tap water when needed.	Best to avoid carrying heavy cans around. Make up needed bottles in advance of trip and transport in insulated tote-bag with refrigerated gel-pack to keep at safe temperature until needed.	Best to avoid carrying heavy cans around. Make up needed bottles in advance of trip and transport in insulated tote-bag with refrigerated gel-pack to keep at safe temperature until needed.	Speediest feeding on the go. No mixing required—just pop on a clean nipple and serve. Disadvantages: glass bottles can break if not well protected and are heavier than plastic. Advantage: used nursettes are disposable.
Shelf-life (unopened)	Expiration date may be more than 2 yrs.	Expiration date may be more than 1 yr.	Expiration date may be more than 1 yr.	Expiration date may be more than 1 yr.
Shelf-life (opened)	1 month	48 hours when opened can is kept tightly covered in refrigerator	48 hours when opened can is kept tightly covered in refrigerator	Opened bottle is not reusable after baby is done with it. Leftover contents should be discarded.

Every mother, of course, needs to look at her own situation to figure out what is most suitable. If you'll be doing a lot of feeding on the road, consider powder. If you need to save money, then there's no question that powder is the right choice. When time is limited—say you've got to get the formula made and delivered to the daycare center by eight every morning—perhaps the ready-to-feed in cans is for you.

You can rely on different preparation methods for different situations. Use liquid concentrates or ready-to-feed in cans on a daily basis at home, but if you'll be taking the baby out for a few hours, bring along an empty bottle and a measured amount of powder, find a water fountain, and make what you need. On a long and crowded airplane flight, when you don't want to have to wait for a flight attendant to bring you some mixing water, stow a few

---

Money-Saving Tip!

New parents can really save money by signing up for one of the big formula makers' "new baby clubs." The Resource Guide in the back of this book gives information on how to sign up. Formula companies say that new mothers receive on average about $100 worth of formula and other supplies through hospital and doctor's office promotional giveaways, but if she signs up for a new baby club she can double or even triple her savings. Club memberships typically start off with a free case of the formula you choose, and at regular intervals mail you coupons good for one, or two, or even five dollars off your purchases. Unless your baby is wedded to a particular brand, there is no reason not to join each and every formula maker's club to collect the maximum possible number of freebies.

ready-made nursettes in your diaper bag, and you can just pop on a nipple and feed anytime the baby gets hungry.

If your baby will accept chilled formula, travel is made easy by bringing along an insulated bottle bag, a pack of "blue ice" (specially packaged gel that helps cold foods stay cold) and an already prepared bottle.

Warmed or Cold?

Breastfeeding guides often point out the inconvenience of having to warm bottles at home and keep bottles chilled while traveling to prevent spoilage, whereas the milk inside a woman's breast is always at the perfect temperature. You might get the idea from reading a breastfeeding guide that the chilling, storing, and warming of formula will be a constant hassle.

Yes, it can be, but it certainly doesn't have to be. First of all, there is nothing wrong with giving a baby a bottle cold from the refrigerator . . . provided the baby will drink it without protest. It's common for grandmothers and women from many other cultures to believe that it isn't good for the baby's tummy to drink any liquid cold; however, the pediatricians I consulted said, nonsense, that's simply a myth.

If you are starting with a newborn, you'll be doing yourself a favor by giving only cold bottles, so there will be no basis for your baby to prefer any other kind. That way you'll never have to bother with warming.

If you've already started giving warm bottles, or if you started off breastfeeding, your baby will naturally have come to expect it warm; but it will be worthwhile for you to cut down on the warming process by a few seconds each time, until you are serving the bottle at room temperature, and then finally, serving it cold.

Since your ultimate goal is to get your child drinking regular milk poured straight from the refrigerated carton into a cup, anything that advances your baby along that road will save you much time and trouble later on. It's far easier to start changing the habits of a three- or four-month-old baby than the habits of a fourteen-month-old toddler, or worst of all, a headstrong two-year-old.

But for those who don't mind warming or don't wish to enter into a prolonged battle with the baby over the matter, here are some of the most popular warming techniques:

Is Microwaving Safe?

Most cans of formula carry a warning that reads: "Do not use a microwave to prepare or warm formula. Serious burns may occur." Most parents who warmed their formula told me they did not use the microwave, not because of the risk of hot spots, but because they'd heard somewhere that microwaving destroys the nutrients in formula or milk.

However, scientific analysis of microwaved formula or milk has shown there is no nutrient loss. The risk of burning can be eliminated if the microwave is used only briefly and the parent inverts the bottle enough times to even out any hot spots. How brief should the microwaving be? Experts recommend no more than 30 seconds on high for an eight-ounce bottle. (Be sure to leave the nipple and ring off). But if, like me, you prefer to be on the safe side, try shortening the time to 20 or even 15 seconds for an eight-ounce bottle, and 12 seconds for a four- or six-ounce bottle—just enough to take the chill off it.

Take the bottle out of the microwave, put the nipple and ring on, and invert the bottle ten or fifteen times (you don't want to shake it, as that will add air bubbles). *Always* test the temperature by shaking out a drop of formula onto your wrist.

- For those who sterilize: Mix powdered formula or liquid concentrate with water that has been boiled five minutes and has been left to cool to 95° to 99°F (about body temperature, same as breastmilk). Serve the first bottle immediately, cover and refrigerate the rest, and when needed, warm refrigerated bottles by one of the methods below.
- Remove the chilled bottle from the refrigerator and run it under extremely hot tap water for a minute or two. Invert the bottle five or six times to even out the temperature inside the bottle. Be sure the nipple is not too hot from contact with the hot water.
- Remove the chilled bottle from the refrigerator and let it rest in a pot of extremely hot tap water for a few minutes. Invert the bottle five or six times to even out the temperature inside the bottle.
- Use an electric bottle warmer according to its instructions. (See the section on gadgets, page 172.)
- Warm in the microwave, *carefully*.

Bottles and Nipples

Once you've decided what formula to buy, what are you going to put it in? Be sure that the nipples you purchase will fit on your bottles and vice versa. Here are the main bottle choices:

- standard 4- or 8-ounce plastic bottles
- disposable sterile bag inserts that fit inside Playtex plastic holders
- "easy-to-hold" bottle shapes such as the squarish "Kindergrip" bottle by Playtex, or the hole-in-the-middle design by Änsa.
- Johnson & Johnson's angled "Healthflow" bottle

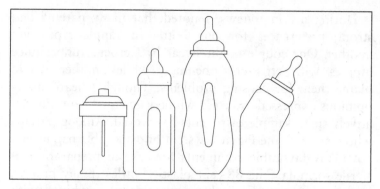

Fig. 4.1. The variety of bottles on the market include (left to right): the Playtex with disposable insert bag, square-shaped Kindergrip, Änsa, and Healthflow.

Here are the main nipple choices:

- rubber (beige or brown-colored) or silicone (clear)
- with or without anti-collapse ridges inside
- straight or orthodontic-shaped
- single-hole, three-hole, or cross-cut opening at the tip
- nipples graduated in size for different ages (newborn, infant, and toddler)
- wide-topped nipples designed to fit bottle holders using a disposable bag-insert system.

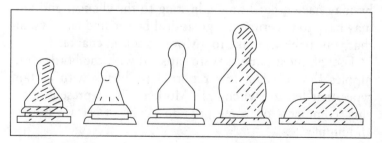

Fig. 4.2. Nipple choices include (left to right): standard rubber, silicon with anti-collapse ridges, Healthflow, Nuk, and Playtex.

During my interviews, I noted that many parents had strong preferences for one bottle or nipple type over another. One couple might swear by Gerber's rubber juice nipples with cross-cut openings, while another would blame them for causing problems. Though I heard many opinions expressed, no clear winners emerged from the relatively small sample of parents I surveyed. Among parents who sterilized, the Playtex system of disposable bag inserts got many favorable comments for ease of preparation of sterile formula. The 88-cent plastic bottles (many brands, but most commonly Gerber and Evenflo) combined with straight, rubber, single-hole nipples (three for 79 cents) got the plurality of votes in my nonscientific poll.

Those who checked with a doctor or lactation consultant were often advised to use "orthodontic" nipples (Nuk, Pur, and Mam are three widely available brands) because the shape is designed to resemble that of a mother's nipple when extended during sucking. Similarly, nipples with three tiny holes were recommended over the single-hole type, because the nursing mother's nipple sprays milk from multiple openings.

Consider what works best for you, and what your baby seems to like. (Of course, when they're young enough, they'll usually accept anything.) If you started off breastfeeding and are now switching over to bottlefeeding, your older baby may have a hard time adjusting to the change, and you may have to experiment a great deal before finding a system that your baby will take to. (More on this in chapter 6.)

Though most parents were satisfied with the bottles and nipples they used, a few reported problems with certain types that led to switching. "Mothers Talk" presents parents' comments on some pros and cons of certain bottles and nipples.

Gadgets

Breastfeeding mothers do have one thing over bottlefeeding

Mothers Talk About Bottles, Nipples, and Paraphernalia

We used to buy the cheap rubber nipples, but every other month the holes would get clogged, and the baby would be sucking and sucking and getting nothing out. My mother told me I should sterilize a sewing needle and use it to expand the hole, but that's too much trouble to go to for a 50-cent item, and besides, I'd rather not have to deal with the problem when the baby is hungry. So now I only use silicone nipples. They cost more, but I've never had one clog up on the baby.

—Karen

My baby likes silicone or rubber nipples equally well. The only problem we've had is with the nipples that don't have anti-collapse ridges on the inside. My son sucks for ten seconds and then the nipple collapses, and he cries. What's annoying is that the bottles I buy come with the cheapest rubber nipples, and I have to buy better, anti-clog nipples to go with every new bottle.

—Florence

What's really irritating is that the nipples come packaged in pairs, but the nipple rings come packaged in threes.

—Rosalyn

My pediatrician recommended Nuk nipples. She said they have a natural shape, similar to a breastfeeding mom's.

—June

My baby has gotten used to those odd-shaped Ansa bottles that the baby holds with both hands. My baby also likes her formula warmed, and we were very pleased with the automatic warmer we received as a gift—until we tried to put an Ansa bottle in it (they're extra wide) and discovered it wouldn't fit.

—Sonia

We received this very clever European design bottle system, called Avent, as a gift. The bottles are indented in the middle, wider than American bottles, with a wider than normal silicone nipple. The bottles also come with screw-on "sippy tops," so you can start training your baby to drink from a cup. Our baby loves the whole set. The problem comes when we're at someone else's house and need to borrow a bottle. Now she really hates to drink from anything except the familiar Avent bottles, and nobody else has got them!

—Wanda

I started using silicone nipples when my first child was born. They're so durable, I'm still using all the same nipples four years later with my new baby.

—Fiona

The best bottles are the 99-cent plastic ones I buy at K-mart. No fancy design, they fit any nipple, you can toss them in the top rack of the dishwasher, they fit in the bottle pocket of my diaper bag, and they last forever.

—Lana

For certain purposes, opaque, solid-colored bottles are useful. If I need to put a cough syrup in the baby's milk, I mix it in one of the blue or green colored bottles. My baby doesn't mind the change in flavor, but she does object if she can see the color change in her milk.

—Ingrid

I had a hard time switching my baby from breastfeeding to bottles, because my breastmilk used to let down very fast, while the single-hole rubber nipples seemed to let out the formula too slowly. Finally, we discovered Pur's "Toddler Fast-Flow" nipples. They're orthodontically correct silicone nipples with a relatively large hole at the end. They don't sell that many in the stores near us. I used to have to ask my mother-in-law in New York to buy them for me at the big discount pharmacy near her house, and mail them to me here [Washington, D.C.].

—Tracy

mothers—they always have their equipment with them and it's easy to carry around. Of course, many breastfeeding mothers still go out and buy gadgetry as well: pumps, nursing pillows, nursing stools, nipple shells, nipple creams, and manual expression funnels.

But all of this is minor compared to the catalogs full of gadgetry available to bottlefeeding parents. Glossy color catalogs such as The Right Start, One Step Ahead, The Orange Elephant, and Hand in Hand (see Resource Guide for toll-free numbers), each devote several pages to nifty items designed to make bottlefeeding more convenient than ever. While it's true that most bottlefeeding parents can get along very well without spending a lot of money on coolers, warmers, and other paraphernalia, it could be that you will discover just the product you've been hoping to find to solve some particular bottlefeeding problem.

Tip! One of the Best Liquids Is Free

Bottlefeeders can start instilling good habits early by introducing the baby at a young age to drinking water. Water has several advantages. On hot days, when a baby needs extra fluid but not extra calories, you can avoid the danger of dehydration by getting your baby to drink a bottle of water. If your older baby (over six months) is still waking up at night, a bottle of water instead of formula will satisfy thirst without adding to the risk of dental caries. Also, you don't have to go down to the kitchen to get the water, and it doesn't fill up the baby's tummy at a time when you want your child to learn to sleep all night without a feeding. A liking for the taste of water will be of great value later in the child's life when so many of his or her playmates are drinking little but sugary fruit punches and soda pop.

Electric Warmers

- *Babytec warmers* hold any size of bottle (even odd-shaped bottles such as Ansa "Easy-Grip" or Playtex disposables). Also good for warming baby food jars. Adjustable thermostat and automatic shut-off. $39.95. #G2666 - Right Start.

- *Nighttime Feeder* is both a warmer and a cooler, keeping two pre-chilled bottles cool for up to 8 hours, until needed for those middle-of-the-night feedings. Just remove a bottle from the cooling section, pop it in the steamer section, and three minutes later it is warmed to a comfortable temperature for baby. Keep Nighttime Feeder on your nightstand or on top of baby's dresser, and you'll never have to stumble around the kitchen at 2 A.M. again. UL approved. $46.95. #1735 - One Step Ahead.

- *Heat & Chill Wrap.* Conveniently sized to wrap around a single bottle, this thermal wraparound pouch contains an activator disk inside a reusable heating pad to warm up a chilled bottle within minutes. To keep the bottle cold, remove the heating pad and replace it with the freezer-pack that comes with the set. Keeps bottles at the desired temperature for hours. Simple, safe, non-electric. $24.95. #G321 - Right Start.

- *Auto bottle warmer.* This handy gadget is the answer for babies who want warm formula on long car trips. Take a bottle from your cooler and slip it into this adjustable wrapper, then plug into your car's cigarette lighter. When not in use, hang it from a knob on your dashboard or stow it away in the glove compartment. Also works in boats and RVs. $12.95. #G261 - Right Start.

Coolers and Bottle-totes

- *Stroll'r Hold'r.* Hooks over the push-bar of your stroller to give you a cup-holder for your baby's bottle or your own can of soda. Also snaps onto a shopping cart or bike handle. $7.95. #1177 - One Step Ahead.

- *Hot 'n' Cold Bag.* Compact zippered pouch lined with Thinsulate comes with a reusable gel-pack which can be frozen or heated to help keep cold bottles cool and warm bottles warm. 11" x 7½" size is just large enough for two bottles or one bottle and three baby food jars. $8.95. #G111 - Right Start.

- *Bottle insulator.* Single 8-ounce bottle holder made of insulating closed-cell foam keeps a chilled bottle cold or a warmed bottle warm. Also fits three baby food jars or two 4-ounce bottles. Includes carrying strap. Does not use a gel-pack. Available in royal, teal, or fuschia. $9.95. #2386 - One Step Ahead.

- *ThermoBottle.* This 8-ounce insulated bottle keeps warm liquids warm or cold liquids cold for up to four hours. Shatter-resistant, compact, lightweight, and portable, comes with nipple, ring, and protective cap, which also converts to a drinking cup. Dishwasher safe. $7.95. #03606 - The Orange Elephant.

- *Tote-a-Bottle.* Slip an 8-ounce bottle, warmed or chilled, inside this insulated bottle bag, zip the top shut, use the Velcro strap to attach to your belt or stroller, and off you go, hands-free. $6.95. #03603 - The Orange Elephant.

- *Mini-Fridgy.* Thinsulate-lined cooler, 9"H × 6"W × 5"D, holds six 8-ounce bottles, or one or two bottles and lots of food. Comes with reusable cold-pack. In purple or teal. $11.95. #G320 - Right Start.

- *Powdered milk container.* This small, three sectioned plastic container is a handy little item. Measure out enough powdered formula in its three compartments to make up three bottles, toss it into your diaper bag along with an empty bottle, and you can make formula in an instant, wherever you go. Or carry powder for one bottle and Cheerios or some other snack in the other two compartments. Compact and versatile, at $4.95, you can't go wrong. #2451 - One Step Ahead.

Storage and Cleaning Products

- *Bottle dryer rack.* Countertop rack holds twelve bottles (six large, six small), nipples and rings upside-down on rods for sanitary air-drying. $11.95 #G-130 - Right Start.

- *Microwave sterilizing system.* Sterilize three 4-ounce bottles, nipples, rings, and tops without waiting for a pot to boil. Place items in microwave pan, add a small amount of water, put cover on, place inside your microwave, punch in 7 to 9 minutes, and that's all.

Comes with two 4-ounce Avent bottles. $29.95.
#4015 - One Step Ahead.

- *Dishwasher baskets.* This item is indispensable for
any bottlefeeding parent with a dishwasher. It solves
the problem of how to wash all those tiny parts—nipples, rings, sealers, and bottle tops and make sure they
stay safely in place in the dishwasher all the while.
Two-tiered plastic basket holds nipples on top and
other parts on bottom. 4"H × 8"W × 4¼"D. Set of
2, $7.94. #4126 - One Step Ahead.

- *Formula stain remover.* If you've ever had a formula
stain set in your clothes you know it's one of the
toughest to remove. These cleansers are designed to
eliminate stains from formula, and also do a good job
on fruit juice, baby food, coffee, wine, and other protein stains. Formula I is meant for white or bleach-
safe washables. Formula II is for colored clothes,
silks, and wools. Set of 2 cleansers, 8-oz. size, $9.95
(#29791) or 16-oz. size, $18.95 (#31559) - Hand in
Hand.

Bottle Attachments and Cup-Trainers

- *EZ Sips.* Turn any ordinary bottle into a training cup
with these sipper-spouts that slip on using ordinary
nipple rings. Top-rack dishwasher safe. Set of 6
spouts, $4.95. D150 - Right Start.

- *Adjustable-flow training cups.* Lets you change the
flow-rate so that baby can adjust gradually to cup-
drinking. Spill-resistant design with snap-and-twist lid
prevents accidental openings. Top rack dishwasher
safe. Set of 2 for $7.95. #29835 - Hand in Hand.

- *Spill-proof tumblers.* Babies often learn straw-drink-
ing before they can handle cups. Here's a lidded cup
with a reusable straw that baby can turn upside down
or leave on its side without spilling a drop. Dish-

washer safe. Set of 3 for $14.95. #31516 - Hand in Hand.

- *Flip'n'Sip.* Ten-ounce thermal cup with top that flips open to reveal a sipper-spout. Seals tight for travel. Has carrying strap and easy-hold handle. Dishwasher safe. $4.95. #03605 - The Orange Elephant.

- *Bottle thermometer.* Take the guess-work out of warming. Features a "ready-zone" cap that indicates when formula is heated properly. Dial thermometer measures accurately within two degrees Fahrenheit without mercury. Microwave, boiling water, and dishwasher safe. Fits standard 8-ounce bottles. $12.95. #07001 - The Orange Elephant.

- *Powdered formula mixer.* Get the lumps out of your powdered formula bottles the easy way with this handheld, battery-operated mixer. Inserts right into the baby bottle. Comes with two mixing wands and is powered by two AA batteries (not included). $9.95. #G211 - The Right Start.

- *Bottle burper.* Here's how to make sure your baby is getting all the formula out of those disposable plastic bottle inserts and not getting any air: Just push on the end of the bottle with this small plastic handle, and out go the air bubbles. $3.95 for a set of two. #2216 - One Step Ahead.

- *Water bottle adapter.* Turn any brand of bottled water into a baby bottle with this ingenious adapter set. Screw on the adapter ring to any bottle of Evian or other brand of bottled water, and then screw on a standard nipple and ring. Set includes two adapter rings and one standard silicone nipple and ring. $3.95 per set. #4490 - One Step Ahead.

CHAPTER 5

Working Mother, Hungry Baby

One of the most common reasons for mothers to choose the bottle for a newborn or switch to the bottle after a few weeks of nursing is that the conditions of her workplace make breastfeeding difficult. Breastfeeding, even under the best of circumstances—at home, with housekeeping help, without other children who need time and attention—can still be overwhelming for many mothers. Add to that the pressures of the workplace—having to hand a child over to a caregiver at 8 A.M., get to work, pump milk, (or make runs to the daycare center to feed)—it's usually too much for all but the superwoman.

I did hear from a few women who somehow managed to combine a full-time career with breastfeeding, but I heard from many more who tried it for a few days, a few weeks, or at most a month, and found themselves drained, not just of milk, but of energy by the end of the day, leaving them little time for enjoyment of their babies when they were at home. Many babies, too, appeared to have difficulties adjusting; after being offered bottles all day by the caregiver, they would frequently start refusing the breast, and quickly wean themselves to an all-formula diet.

Those few mothers who were able to keep up breast-feeding while on the job had one thing in common–a congenial and supportive environment at work. This included:

- a female boss who had nursed her own children, or a male boss whose wife had nursed his children, or a boss who believed mothers should be able to nurse, if they so wished;
- co-workers who were supportive of a nursing mother's needs for time and privacy and were not critical if they happened to see a milk-stain on a blouse or hear the whirring of an electric breastpump;
- a private office or a clean, well-lighted and comfortable lounge area where the mother could express milk in comfort, without interruption or disapproval from anyone;
- three or four breaks of 15 to 20 minutes each, to allow time enough to pump out a full bottle at each break, clean the pump, and label and store the milk properly;
- a locker or closet to store a change of clothing (if milk leaks and stains), and (optimally) facilities for showering;
- a place to store the breastpump when not in use, and a refrigerator in which to keep the pumped-out milk;
- no need for the "power-suit" mode of dress—instead, acceptance of loose sweaters, or cotton shirts and jumpers that provide easy nursing access.

That so few places of employment encourage nursing is a shame, and breastfeeding advocates have rightly rallied and lobbied to improve conditions and change the attitudes that foster those conditions. No woman should have to give up nursing her baby when she'd like to continue (provided her baby is thriving), simply because her employer is uncomfortable with the arrangement. Still, we live in a far from ideal world, and many women do in fact end up weaning, because they know, given the way things work at their jobs, that it is too hard to keep up with their duties and keep the milk flowing at the same time. (For stories of how mothers dealt with infant feeding upon their return to work, see "Mothers Talk" page 185.)

I also heard from women who weaned their babies for their own reasons (breast pain, problems with latch-on, prior breast surgery, or any of the other reasons listed in chapter 1), who happened to work in an environment in which breastfeeding was the norm. When many colleagues have breastfed successfully on the job, the mother who doesn't may feel like the odd woman out. When her maternity leave is at an end and she turns up without a breast-pump, she finds herself criticized and treated as if she's ignorant of the benefits of nursing. This was the case for a few nurses I interviewed who worked in hospitals that provided pumping rooms; lactation consultants on staff sometimes reacted as if these mothers had rejected breastfeeding intentionally, to set a bad example.

Just as some working mothers were ostracized for bottle-feeding, other mothers have been criticized for breastfeeding on the job. A few of the bottlefeeding mothers I interviewed noted that they had had to cover for breastfeeding mothers who took long breaks to pump milk or made trips to the daycare center to nurse. However, I found such complaints by bottlefeeders against breastfeeders were rare and generally good-humored. Not one woman suggested that their lactating fellow workers should be denied the time off or be pressured to wean. They did want some appreciation for taking up the slack.

Most of the bottlefeeders who completed the workplace policy questions on my survey stressed that the breastfeeding choice must be supported and protected. Many added that it was a good idea for employers to provide comfortable accommodations to encourage the nursing mother to continue.

Can the System Be Reformed?

It's clear from even brief conversations with new parents that in America it's harder than it ought to be to work full time and bring up children. The ability of each mother to make a feeding choice that suits herself and her baby is constrained, causing stress and discomfort not just to new parents and their babies; this stress reverberates through society. It is to *everyone's* benefit to have children brought up by parents who have the confidence and freedom to do what they think is best. Is there any way to bring about maximum freedom of choice in infant feeding for working parents? Or must each company's employees be left to lobby their own employers for piecemeal change?

Congress could mandate along the lines of the Family Leave Act that all large companies (say, 50 employees or more) must provide lactating workers with adequate facilities and time off for pumping. Realistically, in a country without mandated healthcare access for its citizens, we are politically very far away from the time when the right to breastfeed on the job will be secured for working mothers. In the current economic climate, when cost-cutting is the most praised activity in both business and government, society is not about to accept a change that would force businesses to take on costs that most economic analysts say benefit only a few. Barring some great political turnaround in the future, it is safe to assume that the interests of large corporations carry more weight with Congress than those of financially strapped parents of infants.

Breastfeeding advocates will point out that legal protection for breastfeeding on the job might save money by reducing the need to care for sick children (if you believe there is a causal relationship between continued breastfeeding and fewer childhood illnesses). There might be truth to this, but costs of caring for sick children are felt primarily in incrementally increasing health insurance premiums that are borne by millions of consumers; while the bill for constructing nursing facilities and covering for lost work-time during pumping breaks would fall on each employer in a burdensome lump sum.

Those who care about individual choice say money is not the real issue—that every mother should have the freedom to do what she thinks is right for herself, her child, her body, and her family. It's no cop-out to say that the problem is complicated, and that there are no one-shot solutions, no magic formula (bad pun intended!) to deliver happiness and health for all.

Mothers Talk about Infant Feeding and Employment

With my first child I returned to work full-time six weeks post-partum (after a C-section!). The baby nursed every hour around the clock. I tried to pump milk out at work, but there were no facilities, and I was exhausted all the time and not drinking enough liquids for adequate milk production. I suffered through mastitis, but what really put an end to it [breastfeeding] was a business trip to Canada, when the baby was eight weeks old. I was miserable and depressed over the whole situation, and realized, as I cried in my Canadian hotel room, that the "dairy farm" had shut down. With our second child I did the whole parenting thing differently: stayed home, worked part-time from home, and nursed for a year, when I was satisfied and happy to wean.

—Carla

There haven't been any nursing mothers here [at her workplace], but I don't think the bosses really want to accommodate nursing mothers at all. Even though I chose not to nurse, I think nursing mothers should be encouraged to feel comfortable, wherever they want to feed the baby, whether it's in the mall or the lunch-room. They aren't doing anything lewd. I think this [so-cietal] hang-up about nursing is ridiculous.

—Anne

My workplace doesn't make any accommodation for the breastfeeding mom. I have no idea where I would have pumped [if she hadn't weaned her baby already]. The on-site daycare center here does not allow visita-tion during the day, so I assume breastfeeding there was not allowed. It's a shame that even with on-site daycare, moms can't breastfeed.

—Susan

I haven't nursed for almost five years, and I don't miss it a bit. . . . I had a real challenge with my older son, who was seven weeks old when I had to return to work full time. For six months I nursed him for three of his five feedings a day. I pumped milk for one of his two feedings when he was at daycare, and used for-mula (yuck, the spit-up was hard to wash out—the main reason I don't like formula) for the other feed-ing. Eventually, I found that my entire life was just working, nursing, and pumping, and it wasn't putting me in a good frame of mind.

—Alicia

I knew a lot of women who nursed for a few months and then switched over to formula when they went back to work. For me, the hardest part [about working and breastfeeding] was expressing milk in the grungy bathroom at work. So I finally decided on half and half. I nursed first thing in the morning, and after work, and again at bedtime. My daughter got two or three bottles [of formula] a day. It seemed the easiest thing, and I really felt like she was getting all the benefits of breastfeeding, yet I had the convenience of formula. It drives me crazy when I hear mothers say (in kind of a self-righteous way) "My baby never had a drop of formula, nothing but breastmilk till she was three." I don't think formula's a poison—it just makes life easier, like disposable diapers.

—Sally

I found it difficult to breastfeed and work in the home at the same time. Since our son does have to spend twelve hours a week at the sitter's (where he is bottlefed), and since I was getting very little work accomplished at home with a baby constantly at the breast, I decided to wean him to a bottle at the age of six weeks. For the first few days, I alternated between bottles of formula and nursing at the breast, but it became obvious that it was difficult for him to do both, so we went to bottle only. I do pump a couple of times a day, but for the most part, he is fed formula. Full-time breastfeeding was not only draining me physically, making it difficult to work without falling asleep, but it was also difficult to keep up with our three-year-old daughter when she got home from daycare. Since I stopped breastfeeding, my stamina has increased immensely, and I'm a much happier mother than I was just a couple of weeks ago.

—Brittany

I tried a battery-operated pump but found it incredibly painful. I was fortunate in being able to arrange to have my husband bring our son to me at my office for lunch, and also fortunate to learn about the huge superiority of rental breastpumps. I think that all companies should give breastfeeding women access to a small room with lockers, a small fridge, a comfortable chair, and an electric outlet—plus a lock on the door. Few do, in spite of the savings in [reduced] employee absenteeism, due to less illness among breastfed babies.

—*Jackie*

I have been back at work for six weeks and have been pumping during my lunch break pretty unsuccessfully, due in part to the lack of support at my job. My boss asked me if I felt perverted! Now I have resolved that it does not matter how much I can pump, as long as I can maintain the production to feed my baby when I'm home. I'm supplementing [with formula] during the day, but am worried that my supply will dry up completely.

—*Mimi*

My original intention was to go back to work full time when my baby was five months old and leave bottles of expressed milk with my daycare person, but it hasn't worked out that way. I've had to go to morning and evening breastfeedings with bottles of formula in between, because it turned out that it took too much time to pump out the 24+ ounces of formula he needs per day, and I do not have the kind of job that allows me to schedule my pumping breaks. Also, I found there was no convenient, private, nearby place to pump. What I would really prefer to do (and so would most of the working mothers in my office, according to the mini-survey I conducted) would be to work part-time in the office and "telecommute" from home the rest of the time. However, when mothers have raised this idea within the company, we've been told that our jobs aren't the type to allow that, and if we did so, it would severely hamper our careers.

—*Holly*

What extremes must an employer go to? La Leche League and other breastfeeding organizations believe no expense is too great, but that's not the reality. Every choice we make has its consequences and costs. Returning to work while breastfeeding also has consequences. Each mother has to carefully evaluate her own work situation when deciding how to feed.

—*Kate*

Daycare Centers, Nannies, and Au Pairs

For most working mothers the key question is how to find loving, reliable, affordable childcare. In this the bottlefeeding mother is at a decided advantage. The woman who breastfeeds and wants to use a daycare center must first find one close to her place of employment that allows for drop-in visits by nursing mothers (not all of them do); alternatively, she must supply the center with her pumped-out milk in bottles and trust that center to handle the milk properly. Breastmilk, if frozen, must be carefully thawed and fed to the baby within an hour's time. If other babies at the center are on formula and one child grabs another child's formula bottle, germs may be passed from one child to the other, but the formula itself is easily replaceable—no big deal. Not so with breastmilk: When each four-ounce bottle may take a good half-hour to produce, the mother would be rightly angry if the center does not ensure that her milk goes exclusively to her child. Because of the extra care required in the handling and supervising of bottled breastmilk, some daycare centers will not accept breastfed children, while others will accept the children but will take no responsibility for the milk.[1] While they're under the center's charge, the children must drink formula, the same as all the others.

Nursing mothers who use in-home caregivers (nannies or au pairs) may be troubled by lack of support from the caregiver. Vicky and Amanda were two nursing mothers who talked to me about their different problems with in-home childcare.

Vicky went back to her part-time job as a teaching assistant at a university when her baby was six months old. She hired a gentle, grandmotherly woman to live in and look after her baby. Sometimes Vicky left bottles of breastmilk for the baby; at other times she came home to nurse. Vicky's baby seemed to love the nanny, and Vicky was pleased at the way the nanny handled her job. The trouble stemmed from the fact that Vicky's baby was on the small side. She'd been just six pounds at birth, and although her pediatrician said she was developing normally, to the nanny she seemed small compared to the other babies that age. Not a day would go by that the nanny didn't make some remark: "She's so little, this baby—are you sure she's getting enough milk?" or "Can't I just give her one little bottle a day, to help her fill out a bit?" Vicky tried to get the nanny to drop the subject, but she never took the hint. The nanny, who was about sixty and had some forty years of childcare experience, could not understand why Vicky, who was in her mid-twenties, would not defer to her greater wisdom. Vicky's solution in a moment; but now for Amanda's dilemma:

Amanda, who was bilingual in French and English, was very happy to be able to bring over from France a twenty-year-old au pair who would speak French to her three-month-old baby. What she hadn't bargained on was that the au pair would have some very French ideas about how babies are to be fed. It seems that where the au pair grew up, it was the custom for babies to start on solid foods at three months. The mothers would typically puree all kinds of table foods and spoon-feed them to the baby, being pleased when the baby developed as broad a palate of favorites as quickly as possible. It would not be unusual to see a five-month-old eating a salmon mousse or a bit of duck pâté—something most Americans won't appreciate until after college. But such a practice is completely against the advice of most breastfeeding experts, who say to hold off giving any solids until six months, at a minimum, and introduce each new food slowly, no faster than one a week, starting with something simple and bland, such as rice cereal. If a baby starts eating solids too early, the prevailing theory goes, the baby will nurse less, and the mother's milk supply will dwindle. Amanda explained to the au pair why she did not want the baby fed any solids, but one day when she happened to return from work mid-day, she found the au pair allowing the baby to share her own lunch of cream of mushroom soup.

What did Amanda do? She did just what Vicky ultimately decided to do: She fired the caregiver. Both these mothers concluded that the loss of a warm-hearted and well-meaning caregiver was justified, to make sure that their babies were fed the way they felt was best.

Such problems occur not only when a breastfeeding mother leaves her baby with a nanny; formula-feeding mothers have had their share of difficulties in getting caregivers to follow their instructions. The two stories I'm about to tell were also resolved by changing caregivers. Later, I will tell you how to avoid such a situation altogether.

Meredith told of hiring Annie to care for her six-month-old son. Annie had previously worked for a family with a bottlefed baby, and said she'd always prepared the baby's formula and handled feedings without problems. Meredith assumed that such an experienced caregiver might be insulted to be told how to feed the baby, so she didn't walk her through the process. Then one weekday Meredith stayed home with a toothache and happened to see Annie making up the day's batch of bottles. Annie had just emptied the kitchen trash and didn't wash her hands before she went to get the ready-to-feed can, nor did she shake the can, nor did she rinse the top before punching the holes with the can opener. She made up six bottles, gave the baby one, and put the others back in the refrigerator—all without bottle-tops. Later, when it was time for the baby to have another, she took a cold bottle from the refrigerator, popped it in the microwave without first removing the nipple, hit one minute, and then gave the warmed-up bottle straight to the baby, without having shaken it up nor tested the temperature. When Meredith told Annie that she wanted things handled differently, Annie retorted, "I've always done it this way, and it's always been fine." Meredith told her, "It's *not* fine with me," and promptly dismissed Annie from her job.

Alison told another story. Her nanny came from Eastern Europe, spoke little English, and had little familiarity with American baby-feeding methods. Though she seemed caring and very intent on learning how Alison wanted things done, the nanny still made some critical mistakes. She was extremely frugal with all things, including formula cans that had passed their expiration dates; she just could not bring herself to throw out anything that looked and smelled to her like perfectly acceptable food. Nor did she appear to grasp the importance of mixing up the powdered formula with exactly two ounces of water for each scoop of powder. She sometimes made it much weaker than recommended— perhaps, Alison reflected later, with the intention of making it go farther to save money. Though Alison explained the danger of this false economy as best she could, she was never sure that the nanny, with her limited English, got the message. Still, her baby seemed to love the nanny (and her rates were reasonable), so Alison was motivated to work with her to improve her skills . . . until the time that her baby was up vomiting all night. Alison stayed home from work the next day to take him to the pediatrician.

While in the pediatrician's waiting room she happened to see a neighbor who had a baby of about the same age. The neighbor said, "Your son probably drank from a bottle that was out in the sun too long. I was wondering if I should tell you this, but I was at the playground yesterday around noon, when it was really hot out. Your nanny was there with your son. They weren't in the shade, and she kept offering him the same bottle from her bag. It wasn't in any kind of insulated cooler. When I knew it had been more than an hour, I tried to tell her the bottle was no good, but I don't think she understood me."

The pediatrician said he thought spoiled formula could easily have caused the baby's symptoms. After that, Alison didn't feel safe leaving her baby with the nanny, and had to use up a week of sick leave while she searched for someone better versed in the basics of hygiene.

Could Meredith or Alison have prevented these mistakes from happening? Not all misunderstandings are preventable, but childcare experts generally recommend that all employers of nannies do the following:

1. Stay at home with the nanny the first few days or perhaps as long as one week, to let her see exactly how you want things done. On the first day the nanny should simply observe.

2. On the second day, let the nanny do everything, while you watch and make sure you approve. If the nanny seems to resent being told how you expect the formula to be prepared, or says: "In my family we always did it *this*

way and never had any problems," take that as a sign that
the nanny is going to end up deviating from your wishes.

3. Make it clear from the outset that you are very particular about the way you want feeding handled, and that
doing it your way is a requirement of the job.

When bottlefed children are in daycare or in a shared-
nanny situation with other bottlefed children, another
problem commonly arises: How do you make sure that
your child gets only bottles meant for your child (to limit
the germs going back and forth)? This is especially important if your child has any sort of allergy and is on soy formula or a hypoallergenic variety, while all the other children are drinking formula made from a cow's milk base.

Solution: Choose oddly shaped or colored bottles to
send to daycare with your baby. Caregivers are less likely
to grab the wrong bottle if it looks and feels different from
all the others. Although most daycare centers will ask you
to mark your child's name on his or her bottles, that won't
do a thing to stop your child from taking a sip of someone
else's bottle, since your baby can't read! But a baby will
very soon get used to the shape of his or her own bottle if
it's one of those double-grip Ansa bottles or one of the
squarish-shaped Kindergrips, or is the only one with a big
Mickey Mouse on it. Also, other children will be less likely
to want to drink from your child's bottle because it will
have an unfamiliar feel to it.

The Role of the Father

Stay-at-Home Dads

You might think that stay-at-home mothers would applaud
any father who makes a commitment to spend the day
with his children while his wife earns the family's living.
You might think there would be acceptance of the use of
formula by fathers, who, after all, are biologically unable

Mothers Talk About Childcare Arrangements

After some initial difficulties getting started, I breast-fed my daughter exclusively for the first five months. After that I went back to work part-time and put her in a daycare center for a couple of hours a day. The daycare center operator was not big on breastfeeding, but by that time, my baby was completely resistant to the bottle. It took me a while to work out a solution of sorts, a compromise of solid foods and short daycare stays.

—Lou-Ann

I bottlefed from three weeks on because of difficulties in milk supply. When I went back to work at four months, I found a shared childcare situation. Another mother of a four-month-old and I share one nanny, who looks after both children at my house or the other child's house, alternating weeks. The other mother breastfeeds and pumps out milk, though the nanny uses formula sometimes when there are not enough breastmilk bottles to get through the day. So far it's worked out very well. We've had no problems with mix-ups of bottles. The other mother is very laid back about feeding. She's never compared our kids' health—though her child has had as many colds as mine. (In fact, they always get sick together.) Both kids are growing well, though they're both on the small side. I'm hoping to continue this arrangement till both children are in preschool.

—Bess

I bottlefed from day one, partly because I knew I'd be going right back to work six weeks after the birth.

Carrying milk back and forth from my office to the daycare center would have been one more thing to have to keep track of, and I felt I already had too much going on. Although the daycare staff didn't actively discourage mothers from bringing breastmilk, I definitely got the impression that they were more comfortable with formula. I know they had a discussion at one point about whether they should wear gloves when handling breastmilk to prevent the spread of infectious diseases. They didn't wear gloves when my son was in the center, but then I don't think any of the other babies there were on breastmilk at the time.

—*Norma*

An Anti-Daycare Opinion

Though I heard many positive things from working mothers (both breastfeeders and bottlefeeders) about their childcare situations, I also came across the following opinion from a pediatrician adamantly opposed to daycare (quoted approvingly by La Leche League in its publication, "The Breastfeeding Rights Packet," Publication No. 78, July 1986, p. 19.)[2] I include it here because it exemplifies an underlying anti-working mother theme that exists in much of the breastfeeding literature I reviewed.

As a pediatrician I know that we do not know enough about nurturing to be able to tell mothers that if they find a person or institution that meets such-and-such standards, that this will be an adequate mother substitute. We can list people's credentials, pinpoint the standards for a daycare center, but just as breastmilk cannot be duplicated, neither can a mother. We cannot put mothering into a formula and come up with a person who has the special feeling for your child that you do. . . . [ellipses in La Leche League pamphlet's quotation] Just as everyone but a mother is excluded from nursing a baby, so they are excluded from those immense feelings of satisfaction and inner unity with the child.

—*Sally E. Shaywitz, M.D.*

to breastfeed. You might think that fathers would be welcomed into daytime playgroups for stay-at-home parents, as they provide a positive male role model in a world that needs more nurturing men.

If those are your assumptions, then you'll be surprised to learn what stay-at-home fathers are running into as they go about their business, mainly from militant breastfeeding women. Consider Tom, who lived in a large, state-subsidized housing complex in New York City. His wife earned barely enough to support the family, but he was determined that his child get the benefits of one full-time stay-at-home parent. His apartment complex had a meeting room set aside for uses that the housing authorities wished to encourage. One of those uses was the stay-at-home mothers group, which held frequent get-togethers so that babies and toddlers could play together, and the parents could share parenting tips, enjoy the company of other adults, and learn from one another.

Tom was the first man to be a stay-at-home parent in the apartment complex. Since the building was government-run and the meetings were therefore government-sponsored, he assumed there could be no discrimination on the basis of sex. Actually, he didn't just assume lack of discrimination; he expected that he would be welcomed for bringing an interesting, different perspective on home parenting. Instead, he was subjected to rude remarks and told he should not return.

Actually, the group was about evenly divided on whether he should be allowed to join. Opposition to having a man join the group came mainly from breastfeeding militants. Breastfeeding, they said, was a special, private thing for women only. They were uncomfortable exposing themselves in front of a man. (Curiously absent in this case was any of the usual rhetoric of the breastfeeding movement about the right to breastfeed in public, or the assertion that the exposed breast has no sexual significance when a woman uses it to feed a baby.) The man sued for his rights and won a victory in the courts, but unfortunately, could not win over the hearts of those women who still refused to accept him for what he was—a caring, devoted full-time parent who, just like any mother, was seeking companionship and support for the too-often undervalued job he was doing.

Now consider the experience of Rob, who split childcare duties fifty-fifty with his wife, each working about 30 hours a week, each handling the baby-care while the other was at work. While in the store buying formula, a woman came up to him and criticized him for not making sure that the baby was fed breastmilk. Though taken aback about this advice from a complete stranger, Rob explained that with his wife's work schedule, pumping had proved impractical, and added, "Obviously, I couldn't breastfeed"—and so formula was the only choice.

Undaunted, the woman persisted, "But if it's not too late, your wife really should give pumping another try."

Rob sputtered wordlessly, picked up his formula purchases, and left the store. Months later, in a telephone interview with me, he said, "I wish I'd been a quicker thinker. I would have loved to have seen her reaction if I had told her I was a widower . . . or better yet, that I was part of a gay couple and we'd adopted our baby."

Fully involved fathers encounter criticism wherever they happen to be, I discovered. I heard from another father, Mark, who was fortunate enough to be offered six weeks' paternity leave. He decided to use it after his wife's maternity leave (also six weeks long) had run out. Though his wife had breastfed her newborn during her time at home, the baby was quickly weaned to formula before Mark's stay-at-home period began. The couple's plan was to have Mark go back to work when his six-week leave was up, and then have a full-time nanny look after the baby.

Shortly after the baby was born, Mark and his wife and new son moved into a new house, and were welcomed to the neighborhood by the woman who lived across the street. After first asking Mark's wife if she was breastfeeding, and nodding in satisfaction at the affirmative response, the neighbor's next question was how long she planned to be at home with the baby. On hearing that the mother intended to wean at six weeks so that her husband could stay home with the baby while the mother worked, the neighbor told Mark, "It's a shame you can't give up your six-week leave to your wife, so that the baby can get at least twelve full weeks of breastmilk." The neighbor added that she had nursed both of her children past the age of three, and wouldn't have dreamed of taking outside employment before they were in school full time. Needless to say, that's one neighbor relationship that got off to a rocky start!

Even when the working mother is intent on breastfeeding, the father may still be in for a hard time. Here's what happened to one couple, Jim and Krista, who decided to keep on feeding breastmilk after Krista went back to work and Jim stayed home. Krista was fortunate to have a liberal, understanding boss (a man whose wife had breastfed their two children) who allowed her ample time off to pump. The trouble was that Krista found pumping difficult and would have to spend thirty to forty minutes to produce a few ounces. She bought different pumps, to no avail, and even after she tried renting an expensive, hospital-quality pump, she found she still wasn't keeping up with her baby's demand. Towards the end of every work-day she would get a frantic phone call from Jim, telling her he had run out of bottles, and could she please pump out another. A few times he even rushed over with the baby in the car, so that she could breastfeed the baby in her office. The baby was screaming and miserable much of the day, wanting more milk, when there wasn't any left. After several miserable weeks, this couple, who had started out deeply committed to keeping their baby on an all-breast-milk diet, decided the only way for their childcare arrangement to work would be to give the baby formula once the day's supply of breastmilk bottles was done. After that, Jim's days with the baby were easier for everyone.

The Working Father

A father need not stay home full-time or part-time to play a major part in feeding the baby. Indeed, only a tiny fraction of fathers ever take more than a day or two off from work for childcare.[3] However, the great majority of fathers of bottlefed babies handle some of the feedings, allowing mothers who have frequently spent all day with a fussy, demanding baby, to get some sorely needed rest. When both parents work and share equally in the burden of providing income for the family, it's only fair to expect the father to share equally in the burden of caring for the baby when both parents are home. Of course, in most American households, the job of childcare still falls largely on the mother, working outside the home or not—but in the bottlefeeding home, there is at least the *possibility* of dividing the feeding chores equally between the two.

A common strategy adopted by my respondents is to have the father handle the middle of the night feeding, allowing the mother to get a full night's sleep. A few couples worked out timetables calling for the father to feed at certain times, the mother to feed at other times. Weekends were more likely to see the father handling feedings. Among those women who breastfed for the first few weeks or months were some who made a point of reserving certain times of the day for the father to do a feeding—either of expressed breastmilk in a bottle, or one bottle of formula a day. By so doing, these mothers were not only relieved of the full responsibility for all feedings, but fathers were provided increased opportunity to cuddle the baby and experience the one-on-one intimacy of the feeding relationship. An additional benefit reported by both mothers and fathers is that the baby early on learns to trust and love someone besides the mother.

Of course, in the eyes of breastfeeding militants these are not benefits at all, but drawbacks to the development of the primal, exclusive mother-baby "dyad" that springs from the act of breastfeeding. A young infant, the militants assert, suffers trauma at every separation (no matter how transitory) from the biological mother, even if left with its biological father to feed. I saw these views expressed in the e-mail replies to the breastfeeding mother who posted a query asking if it would be all right for her husband to offer one bottle of formula a night. A chorus of no's boomed back at her, some sternly reminding her of her duty to "be there for her baby" day and night and do her biological duty—the one thing a man can never do, and that is breastfeed. See "Fathers Talk about Feeding Their Babies" for a sample of the advice she received.

When I heard from fathers themselves about their feelings when they fed their babies, I was surprised myself at the depth of their emotions. Perhaps I had unwittingly absorbed some of the attitude that a man can't *really* feel what a woman feels when she gives nourishment to a baby. But the fathers who told me of their joy at bottlefeeding used so many of the same expressions of awe to describe their feelings as they watched their tiny babies sucking that I would bet, if I removed the names from their quotations, no reader would be able to tell which were spoken by a bottlefeeding father and which by a breastfeeding mother.

Fathers Talk About Feeding Their Babies

I have two children, a son, three-and-a-half, and a daughter, ten months, both adopted, and of course they were bottlefed. Right now my wife is working full-time, and I'm working part-time, mostly at home, and I do all the daytime childcare, except in the mornings, when my son is in preschool and my daughter is in daycare. I would say without a doubt this is the most enriching year I have ever spent. I'm starting up a new business now, and when I get it better established, I hope to be working at it full time, and when that happens, we'll probably hire a nanny—but I know I'll really miss the everyday closeness with the children. My only complaint is that when I take them to the playground or pick them up from their schools, very often some mother smiles condescendingly and asks if I'm "filling in" for my wife. They just don't know what to make of a man who does what they do. They always assume I'm just a reluctant substitute for a mom.

—Charles

There's nothing I enjoyed more than giving a bottle. I always did the early morning feedings, because I'm up early, and my wife liked to catch up on a little sleep then. I came to know my babies in large part through holding them during feedings. It's been one of life's great pleasures for me. I'd have a third, and do it all over again, except for the fact that my wife swears she never wants to be pregnant again.

—Matthew

I know my wife was terribly disappointed when she couldn't breastfeed, and I felt badly for her, but at the same time, I could see how exhausted and miserable she was, and how much better things were for all of us when the baby started on bottles. On weekends when I didn't have to get up early for work I usually did the middle of the night bottle, so she could get some sleep. For me feeding was a very important part of my relationship with my daughter. I'd hate to think that I'd never have had that [if his wife had ended up exclusively breastfeeding].

—Steve

My wife belonged to a mother's group, where they all were down on bottlefeeding. But at the same time my wife said there was a lot of resentment against the fathers for not being able to feed the baby. During the time she was a stay-at-home mom I know she enjoyed the company of the other mothers during the day, but it used to get to me a bit that so many of them were so negative about the fathers. It was like the father was an outsider handling "their" baby. I never felt that my children were more "bonded" to my wife than to me—even when she was breastfeeding. I always felt they were part of me, part of her—our babies. Anyone who loves a baby can be nurturing—whether you have breasts or not.

—Luke

When a breastfeeding mother posted a message on a parenting forum saying she was considering giving her baby an occasional bottle so that the father could do some feeding, she received several replies from militant breastfeeders very down on dads' feeding. Here is a representative sample of the advice she received:

I have to put in my two cents worth on this subject of introducing bottles so that dad can feed the baby too. Lots of babies have warm, close relationships with their daddies without the symbolic bottle binding them together. . . .The reality of it is, after the novelty of it wears off, mom will end up doing most of the feeding anyway, be it bottle or breast, unless, of course, she is not home with the baby most of the time. So I don't think it is worth risking nipple confusion so that dad can "participate" in feeding and somehow "bond" better with the baby. . . . There are many ways dad can "participate" in breastfeeding, at least to the point of feeling involved: e.g., bringing the baby to mom, being in charge of burpings in between breasts, cuddling mom and baby while the baby nurses, etc.

—*Joni*

Here's an interesting observation about the value of letting other members of the family feed the baby, from a mother who both breastfed and bottlefed:

I was lucky (and I do believe that there is an element of luck involved) in being able to nurse my three kids fairly easily. However, all of them took bottles, too. With our last one, we introduced the bottle fairly early (mainly because the other two had been rather resistant) and once we did, everyone wanted to feed her! I think bottlefeeding really helped integrate her into the family, especially with my son, who was three at the time. I have very fond memories of my son holding his baby sister in his lap, giving her a bottle. When they're infants, feeding seems to be their biggest interaction. . . . I certainly didn't feel selfish for having let others relieve me of some of the feedings. I think that, given the circumstances, I would have felt selfish if I had kept that special kind of closeness all to myself, and deprived my husband of the pleasure of it. Still, everyone needs to do what works for them.

—*Grace*

What does La Leche League think about having the father play a primary role in childcare? The breastfeeding advocacy group's "Breastfeeding Rights Packet" (Publication No. 78, July 1986) describes with approval the views of British child psychologists James and Joyce Robertson (page 19)[4]:

> James and Joyce Robertson have demonstrated what many other childcare experts have known: that infants and very young children have emotional needs that can be met only by a mother or mother substitute who will buffer them from a sometimes overwhelming world and support them on a daily basis. But the Robertsons take their message a step further. A mother substitute really won't do, they say. It should be the child's own mother who cares for him or her in those crucial first three years. Even the baby's father is only second-best as a caretaker, the Robertsons believe, at least until the infant is about eight months old. In short, they say, daycare is bad for very young children. . . . The Robertsons have seen all the problems with infants who were not adequately mothered.

CHAPTER 6

Problem Solving

Although few babies have any difficulty mastering the technique of sucking formula from a bottle, that doesn't mean that bottlefeeding will always be problem-free. While breastfeeding couples have available over *forty* different guides to answer their questions, bottlefeeding parents have mostly been on their own, and have had to use trial and error to find what works best for their babies. When I interviewed bottlefeeding parents, I always asked them what, if any, problems they encountered, and got their best tips for problem solving.

This chapter presents the most common problems and suggests possible solutions. Keep in mind that all babies are different, and what works for one parent might not work for you. And, as always, if you have any doubt about the appropriateness of any problem-solving technique for *your* baby, talk it over with your pediatrician first.

Q. I've been trying to wean my baby off the breast and onto bottles, but she's never been anything but breastfed till now (four months), and she seems to hate the bottle. She screams and turns her head away every time I offer it.

I'm starting work in less than a month and won't be able to leave work to breastfeed her at the daycare center. Help!

A. You have two separate problems to solve: 1) To get the baby to accept an artificial nipple; and 2) to get the baby to accept the taste of formula instead of breastmilk. If you have time, it's best to concentrate on the first problem before tackling the second. Express your milk into bottles and let someone else try the feedings. That way, your baby won't sense your breasts nearby, the constant reminder of the preferred method of feeding. You also won't have to listen to her cry and feel like giving in and offering a little nursing for comfort. The bottlefeeder (whether Dad or a familiar babysitter or relative) may have to experiment with nipple shapes to find one that the baby will accept.

When I weaned my first child off the breast, I found it easiest to get her to accept the silicone "orthodontic" shaped nipples (common brands are Nuk, Pur, and Mam). Some of the orthodontics come in different sizes, marked "newborn" (0 to 3 months), "infant" (3 to 6 months), and "toddler-fast-flow" (6 months and up). Since a breastfeeding mother with a well-established milk supply can provide a very fast flow of milk from the multiple openings in her nipples, the formerly breastfed baby will probably be happiest with a fast-flowing nipple—even if under 6 months old. But do experiment to find which nipple is best accepted by your baby.

Keep in mind, too, that when a baby is finally hungry enough, she *will* drink from a bottle, even if with much resentment over the loss of your warm breasts. Of course, waiting for her to give in will feel like a form of torture, but be thankful that infants' memories are short.

Once your baby has accommodated herself to the idea that hunger can be abated by sucking from something other than mommy's breast, then try getting her used to the taste of formula. Having become accustomed to drinking milk at body temperature, she will certainly prefer her formula warmed (see chapter 4 for descriptions of the different warming methods). If your baby rejects the taste of warmed-up formula, you might try giving her mostly expressed breastmilk in her bottle, topped off with a little formula; then each day, add an ounce more formula to the mixture until at last she is drinking all formula and no breastmilk.

If you find this advice too slow-going, or if you find yourself having trouble pumping out the necessary bottles of breastmilk, then try offering an all-formula bottle right from the start, but experiment with different types and brands of formula to see which is most easily accepted by your baby.

Q. I'm in the process of switching over to bottlefeeding, and my baby seems to be adjusting fairly well; however, my breasts aren't. Is there anything I can do to prevent the incredibly painful bouts of engorgement I'm experiencing several times a day?

A. The key to avoiding engorgement is to wean *very slowly*. Making the change very gradually is also important for those whose babies are highly resistant to anything new. Many experts recommend extending the weaning process over a period of six or more weeks. You begin by eliminating just one nursing the first week, substituting a bottle for the midday feeding. The following week offer a bottle instead of the breast at the mid-afternoon feeding, and the week after that give a bottle at the mid-morning feeding, and so on, week by week, until you are down to nursing just twice a day, once just after the baby wakes up, and once again, before putting the baby down for the night. How you handle elimination of the last two nursings depends on your baby's schedule and personality. If you think your baby will find it hard to go to sleep without a nursing, you might want to keep up the bedtime nursing for some time to come (how long is up to you and your breasts). If *you* find it uncomfortable to wake up in the morning with milk-filled breasts and not empty them through nursing, then for your own sake, make the first-thing-in-the-morning nursing the last one to go, before your child is finally, completely weaned.

Following this very gradual approach should allow your breasts time to adjust. However, if you're already too far along the road to weaning to follow this advice, then go ahead and wean your baby completely to bottles, and use a breastpump, or your own fingers to express milk whenever you feel your breasts becoming overfull. Pump out only as much milk as you need to feel comfortable again. Longer pumping will only stimulate more milk production and prolong the time it takes for your glands to get the message that no more milk is needed. To combat the pain of engorgement that you might still occasionally experience, try aspirin or Tylenol, and frequent long, hot showers.

Q. Ever since I introduced juice into my son's diet, he's refused formula. He fusses till I break down and give him an apple juice or orange juice. My doctor says he needs formula until he's at least a year old. He's only nine months. How can I get him back on formula?

A. Here are three possible solutions: The Tough Guy Method, the Softie Solution, and the Tricked-Ya Approach. (Your pediatrician will probably endorse only the Tough Guy way, but if you find yourself without the necessary stomach for it, then talk with him or her about the feasibility of the other two approaches.)

Tough Guy: Ban all juices from the house until your baby is securely back on formula. When he's thirsty enough, he'll drink it. Do not let him see anyone else, adult or child, having a juice drink, and if possible, avoid situations in which other babies are drinking juice. He must be led to think that that white stuff is all that exists to fill bottles anymore.

Softie: Don't fight about it. Give him calcium-fortified orange juice and make sure you're compensating for the loss of the milk-based nutrients through wholesome meals, including lots of cheese, cottage cheese, yogurt, eggs, meats, and vegetables. If your child is a picky eater and does not like cheese or other dairy products, then do *not* try this solution.

Tricked-Ya: For a few days make the formula into a milkshake by adding ice-cream, vanilla or chocolate flavoring, or possibly some fruit, such as pureed strained strawberries or bananas (whatever your child likes best). If the formula milkshake is accepted, then start cutting back very gradually on the extra ingredients until you are finally down to plain old formula.

Another trick to get an older baby to drink formula is to give him a snack-sized bag of potato chips or a serving of French fries or some other salty food, which will make him thirsty—then give him the bottle of formula. And if that doesn't work, try this one: Put the formula in an opaque, colored bottle (so he can't see that the contents are white) and put in a few drops of orange extract flavoring, and *tell* him it's orange juice. Some babies care less about actual taste than about winning the battle. If he *thinks* he's getting orange juice, that may be all he needs to be content. Of course, you'll be teaching the lesson that all he has to do is fuss to get his way, and if that is something you dearly want to avoid, then the Tough Guy Method is the only way to go.

Q. My baby is over six months old but still wakes up at night for a bottle. My pediatrician says she has no need for night feedings anymore. How can I help my baby learn to sleep through the night?

A. A cold-turkey approach will usually just frustrate and anger a baby. Babies can't understand why something that used to happen regularly, like getting a bottle at night, has to change. In most situations involving a baby and something new, the best course is to introduce the desired reform so gradually that the baby won't notice anything's different until the change is virtually complete. Let's say you've been giving a 2 A.M. bottle of four ounces of formula each night. The first night you should make up the bottle with three ounces of formula to one ounce of water. (You might want to keep that up for the next night or two, as well.) Then offer less liquid overall, just three ounces in the bottle, only two of which are formula. Continue that mixture for a few days, before changing to two ounces of liquid, half formula, half water. Over the next week or two, you will keep increasing the ratio of water to formula, and continue reducing the overall volume of liquid in the bottle, until at last your baby is drinking only water in the nighttime bottle, and only an ounce at that. Now when your baby wakes up at night, it isn't to satisfy hunger, since you've eliminated the formula, and it isn't to satisfy thirst, since you're only giving a total of one ounce of liquid—it's just that the baby is used to waking up and having a parent's presence for a short time.

When you reach this point, you're ready to try going in and just rubbing the baby's back for a minute in the dark. (By the way, all those night feedings should be done without turning on lights, and the baby should be put back in the crib as soon as she's done sucking, even if she hasn't finished the bottle, after which you should tiptoe back to your own bed.)

Once you're no longer giving a bottle at night, your baby may begin sleeping uninterruptedly. If she doesn't, it may be that she's napping too much during the daytime, or that she needs more exercise and activity in the late afternoon or early evening to make her feel tired enough for a long sleep. Or she may just need some familiar objects in her crib—a special blanket or stuffed animal—to help her comfort herself back to sleep. If she uses a pacifier during the day, you may find it worthwhile to scatter five or six of them near her mouth in the crib, so that she won't have any trouble finding something comforting to suck on when she wakes up in the middle of the night.

Many parents have found useful strategies for eliminating their child's wake-ups in a book by sleep expert Dr. Richard Ferber, *Solve Your Child's Sleep Problems* (Simon & Schuster, 1986).

Q. My baby is in the habit of falling to sleep with her last bottle of the evening. I know it's bad for her, but how do I change her habit? If I don't let her have one last bottle in her crib, she just stays awake and cries.

A. Try making her last bottle of the evening a water bottle. You can phase out the formula at bedtime in the same gradual method described in the question above for phasing out the middle-of-the-night feeding. If that doesn't work, you could also experiment with changes in her bedtime ritual. Give her her bottle an hour before bedtime, and then let her wind down with a warm bath, or stories, or lullabies. Just to help her over the transition, you might try rocking her to sleep in your arms in a rocking chair, and then moving her to the crib. Be warned that this will probably lead to dependence on the rocking chair to go to sleep, and then you'll have to find some technique to phase *that* out—but at least being rocked to sleep doesn't cause cavities!

Q. I've always warmed my baby's formula, but I think it would be a great time-saver if I could get him to take his bottles cold from the fridge. Any suggestions?

A. Warm the bottle a little less each time. If your baby is nine months or under, you'll probably be able to get him to drink his formula cold within a week or sooner. If your baby is older and stubborn (as mine was) you may need to try a few different tricks. Is he allowed to have fruit juices yet? Accepting one cold liquid, fruit juice, could lead him into accepting formula cold. For a limited time, try offering some formula-fruit juice "smoothies" (chilled, of course). Mix some formula in with banana-apple juice (Gerber makes it), or puree some strawberries, strain out the pulp, and add it to the cold formula. You can make the mixture even more tempting by adding a drop of vanilla extract and a little ice cream. Once your baby will accept any cold drink mixture containing formula, waste no time in altering the mixture to start moving toward getting your baby back onto an all-formula diet. You do not want to get yourself sucked into preparing time-consuming and overly sweet formula mixtures on a regular basis.

Yet another approach is to wait until the hot part of the summer, take the baby outside and let him play until he's thirsty, and then give him his bottle cold from the fridge—you may well find that he'll love it that way from the first gulp.

Q. My daughter has turned one, and my pediatrician says it's time to switch her over to cow's milk, but she's so used to formula, she won't drink anything else. Am I ever going to get her off the can?

A. I have never heard of a case of a kid still on formula in high school, so your odds look pretty good. The gradual change method works this way: First week, make up some eight-ounce bottles with five to seven ounces of formula plus one ounce of cow's milk. Next week, add another ounce of cow's milk, and one less ounce of formula. By the end of six or seven weeks your child should be all on cow's milk without noticing a change.

Well, maybe not . . . Some very perceptive toddlers might see you taking out a carton of milk and pouring it in the bottle. "Hey!" that little brain thinks, "that's not formula from a can! What's going on?" Your little Sherlock Holmes then refuses the bottle, even though it may taste no different than yesterday's bottle. You might be able to out-wit such a toddler by not doing bottle preparation in front of him or do what one clever mother, Margaret, did: She secretly poured whole milk into little glass nursette bot-tles—the kind she used to give the baby when the family went on vacation, since the four-ounce, ready-to-feed for-mula bottles were so convenient for travel. Her baby loved the taste of the formula in nursettes, and immediately assumed, when handed a nursette bottle full of milk, that she was getting her favorite formula, and so sucked it down with gusto. The only trouble was that the toddler would then only drink her milk in those four-ounce glass bottles, and getting her to accept drinking from a cup was another long story.

Q. My baby's been on soy formula. Now that he's over a year old, am I supposed to take him off soy and start giv-ing him whole cow's milk?

A. If you were giving him soy because of a milk allergy, no, don't switch to cow's milk. You might try one of the new toddler formulas, Next Step® Soy, or you might trade in the formula for calcium-fortified juice—but only if you can ensure that his diet includes lots of sources of protein, minerals, and vitamins to compensate for the nutrients he won't be getting from milk. If you originally chose a soy formula based on a family history of intolerance to lactose (the sugar in milk), then switch him over to a lactose-free or lactose-reduced milk (most supermarkets carry brands such as Lact-Aid or Dairy-Ease). You could also buy lac-tose-reducing drops and add them to each carton of whole milk that you buy.

If you originally chose a soy formula because your baby seemed gassy and colicky on milk, you may find, now that he's older, that his digestive system has matured and he's perfectly capable of handling cow's milk. Try it out for a day or two and see how he reacts. If he's been okay with cheeses, ice cream, and other milk products for the last month or so, he'll probably be fine with cow's milk. When in doubt, talk to your pediatrician first.

Q. I have friends who breastfed their children for more than a year. If breastmilk and formula are nutritionally comparable, why shouldn't I go on giving formula as long as my friends go on giving their children breastmilk?

A. Your friends don't *need* to give their children breastmilk past one year. If children eat well-rounded diets, they could get all the nutrition they require from the foods they eat and cow's milk. They probably derive emotional satisfaction from the nursing relationship. On the other hand, if your toddler seems to get a lot of comfort from sucking on a bottle, and likes the taste of formula (and you don't mind paying formula prices), then there is no harm in continuing to give formula in bottles past the one-year mark. There is nothing magical about the first birthday that dictates an end to formula—just know it is no longer medically necessary. If you'd like a compromise between formula and milk, you might try one of the toddler formulas now on the market.

Q. My baby is eight months old but still doesn't hold her own bottle. Is there something I can do to teach this skill?

A. Is your baby holding other objects—toys, spoons, teething biscuits—and manipulating them with any degree of skill? If not, talk to your doctor about investigating the cause of a possible developmental delay. If the baby is able to hold other things and bring them to her mouth, then it could well be that she simply prefers mommy to hold her bottle for her, proving to her satisfaction that you are there when she wants you. This was the case when I weaned my breastfed daughter to the bottle. She was so shocked by the fact that my breasts were no longer available, she needed the reassurance that I would still be there to hold the bottle for her. She did not hold her own bottle until she was fourteen months old (an age at which most other bottlefed babies had long ago accepted the switchover to cups).

If it's a question of the baby's preference, and you don't mind continuing to play bottle-holder, then just wait her out, and she'll eventually see the advantages of being able to hold her own bottle. If you have run out of time and patience, then start the bottle-holding lessons without delay. Fold her hands around the bottle correctly and assist her into tilting the bottle to the right angle for drinking. If she lets it slip down or drops it, repeat the lesson until she begins to keep it there herself. After the first three or four attempts, however, sit back and don't intervene when she has difficulty. Let her try to figure it out on her own for a minute before you offer help. Each time you step back and don't help, wait longer and longer before you come to her aid. Remember to use praise and sound thrilled each time she holds the bottle right, or gets closer to doing it right. Don't express displeasure over failure, but make sure she sees a definite change in your expression for the better when she is trying to get it right. If she's actively resistant to the idea and is throwing the bottle down or screaming, then quietly but firmly say, "No, that's not right," and stop the feeding, resuming it only when she's stopped fussing.

Put her in contact with babies who can hold their own bottles and let her see how they do it. Consider leaving her for a whole day with a sitter or relative whose child holds her own bottle, and see if she can pick up the skill under someone else's tutelage. (She just might be too stubborn to give in and do something on her own, while mommy is sitting there so obviously *able* to help but unwilling to do so.)

Q. My baby is over two years old but still isn't drinking from a cup—not even a "sippy cup" with a lid that has small holes in it. All the children in his playgroup have long since given up the bottle. Yet every time I give him a cup he just turns it upside-down on himself or throws it across the kitchen. I'm tired of cleaning up the mess, but I'm even more tired of washing bottles and nipples—not to mention having friends say, "Isn't he a little *old* for bottles?"

A. Let's take your last complaint first. Just as when strangers ask a bottlefeeding mom, "Why aren't you breast-feeding?" people should know that questioning a parent's feeding style is intrusive, rude, and unwarranted. You need not defend your bottlefeeding practices—but do let others know they are not allowed to attack you.

Once you've freed yourself from caring how it *looks* to other people, then ask yourself in private and consider the needs and personality of *your* child: How do *you* feel about a two-year-old with a bottle? Is it really so terrible? Does he get comfort from it? Are there changes in his life causing stress? (A new sibling? A change in your childcare situation? The start of preschool? Or toilet-training?) If that's the case and you have a child who doesn't adapt eas-ily to change, you might just want to back down on the bottle issue, until you hit an uneventful time in the child's life, and the child has the vocabulary and understanding to discuss the change and be prepared for it.

Think of it this way: Lots of breastfeeding mothers con-tinue to nurse a child past the age of two, because the child appears to need the comfort; bottlefed children may have their psychological need for comfort met by sucking, just the same way.

However, if you are determined to make the child accept the cup sometime soon, here is an approach you might want to try: Set certain hours and/or situations in which only cups will be used. For example, you could tell your child that he is allowed to have three bottles a day: one upon waking, one just before naptime, and one just before bedtime. At all other times, you will explain, his milk and juice will be given to him in cups. If your child spends the day or part of the day in a preschool or daycare center or in any type of group situation, you might say that when in the group, drink from cups; he can still have a bottle at home. This way mommy and daddy don't appear to be forcing the change, and daycare staff or sitters appear to be invested with the authority to enforce the cup-only rule. Small children generally have an easier time accepting rules if they know that's the way things are done someplace else, and they see all the other children living by those rules too.

Some parents have found that with a two-year-old there's no use trying to reach compromises. You just have to make it clear that there is no alternative but to do what the parents say. If you agree with this philosophy, then try this: Pick a day about three or four days away and declare that to be No-More-Bottles-Day. Tell your child several times a day for those three or four days that the time is fast approaching when he will be too old for bottles, and that by decree, all the bottles must be thrown out on that day. You might want to add that he will receive a present of a new cup, and (especially if you think he'll have a hard time getting to bed without a bottle the first night) a new toy or stuffed animal, to celebrate his first all-cup day.

When Bye-Bye Bottle Day arrives, upon waking, let him help you prepare the bottle. Let him drink it. When he's done, take that bottle, and every bottle in the house, and let him take out a big plastic garbage bag and throw all the bottles, nipples and rings inside. Then let him see you put a twist-tie around the bag, and let him help you carry the bag out to the trash can in the yard (or out to the trash-room of your apartment building).

(If you are planning to have more children and don't want to see all those bottles go to waste, then go back after your child is asleep and retrieve the sealed bag. Wash all the bottles and store them safely where you know your child can't find them).

It's essential that your child *believe* that all the bottles are gone forever, and that there is no chance to retrieve

Tip! From Bottle to Cup

Children who have trouble with or are resistant to cup-drinking are sometimes good with straws. You can buy fun straws that are twisted in different shapes, or have animal-holders attached to them. You can also buy juice-boxes or milk-boxes in four- or six-ounce servings that come with straws (they're also great for travel). Or you can buy little thermoses that come with a flip-up straw attached. Most baby product catalogs offer choices with child appeal. See Resource Guide for toll-free phone numbers.

them. He will probably like being involved in all this activity and ceremony . . . that is, until he's thirsty. Then he'll ask for a bottle and need to be told, again and again, that there are no more bottles in the house—only cups. The first two or three days, especially for those who have a strong-willed child, will be hellish, messy, tearful, and tantrum-filled. By the fourth day at the latest, I promise you that your child *will* have accepted his fate.

Q. After I take out a bottle of formula from the fridge, how long before the formula goes bad?

A. To be on the safe side don't let your baby drink from a bottle that's been left out longer than an hour—or less, if you're outside and it's a hot day. Keep formula bottles out of direct sunlight, and never put the unused portion back in the refrigerator. Once your baby's mouth has touched the nipple, germs can start breeding in the formula, even after it's in the refrigerator—so always throw out whatever is left over after your baby is done drinking.

> **Important Safety Rule for Formula**
>
> When in doubt, throw it out!

Q. I like to make up bottles of formula one at a time. How do I store the unused portion of the can?

A. Cover the top of the can with a piece of tight-fitting plastic wrap, or use plastic can-tops that you buy in a drugstore or supermarket. Put the covered can in the refrigerator, but be sure to use the rest within forty-eight hours, or you must throw it out. With powdered formula, once you've opened the tub, you must use up all the powder within 30 days or throw it out.

Q. After a few weeks of use I've found that the little holes at the end of the rubber nipples tend to get clogged. Should I throw the nipples away and get new ones?

A. You don't have to. Sterilize a needle over a flame or by wiping it with an alcohol swab and use it to unclog the nipple holes. Rubber nipples tend to clog frequently, while silicone ones don't, so you may just want to switch nipple types. Also, frequent dishwashing tends to make rubber nipples lose their shape and create an imperfect seal with the nipple ring, causing leakage; silicone nipples (they're the clear type) tend to have greater longevity—so many mothers report.

Q. I wanted to continue to breastfeed my son twice a day, so I introduced the bottle gradually into his feeding schedule. But once he was getting more than three bottles a day, he just seemed to lose interest in nursing, and refused my breast. What happened? Could I have prevented this early weaning (he's four months old) by handling things differently?

A. Possibly not. Each baby is different, and some easily adapt to both kinds of sucking, while others develop a strong preference, and once introduced to the ease of sucking from an artificial nipple, decide that's all they want. There's no point in kicking yourself for having introduced the change, because you had no way of knowing in advance how your baby was going to take to it. If you still want your baby to have breastmilk twice a day, you can maintain enough supply to provide him with breastmilk in bottles through the use of a breastpump. You might miss the warmth and closeness you felt while nursing, but keep in mind that if your baby wanted that, he wouldn't have gone so eagerly for the bottle.

Q. My baby seems prone to mild diarrhea. Could it be a reaction to the formula I'm giving him?

A. Possibly, but talk to your doctor about it. He or she may suggest a switch to a soy-based formula, a lactose-free formula, or one of the hypoallergenic varieties. You might also discuss the possibility of adding certain diarrhea-preventive bacteria to the milk formula. *The New York Times* reported a study that showed that breastmilk contains natural bacteria that help prevent infant diarrhea, but that babies who drank formula to which these "good" bacteria had been added had equally low rates of diarrhea as the breastfed group.[1] A powder containing the diarrhea-preventing bacteria is sold under the brand name Lactinex and is available at most health food stores.

Also keep in mind that many babies get mild diarrhea with every new tooth they cut, as they drool excessively, and the swallowed saliva irritates the digestive tract. Any time an infant has mild diarrhea that lasts more than a day or two, or has moderate to severe diarrhea for even one day, a call to the pediatrician is warranted.

Q. My baby is obese. She's in the 95th percentile for weight but only 50th for height. Should I dilute her formula so that she won't be so fat?

A. No. Never tamper with the formula mixture unless directed to do so specifically by your pediatrician, and then follow his or her directions exactly. Most babies like yours just put on a lot of baby fat, and once they're eating solid food and on cow's milk, they start to even out. Also, don't put your child on nonfat or lowfat milk when you switch to milk at one year. Children need the fat content for growth and development. The time to switch to lower-fat products is after age two. A safe way to promote a leaner baby would be to ensure that she's not too sedentary, and that she has plenty of activity to burn off calories during the day.

Q. My baby is too skinny. She's in the 75th percentile for height but is only 35th for weight. Can I mix up a richer formula to help her fill out a bit?

A. No. Never tamper with the formula mixture unless directed to do so specifically by your pediatrician, and then follow his or her directions exactly. Lots of babies grow vertically before they start growing horizontally. Babies come in all different body types, and hers could just be the slender sort. If she's drinking her formula well each day and appears to digest it properly (no diarrhea or signs of any digestive disease), you shouldn't worry.

Q. I bottlefed my first child, who is now three and a half. Soon I'll be having a second child, and I intend to breastfeed. Should I explain to my older child what I'm doing when I'm nursing? What should I say when my child asks me how I fed her? (I didn't breastfeed because I needed to go right back to work after her birth, and it would have been too difficult to pump at my job. This time around I can afford a six-month leave of absence.)

A. Yes, of course let your child see what you're doing when you nurse and explain that that's one way of feeding a baby. Be sure to tell her that there's another way, bottle-feeding, and that's how you fed her. If you were bottlefed yourself as a baby, or your husband was, add that that's how Grandma fed you or Daddy. Sometimes mommies like to use their breasts to feed their babies, and sometimes they like to use bottles. Explain that when she was a baby, you wanted Daddy and Nanny [whoever looked after her] to be able to feed her when you couldn't be there, but that breastfed babies can only be fed by Mommy. If she asks you to let her nurse or taste your milk (and she probably will), it's up to you to decide whether to let her try it. If

---

Tip! Ease the Pain of Sore Nipples

One of the most common reasons for women to wean is to eliminate the pain of sore nipples. If you've weaned for this reason but are interested in trying to nurse your next child, the following remedy should be of interest. It came from a mother who was about to stop breastfeeding, until a lactation consultant told her about this preparation, which worked well enough to allow her to keep breastfeeding. Here's the recipe:

Mix 1 tablespoon of baking soda with 8 ounces of comfortably warm water in two empty margarine tubs, or in two Pyrex custard cups.

Lean forward over a table so that your breasts are hanging in the mixture for 4 minutes.

Dry with a hair dryer on the gentlest setting.

Follow this procedure three times a day. Before nursing be sure to wipe your breasts with a clean, wet washcloth to remove any residue.

you're uncomfortable with the idea of letting her satisfy
her curiosity like that, explain that breastfeeding is just for
babies, and she is a big girl who gets to drink milk from a
cup.

Q. My first child was breastfed until almost two. I intended to breastfeed my second child as well, and told my
first child, who's now four, all about how I'd be feeding the
baby from my breasts. Unfortunately, I became ill soon after the baby's birth and was put on medication that made
breastfeeding inadvisable. Now what should I say to my
older child who is wondering if I told the truth?

A. A four-year-old is old enough to understand that
things don't always work out the way we plan. Give a simple but truthful account of your illness, emphasizing, of
course, that you are fully recovered, so that your child
doesn't worry about your health, or get the idea of blaming
the new baby for making you sick. Explain that most
mothers do feed their babies from their breasts, but that
lots of mothers also feed babies from bottles, and that's
just fine, too. Your four-year-old might actually enjoy being
your helper in the making of formula, and could pick out
the bottles for you to use, hand you the can opener, and if
closely supervised, even hold the bottle for the baby. Your
child might also enjoy having a baby doll that can be fed
from a toy bottle, so she can feed along with you and the
new baby.

Q. I'm not planning to breastfeed, and my doctor says
I'll get a shot of Parlodel after the delivery to dry up my
milk. I heard a news report that Parlodel isn't a good drug
to take. What's the story?

A. In September, 1994, the Food and Drug Administra-
tion issued a warning against the use of bromocriptine
(brand name, Parlodel) as a lactation suppressant in women after childbirth, based on two concerns: first, that the

drug has been known to produce some serious side effects, including dizziness, headache, seizures, postpartum psychosis, heart attacks, and stroke; and second, that the drug is largely ineffective and unnecessary for mothers who do not want to nurse. Parlodel may temporarily reduce milk production, but as soon as the shot wears off, the milk ducts begin to produce again. On the other hand, there is a highly effective and safe way to curtail milk production, and that is simply to avoid nursing. Without a sucking baby to stimulate the production of milk, the glands will quickly get the message that none is needed. Should the non-nursing mother experience some initial engorgement, she can use a pump or hand-expression to let out enough milk to relieve the pressure. A hormonal milk suppressant may only put the engorgement off till a later date. While Parlodel was commonly prescribed in the past, now even its own manufacturer, Sandoz Pharmaceuticals, is advising against the use of its product by postpartum women.[2] However, there are some doctors who feel Parlodel has been unfairly maligned, and that it is safe. If your doctor is one of them, consider seeking a second opinion.

Q. My baby seems to have no limit for bottle drinking. I give him an eight-ounce bottle, he downs it in a few minutes, and then can polish off another one of four or six ounces. He's seven months old and is drinking 50 ounces of formula a day. Of course he's off the charts in height and weight. Is this normal?

A. If your pediatrician's not worried, and your baby is not fussy or cranky after these marathon feedings, you needn't worry either. Of course, there would be no harm in *not* giving him the second bottle after he's finished that first eight-ouncer. Perhaps he's drinking so much because he's thirsty, and would be just as happy getting some water in place of a few of those extra bottles. Perhaps he just likes to suck and would suck on a pacifier if he had one. He might be drinking so much because he's not getting as much solid food as he'd like, or because he's bored and needs to be distracted away from the bottle by more interesting activities. If he's only recently become such a big drinker, he's probably going through a growth spurt, and his appetite should become more normal in a week or two.

Q. My baby is very allergic, as I was as a child. I can't help feeling that she would be less affected if I were breastfeeding.

A. You'll never know, and it's also entirely possible that your baby might have been *more* affected if she were ingesting allergens through your milk, rather than being kept on a nonallergenic formula. The tendency to allergy is often inherited, and since you had allergies, there is little doubt that the baby got your genes and would be prone to allergies, regardless of how she was fed. Your best bet is to try to reduce environmental allergens such as dust and pollens by installing air cleaners, using a special vacuum cleaner, keeping the baby away from furry pets, and wrapping the crib in a special hypoallergenic mattress cover. Since you're not breastfeeding, you don't have to worry about eliminating possible allergens from your own diet, but can rely on a hypoallergenic milk-based or soy formula, and introduce solid foods very gradually, watching carefully for reactions, and at a relatively late age (six months is recommended).

Q. I don't have a dishwasher. How do I make sure the bottles and nipples are clean enough for my baby?

A. For complete peace of mind, after a thorough washing you can always boil your equipment in a big pot of water for five minutes, once a day. If you don't want to bother with that, you're probably safe just putting everything in a basin filled with your hottest tap water and a mild detergent and letting everything soak for a few minutes. Rinse really well (the temperature of the rinse water is

not important) to be sure that you've removed all detergent
and milk residue from the nipples, rings, and bottles. Of
course, you should always separate nipples and rings
before washing. To get dried-up milk gunk out of bottles
and nipples that have been left sitting out for a while, use a
special bottle-washing bristle-brush, which you can buy at
any drugstore.

Q. How should I reply to friends who tell me I should
be breastfeeding, or who tell me my children's colds and ear
infections are attributable to the fact that I didn't breastfeed them?

A. The best policy, in my opinion, is not to allow friends
or family to make such personal comments in the first
place. The instant anyone brings the subject up, say, "We
consider this a personal question and would never dream
of letting anyone else tell us how we should live our lives."
You might add (self-deprecating chuckle optional) that
you'll make a deal: If the person promises not to give you
any more advice about how you use your breasts, you'll
promise not to tell that person what to do with any part of
his or her anatomy.

If the critic persists, and attempts to "educate" you by
quoting some study, you might remark that children in
Rwanda are breastfed, and it hasn't seemed to have done
much for their health and well-being, has it? Or conversely,
why is it that that the present generation of Americans is
the healthiest and longest-lived ever, when 84 percent of
them were bottlefed as babies? For those who decline to
get into the game of dueling statistics, just say, "I have
done my own investigation into the matter and reached the
decision that is best for my baby and my family. Thank
you for your concern" (said with finality so that it's clear
the subject is now closed).

For those who cherish the goodwill of the comment-
maker and don't mind revealing their own medical or emo-

tional history, go ahead and make known any details of
your own circumstances that led you to make the bottlefeeding choice. But don't be defensive. Remember, the feeding choice you have made is as valid for you and your baby
as breastfeeding is for someone else. You wouldn't criticize
someone else for nursing; no one should be allowed to criticize you for not.

Q. My sister-in-law, who breastfed each of her own kids
well into toddlerhood, is always comparing her kids against
mine. She thinks hers are smarter, better behaved, and
healthier because they were breastfed. It's true my kids
have had a lot of ear infections and hers haven't. What
should I say?

A. Don't get into this game with her—it's stupid and
pointless and she's only doing it to make you feel bad.
What if one of her "perfect" kids should grow up to be a
criminal? Would that prove that breastfeeding is bad? You
don't want to cut her off or be rude, but neither should
you have to defend your kids or your childrearing practices
to her. I'd say shrug off as much of her nonsense as you
can, by smiling blankly and saying, "Oh, really?" in a
bored tone, or smiling mysteriously but not responding, or
saying, "It's interesting that you see it that way," and
changing the subject. You might also let it get around to
her secondhand (through another trusted family member)
that you find these comparisons improper and unkind.

Q. My mother-in-law is the original earth-mother, having breastfed my husband as a baby as well as all five of
her other children. She's absolutely appalled that I'm bottlefeeding her granddaughter (I tried to nurse for a few
days but my baby just couldn't latch on). I've *tried* to tell
her to mind her own business, but she believes her grand-
children *are* her business.

A. How her grandchild is fed could only be her business if it involved *her* breasts. If she really won't let up on the subject, go to the library and copy two articles on the dangers of resistance to using formula when a newborn is not breastfeeding adequately. Let her see the *Wall Street Journal* article of July 22, 1994, titled "Dying for Milk—Some Mothers, Trying in Vain to Breastfeed, Starve Their Infants" by Kevin Helliker, or get the August 22, 1994, issue of *Time* and let her read the piece by Christine Gorman, "When Breastfeeding Fails." Perhaps if she could imagine her own grandchild in the place of one of the babies left severely handicapped by insufficient feeding, she would come to see your need to turn to formula in quite a different light.

Q. My mother is deadset against breastfeeding (she thinks it turns women into dairy cows) and she propagandized me all through my pregnancy not to try it. Well, I was just as deadset on doing it, and went so far as to tell her that an artificial nipple would never touch my baby's lips. But after weeks of pain and tears and the use of a breastpump and almost-daily consultations with a lactation specialist, my baby was just losing too much weight and there seemed to be no choice left but to go to the bottle. The baby's thriving now, and I'm glad about that, but I've been hiding my bottles from my mother because I so dread hearing her say "I told you so." I still believe breastfeeding is best, and wish I could have made a success of it. Any advice?

A. Many women have told me it's a lot easier to contend with their anti-breastfeeding relatives when they are successfully breastfeeding than when they appear to "give in" and switch to bottles. When you're happily nursing, you can just ignore them, since, by your very actions, you are proving them wrong. It's when you're having trouble with breastfeeding that the unsolicited advice really rankles.

But why should that be so? Shouldn't you be able to shrug off the unwanted comments just as you would if breastfeeding had worked out? It could be that what's *really* bothering you is a lingering feeling of guilt over your "failure." Any time you make the right decision for your baby's health and that baby is thriving, you *haven't* failed as a mother; you've been the best mother you could be. A "failure" would be the mother who puts her own desire to breastfeed above her baby's health and refuses to give formula.

You need to remind yourself that breastfeeding is *not best for all babies and all mothers*. Of course, your mother is wrong to criticize those who do breastfeed, and to try to pressure you into conforming to her personal views on the subject. Let her know that you are an adult woman, capable of forming your own judgment on basic parenting questions, and whether you breastfeed or bottlefeed is a matter to be discussed between you, the baby's father, and your doctor. Go ahead and take your bottles out of the closet and feed the baby . . . but be sure to tell your mother you don't want to hear her non-medical opinion about infant feeding.

Q. I'm in a mother-baby playgroup. The group leader has asked us not to bring in bottles for our children, so that they don't grab each other's bottles or fuss because one child has something the others don't have. She has not asked those nursing mothers not to breastfeed during the hour and a half session. I think this is unfair. The playgroup meets mid-morning, just when my baby is used to getting her second bottle of the day. Why should my baby go hungry when a breastfed baby can be fed?

A. I'm with you, but the question is, what do you want to do about it? You don't say how many mothers are in the group or if most are nursing or bottlefeeding. If there are several other like-minded bottlefeeders in the group, you ought to band together and press for a change in the rules. If you're all alone, the simplest solution is probably to drop out of that playgroup and find (or organize yourself) a less rigidly run playgroup with equal treatment for bottlefeeders.

Q. There's a teacher at my child's preschool who says she can always tell which kids were the breastfed ones, because they're the healthiest and most emotionally secure. I'm afraid that my child (who was bottlefed from day one and by the way is impeccably behaved) will end up being a victim of this teacher's prejudice.

A. You're right to be concerned. I would not want this teacher at the head of my bottlefed child's class. Yet switching around preschools once the school-year has started can be traumatic for a child, and besides, you'd probably have to forfeit some tuition (I know how steep those preschool fees can be!) There are two ways you can approach this problem: 1) Allow the teacher to assume that your impeccably behaved child was breastfed (since she probably has no idea, despite what she believes); or 2) If you think this teacher somehow *has* learned which children were breastfed or bottlefed, then carefully and gently bring up the subject with the teacher. Don't be hostile or confrontational. If you can, emphasize the positive of the situation rather than the negative (that is, focus on your child's sunny disposition, rather than the teacher's disapproval of bottlefeeding): "I know you're a great advocate of the benefits of breastfeeding, but you know Jenny was a bottlefed baby, and we think she's turning out to be a pretty wonderful kid." If the teacher is not a total bigot, she'll agree with you and quickly backpedal, saying she didn't mean to imply that anything was wrong with your child. If she criticizes your child, in your view unjustly, then you know you've got a big problem with this teacher, and you should discuss the teacher's attitude toward your child with the director of the school. You may indeed need to make a change of schools if the teacher's attitude manifests itself in any actual instances of prejudice toward your child.

To show just how outrageous such a comment is, imagine that the teacher has made the remark in the reverse, and asserted that bottlefed children are better, or suppose she had made a judgment based on some other difference in feeding method: that children raised as vegetarians are superior to meat-eating children—that would offend most people wouldn't it? Now think what the reaction would be if she'd voiced her comparison about children brought up in homes observant of Jewish or Muslim dietary values, and you can see what harm can come from making assumptions about a child's character based on the family's feeding practices.

Yes, the prejudice in favor of breastfeeding really is a form of discrimination! And we bottlefeeders do need to speak up for our rights!

CHAPTER **7**

Your Future,
Your Choice

Many considerations go into making a choice about how to feed your baby, and each new mother needs to take stock of her own unique circumstances to choose what's best for herself and her child (not what some book or "expert" tells her is best). This chapter is for those who have not decided yet. If you are pregnant and you can see the pros and cons in either method, breast or bottle, the quiz that follows may help you sort through your feelings. Even those who are fairly sure they will bottlefeed, or fairly sure they will breastfeed, may find the quiz helpful in gauging how their preference will really fit in with their lifestyle.

If you have already breastfed a first child but are considering trying bottles the second time around, or if you bottlefed your first but are thinking about breastfeeding this time, the quiz may be of help. Keep in mind, though, that no quiz can accurately predict what any individual should do. Nor is this quiz designed to. I would never presume to tell a woman what she should do with her body. The quiz is just a fun way to elicit your thoughts and feelings, and

put a numerical value on something that is essentially un-
quantifiable. So take your "score" at the end with a grain
of salt. If you count up your numbers, read Interpreting
Your Score, and find that you are a great candidate for
breastfeeding—but when the baby is here you can't do it,
ignore this test! If the test scoring pegs you as a bottlefeeder, but when they place that baby in your arms you feel
moved to put her to your breast and find she latches on
and sucks, and it's great!—then by all means, nurse!

Breast or Bottle:

Which Is Best for You?

Follow directions for each section, then figure out your score (page 257), and read Interpreting Your Score (page 264).

Part I. Physical Factors

Multiple Choice   For each question, select only one answer.

1. While looking at your breasts in a mirror, pinch the nipple gently between your thumb and index finger. If the nipple protrudes, you have normal nipples, if the nipple doesn't change, you have flat nipples, and if the nipple actually indents, you have inverted nipples. Select the statement that best describes your body:

    A. Both nipples are normal.

    B. One nipple is flat or inverted, the other is normal.

    C. Both nipples are flat.

    D. Both nipples are inverted.

    E. One nipple is flat, the other is inverted.

2. If you answered the preceding question with B, C, or D:

    A. I am willing to spend several weeks toward the end of my pregnancy wearing nipple shells to help draw out my flat or inverted nipple(s).

    B. I might try wearing nipple shells to help draw out my flat or inverted nipple(s).

    C. I do not wish to put anything on my breasts while pregnant in an effort to prepare my nipples for nursing.

3. Describe the condition of your nipples:

    A. My nipples feel extremely soft and sensitive. If I rub them with a rough washcloth or tug at them firmly, it feels uncomfortable.

    B. My nipples are not especially sensitive to friction. I can rub them with a rough washcloth or tug at them firmly without discomfort.

    C. My nipples are pretty tough. Not only can I rub them vigorously or squeeze them firmly without problem, but I can sunbathe nude for a reasonable time without worrying about sunburn, and/ or I can jog without a bra without feeling chafing against my shirt.

4. Describe your breasts during pregnancy:

    A. I have large breasts, DD cup (also called an E cup) or larger.

    B. I have average size breasts (A to D cup bra).

    C. I have small breasts (never needed to wear a bra, or wear size AA or smaller).

5. Describe your family history:

A. There is no history of food sensitivities or allergies on my side or on the baby's father's side of the family.

B. There is a history of food sensitivities or allergies on one side of the family (either on my side or the baby's father's side).

C. There is a history of food sensitivities or allergies on both sides of the family. Both the baby's father and I have had problems with reactions to certain foods, and/or several other close relatives (my siblings and/or the baby's father's siblings) have had problems with allergic reactions to certain foods.

6. If you checked B or C in the preceding question: If I need dietary restrictions to protect my baby against reactions to allergens in my breastmilk, I will most likely:

A. Try the dietary restrictions as directed by the baby's doctor for as long as necessary to see improvement in my baby's reaction to my milk.

B. Try the dietary restrictions out for a certain amount of time, but if the restrictions should prove too burdensome, or I did not see substantial improvement, I will consider weaning.

C. Not want to put the baby or myself through a trial-and-error process that might never solve the problem. I'd try a hypoallergenic formula, and if that worked I would definitely wean.

7. Concerning breast surgery, choose the statement that describes your experience:

A. I have never had any form of breast surgery.

B. I have had breast implant surgery.

C. I have had breast reduction surgery.

D. I have had a lumpectomy or mastectomy on one breast for breast cancer.

8. Read all the statements below and choose the one* that most closely describes your prior infant feeding experience:

A. This baby will be my first, so I have never breast-fed before. I never took care of other babies, so I have no bottlefeeding experience either.

B. This baby will be my first, so I have never breast-fed before. I've cared for other babies who were bottlefed and I have some experience with bottle-feeding.

C. This baby will be my first, so I have never breastfed before. I've cared for other babies who were breast-fed, so I have observed other mothers nursing.

D. This baby is not my first. I breastfed my older child(ren) and considered it on the whole a satis-factory experience.

E. This baby is not my first. I breastfed my older child(ren) and considered it on the whole a less than satisfactory experience.

F. This baby is not my first. I bottlefed my older

*Those who can answer True for both B and C (because they have babysitting experience with both breastfed and bottlefed babies) should chose C. Those who can answer True for both E and F. (because they have an older child who was both breastfed and bottlefed) may choose whichever answer they believe comes *closest* to describing their experi-ence, with hindsight—but not both. Those who can answer True for both E and G (or any other combination of answers) should similarly choose the single answer that comes *closest* to describing their experi-ence, with hindsight. If you are uncertain how to answer because you started out bottlefeeding your first child with your pumped-out milk (with or without some formula supplementation) and then switched over to nursing full time, you should count yourself as having breastfed your first child, and choose D or E, depending on whether you would characterize the feeding experience as on the whole satisfactory, or less than satisfactory. Choose H if you'd call it a little bit of both.

child(ren) and considered it on the whole a satisfactory experience.

G. This baby is not my first. I bottlefed my older
child(ren) and considered it on the whole a less
than satisfactory experience.

H. This baby is not my first. I have tried both bottlefeeding and breastfeeding before, with mixed
results (that is, I've had good results with breastfeeding before—some of the time or in certain situations, and/or good results with bottlefeeding
before—some of the time, or in certain situations).

True/False Below are 30 statements about your current
health or anticipated conditions upon arrival of the baby.
For each statement, choose True if it by and large applies
to you; choose False if not.

1. I am in overall good health. I have no chronic or
acute conditions (such as major physical disabilities, heart
disease, kidney disease, multiple sclerosis).

2. I have had no complications with my pregnancy. I am
not on bed rest now, nor do I anticipate being put on bed
rest later on in my pregnancy. I do not have gestational
diabetes, preeclampsia, toxemia, high blood pressure, or
any other condition requiring special medication, special
diet, or other preventive measures.

3. I have not been warned about any increased risk of
C-section. My baby is not breech, I am not carrying a multiple pregnancy (twins, triplets, or more), the baby has not
been diagnosed as having Intra-Uterine Growth Retardation (IUGR), nor do I have any pelvic or cervical problems,
as identified by my OB.

4. I am planning to have a home birth, if possible.

5. I am planning to give birth in a birthing center, attended by a midwife (may be a certified nurse-midwife).

6. After delivery, I am planning to keep my baby in the room with me overnight (if planning a home birth, choose True).

7. After delivery, I expect to stay in the hospital or birthing center for a minimum of 48 hours (if planning a home birth, choose True).

8. I do not use any prescription or over-the-counter medications that carry warnings against use during lactation.

9. I do not smoke (or feel confident that I could abstain from smoking during lactation without problem).

10. I do not drink alcohol (or feel confident that I could abstain from alcohol during lactation or drink only sparingly, limiting myself to times when I will not be nursing for the next several hours).

11. I am not a big consumer of caffeine. I drink only a cup or two of coffee, tea, or cola a day (or I could easily cut down or cut out caffeine from my diet).

12. I am not a big consumer of foods made with artificial sweeteners—aspartame or saccharine (or I could easily cut back on or cut out such foods from my diet).

13. I live in an area of normal environmental safety: As far as I know, the water, air, and food supply have acceptably safe levels of contaminants.

14. I am under the age of 25 and am aware of a family history of breast cancer on my mother's side (mother, maternal grandmother, and/or mother's sisters have had breast cancer).

15. I could get along reasonably well for a few months on little sleep or frequently interrupted sleep.

16. My mother successfully breastfed me and/or my siblings, and could serve as a knowledgeable source of advice and support.

17. My mother-in-law successfully breastfed my husband or partner, and could serve as a knowledgeable source of advice and support.

18. I have sisters who have breastfed happily, who could serve as a knowledgeable source of advice and support.

19. I have sisters-in-law who have breastfed happily, who could serve as a knowledgeable source of advice and support.

20. I have cousins, friends, or co-workers who have breastfed happily, who could serve as a knowledgeable source of advice and support.

21. I am aware of a breastfeeding support group that meets regularly in a place that's convenient to me.

22. My health insurance will cover the cost (or much of the cost) of a board-certified lactation consultant, if it turns out that I need one.

23. If my health insurance did not cover the cost of a board-certified lactation consultant, and it turned out that I needed one to assist in breastfeeding, I would be able to pay for one without strain to my budget.

24. My obstetrician, pediatrician, or family practitioner has a board-certified lactation consultant on staff or can facilitate the selection of a competent one, if it turns out that I need one.

25. My obstetrician is very knowledgeable about breast-feeding. Most of his or her patients breastfeed.

26. My pediatrician is very knowledgeable about breast-feeding. Most of his or her patients have been breastfed.

27. The hospital or birthing center where I will deliver has support services for breastfeeding mothers (certified lactation consultants on staff, breastpumps available, and classes on breastfeeding pre- or post-partum).

28. I am planning to take/would like to find a class or attend a support group meeting to help prepare me for breastfeeding prior to childbirth.

29. I will be a single parent.

30. I have been/may have been exposed to a virus that is transmissible through breastmilk.*

Part II. Attitudes

Agree or disagree   For each statement, do you:

- **A.** Agree strongly
- **B.** Agree somewhat
- **C.** Feel neutral or unsure
- **D.** Disagree somewhat
- **E.** Disagree strongly

Don't worry if you agree with one statement, and then find yourself agreeing with a contradictory statement later on. Go with your initial "gut" reaction to each statement, avoiding second thoughts or analysis of any pattern that you think your answers may be forming as you take the test.

1. Even if I get little sleep at night, I can refresh myself by taking naps during the day.

2. I am extremely health conscious.

3. I maintain a well-balanced diet.

4. The foods I eat are fresh and wholesome, or if not, I would have no trouble cutting back/cutting out foods with

---

*If you answer True to this question, you need to consult a doctor—preferably one who specializes in the diagnosis and treatment of infectious diseases—before making the infant feeding decision. Especially if you have any of the risk factors for HIV exposure you owe it to yourself and your baby to be tested. If you are not certain whether you have any risk factors for any diseases that may be transmissable through breastmilk, be sure to ask this question of your obstetrician.

222

22

possibly harmful additives (such as artificial sweeteners, colorings, or preservatives).

5. I am, in general, uninhibited about my breasts.

6. I believe in most cases that what's best for the baby should take precedence over what's best for the parents, so if it turns out to be uncomfortable for me to nurse, I would still try to continue, to provide my baby with the benefits of breastmilk.

7. I believe a baby crying means it has needs that are being unmet and the parents should try to meet those needs. Letting a baby "cry it out" is never a good idea.

8. I like the idea of taking my baby into bed with me at night. I would be in no hurry to get my baby to sleep in a bassinet in my room or a crib in a different room.

9. I'm familiar with the childrearing ideas of Dr. William Sears and believe that what he advocates is generally sound and beneficial to children (even if I don't intend to put all of his ideas into practice myself).

10. I believe cloth diapers are better for baby's skin.

11. I don't get embarrassed easily. Finding a wet spot or stain on my clothes is not something that would bother me all that much.

12. In general I would say I'm fairly "laid back." I don't mind that some things take a long time, and I don't get frustrated if it takes a while to learn a new skill.

13. I'm pretty particular about my clothing. I like it to fit well and look nice, as first impressions are generally based on how a person presents herself.

14. I'm a very neat person around the house—sometimes a little *too* neat, others tell me—but I think it's important to keep the house straightened up, even when time is at a premium.

15. I'm able to tolerate some discomfort, or even pain, if it's for something I think is worthwhile.

16. It's my goal to get through labor and delivery without pain-reducing drugs, if at all possible.

17. If I ended up needing a C-section to deliver a healthy baby, I believe I would be bitterly disappointed, having been deprived of what ought to be one of life's most remarkable experiences.

18. I am generally opposed to pacifiers. It's not a good thing for a baby to become dependent on an artificial sucking device.

19. I just love being pregnant. I love the connectedness, the feeling of oneness with my baby.

20. Pregnancy is a special time, no doubt, but it's also a time of aches and pains, tiredness, that awful bloated feeling and lots of heartburn—and I'll be happy when I'm done with the whole business.

21. Breastfeeding has so many benefits for the baby that I think every woman who has given birth should at least give it a try.

22. I believe it's wrong for hospitals to allow formula companies to distribute free samples to their maternity patients. It sends the wrong message to many new mothers, who aren't sufficiently educated to know that breastfeeding is the medical expert's first choice for infant nutrition.

23. I believe the government should ban all formula advertising directly to consumers, so that vulnerable new mothers are not seduced away from breastfeeding by slickly contrived ad images.

24. I am concerned about possible permanent changes in the shape of my breasts—that they might sag or droop more if I breastfed for more than a few weeks.

25. I am concerned about getting my figure back once I

have my baby. I want to get back to my pre-pregnancy weight as quickly as I can.

26. I wouldn't mind having a bigger, fuller figure after childbirth, because it's an outward indication of my transformation from a girlish, less responsible state of being to a deeper, more reflective, more responsible state of being.

27. My family has a tendency to produce overweight children. Whichever feeding style I choose, I will have to be careful that my baby doesn't get overfed.

28. I am concerned about how well my baby might gain weight. Low birth weight, slow weight gain, or prematurity has been a problem for babies of some of my relatives.

29. If I have a son, I would never consider having him circumcised.

30. Though there are advantages to breastfeeding, I can't help but wonder about how practical it might be for me, given my personality, schedule, and/or home environment.

31. It would be convenient not to carry around bottle-feeding supplies.

32. It would be liberating to be able to leave my baby with others to be fed.

33. I'm hoping to still have some time to myself after my baby is born—to exercise, or relax with a good book, or whatever I need to do to take care of my own needs from time to time.

34. Most women benefit from combining motherhood and employment, not just because of the increased income, but because it's important to remain part of the adult world and build on business or professional skills. It's no good for a child to have a mother who would feel trapped and unproductive at home.

35. Too many women put their careers ahead of their children's needs. What could be more fulfilling and enriching than helping your own children get off to the best possible start in life?

36. When I pack for a trip, I am always well-prepared. I take along everything I need, and seldom if ever find myself having forgotten an important item.

37. It's a bad idea for a mother to take a vacation (even a weekend) away from her baby before the second birthday.

38. I'm a spontaneous person. I don't believe in a lot of preparation for most things. If I'm inclined to do something, and there's nothing standing in the way of it, I go ahead and do it!

39. I've always admired the earth mother type.

40. I tend to be a worrier. When trying something new, I can't help but focus on what could go wrong.

41. I believe Nature is on the whole a benign force. Whatever brings us closer to Nature's design is good; whenever a new technology interferes with Nature's plan, it often turns out to be disastrous for humankind in the long run (if not right away).

42. It's fine to say that men and women are equal, but we shouldn't try to deny the important biological differences between us, or deny that these physical differences lead to differences in outlook and abilities in many areas of life.

43. I'm a hi-tech person. I like anything that's well-designed, that saves time, that makes things work better, that solves problems. I believe if we didn't improve our world through technology, we'd still be living in mud huts with a life-expectancy of about thirty.

44. Sexual pleasure is one of the most important aspects of my relationship with my husband/partner.

45. Much as I love my husband/partner, I expect my love for my child to take precedence. If both my husband and my child were trapped in a burning building and I could only save one I would save my child.

46. There is something indefinable and awe-inspiring about the mother-child bond.

47. A man can be a very good, caring father, but he can never match or fully comprehend the special link that exists between a mother and her child.

48. If a mother chooses to stay home full time to be with her baby, it is the father's obligation to provide enough income to support his family.

49. The best thing for a baby under nearly all circumstances is to be raised by its biological mother—even when the mother is poor, uneducated, and single—as long as she loves her child. Placement for adoption is desirable only when a mother is demonstrably unfit (she is abusive or is thoroughly incompetent to take care of her child).

50. It's better for a baby to go to a pair of loving, stable, financially responsible adoptive parents than to stay with a mother who, though she may very much love her baby, lacks the maturity or judgment needed to bring up a responsible child in today's uncertain world.

51. Surrogate motherhood* should be illegal. The State should not enforce a contract that treats a baby as a negotiable commodity.

52. A baby is a baby for a preciously short time. We shouldn't be in a rush to teach our babies new skills, but should enjoy their babyhood while it lasts.

53. Breastfeeding is the norm in my community. I might be regarded as out of touch if I don't breastfeed.

54. If you can just get organized, you'll be able to get a better handle on almost any activity you take up, and life will be a little less stressful.

---

*An arrangement in which an infertile couple seeks out a fertile woman to bear a child. The woman signs a contract agreeing to be artificially impregnated with the husband's sperm and upon childbirth to give up the baby to be raised by its biological father and his wife.

55. Life is meant to be messy; there's no way around it when babies are involved.

Multiple Choice For each question, choose the answer that most closely reflects your attitude.

1. When I see a mother breastfeeding her baby in a restaurant or shopping mall, my reaction is:

    A. Great! This is a mother who is devoted to her baby's well-being.

    B. Neutral. I don't assume anything about a woman's mothering ability based on the way she feeds her baby.

    C. Negative. I have nothing against breastfeeding, but it makes me uncomfortable to see a woman in a public place engaging in what ought to be a private intimate act.

2. When I see a mother bottlefeeding her baby in a restaurant or shopping mall, my reaction is:

    A. Negative. Doesn't she know that breastfeeding is best for her baby?

    B. Curious. Why isn't she breastfeeding? Did something go wrong that prevented her from breastfeeding?

    C. Neutral. I don't think it's anybody else's business how a mother feeds her baby, as long as the baby's basic needs are being met.

    D. Great! This is a mother who hasn't succumbed to the pressure to breastfeed but goes ahead and does what she believes is right for herself and her baby.

3. My husband/partner is:

   A. very supportive of breastfeeding and expects me to breastfeed

   B. supportive of whatever I think is the right choice for myself and the baby

   C. uncomfortable with certain aspects of breast-feeding: doesn't want me to breastfeed in public, has worries about our sexual relationship if my breasts are used primarily for milk-producing

   D. enthusiastic about sharing the feeding duties, and will be disappointed if I decide to breastfed exclusively

4. Should I find myself feeling sexual discomfort (vaginal dryness, loss of libido) as a result of nursing, I probably would:

   A. tell myself this is a temporary thing, and to put up with it for a few months to ensure that my baby has the best start in life

   B. try over-the-counter remedies or speak to my doctor about ways to alleviate the problem. I would not consider weaning unless it was seriously affecting my relationship with my husband/partner.

   C. do whatever I had to do to ensure that my sexual relationship was not damaged—including weaning, if necessary. It would not be good for my family if breastfeeding interfered with our physical love for each other

5. Choose the statement that most accurately describes your attitude toward birth control after the baby is born.

   A. I would like to avoid becoming pregnant again before my baby is six months old. If I am able to breastfeed exclusively, I would welcome the contraceptive effects of full-time nursing. I would probably not turn to an artificial method of birth control.

B. I would like to avoid becoming pregnant again before my baby is six months old. If I breastfeed I will not rely on it to produce a contraceptive effect, but will use another method of birth control.

C. I would not mind getting pregnant again within six months of my baby's birth. I am not planning to use an artificial method of birth control (whether I nurse or not).

D. I would actively welcome a pregnancy after this one. I want to enhance rather than inhibit my fertility.

Part III. Work and Childcare

Multiple Choice For questions 1 and 2, select *all* the answers that apply to your situation.

1. My childcare situation in the first two weeks after the baby's birth will be as follows:

A. I will be taking care of all the baby's primary needs. My husband has no paternity leave (or less than a week's leave), and we have no arrangements for hired help or relatives to help out on a part-time or full-time basis.

B. I will be taking care of the baby's primary needs, but my husband will be taking one week or more of paternity leave.

C. I will have part-time hired help (less than thirty hours a week).

D. I will have full-time hired help (more than thirty hours a week).

E. I will have a relative (mother, mother-in-law, sister, aunt) who is knowledgeable about breastfeeding staying with me or living close by for a period of time and I have confidence that person will be helpful and supportive of me in my first days home with the baby.

F. I will have a relative (mother, mother-in-law, sister, aunt) staying with me or living close by for a period of time, although that person isn't knowledgeable about breastfeeding and may not be especially supportive of the practice.

2. In the first six weeks after the birth, my husband will be available to care for the baby (or to help me take care of the baby):

A. in the evenings

B. in the middle of the night

C. on weekends

D. sharing equally in childcare duties

E. assuming the role of primary caregiver, for a certain length of time or indefinitely

3. Select one statement that most accurately describes your plans.

I will return to work outside the home full-time (more than thirty hours a week):

A. before my baby is one month old

B. when my baby is between one to three months old

C. when my baby is between three to six months old

    D. when my baby is between six months to one year old

    E. within one year, part time (less than thirty hours a week)

    F. I will work full time at home more than thirty hours a week.

    G. I have no plans to seek paid employment while my child is under a year old.

    H. I'm not sure. I'll wait to see how I feel about working once the baby is here.

For those who plan to return to full-time, outside employment within one year of the baby's birth:

    4. Choose all that apply. My workplace has:

    A. a private place for breastfeeding mothers to nurse or express milk, with adequate storage and cleaning facilities available

    B. a daycare center on-site or nearby, allowing mothers to make drop-in visits for feeding

    C. a supportive atmosphere for breastfeeding. Other employees have successfully maintained lactation, and/or person(s) in charge have expressed approval (or have not expressed disapproval) of any employee's desire to maintain lactation while on the job.

    D. None of the above. Breastfeeding is not supported at my job, or is frowned upon.

    5. Choose all that apply. Women who get ahead where I work need to:

    A. appear professional at all times

    B. dress conservatively

    C. be careful that their childcare needs don't take them away too often from their work obligations

    D. None of the above. Dress is relaxed, and allowances are made for parents who must take an occasional day off to tend to their children's needs.

  6. Choose one statement that most closely describes travel in your work. In my work I am:

    A. never asked to go on overnight trips

    B. occasionally asked to go on overnight trips, but I believe I could get my employer to accommodate any reasonable requests I might have as a nursing mother to limit business travel, or I believe I might be able to accommodate my baby through use of a breastpump to keep up my supply on those occasions when I have no choice but to be away

    C. occasionally asked to go on overnight trips that would be difficult for me to decline or postpone. However, trips are generally short, and stays are at modern hotels, so if I were nursing I'd be able to use a breastpump conveniently and hygienically.

    D. frequently required to travel, or occasionally required to travel, but the trips may be to faraway places or to places with poor conditions (that would make it difficult or impossible for me to use an electric pump to express my milk and keep it safely stored, or keep my pumping equipment free of bacteria)

  7. I expect to use the following childcare arrangement:

    A. on-site daycare center

    B. daycare center or caregiver's home, not near place of employment

    C. shared caregiver, three or fewer children (in own home or other child's home)

D. in-home caregiver for your own child(ren) only

E. relative or in-law as caregiver (in own home or relative's home)

F. flexible, depending on what my needs and my child's needs turn out to be

Mothers Talk About Making the Decision

What I'd say to any woman who's not sure what she wants to do is, "Don't let anyone push you around. Do what's good for you. I have nothing against breastfeeding. I'd say, "Try it." *But it's not a religion.* You won't go to Hell for bottlefeeding. The test is the kids. My son was bottlefed and he turned out as well as my breastfed daughter. And most of my generation were bottlefed, and we didn't turn out so badly, in my opinion.

—Jenny

When making one of the zillions of decisions a parent has to make, we try to consider the impact of our decision in five years, in fifteen years. Based on that, some decisions are suddenly not so big, and some are bigger than we'd initially thought. Our son is a year old now—happy, healthy, growing. Now the breast or bottle decision doesn't loom so important anymore. I don't think we'll even remember it five years from now. I don't think his teachers, his future employer, or even his wife will be able to tell he was bottlefed . . . but I think they will all know that he was very much loved. They will see it in his captivating smile.

—Kate

It's a very personal decision. Each mother has to choose what's right for her. There are advantages to breastfeeding, but there are advantages to bottlefeeding, too: time for oneself and for one's older kids; that the father and the grandparents can participate more; and also, the mother who breastfeeds but is miserable and dreads every nursing is not good for any baby.

—Lisa

I had hoped for a lovely, pastoral breastfeeding experience, but when your baby screams in hunger but won't nurse, you change your priorities. I will say that my experience with my son was very emotional [instead of switching to formula, this mother was determined to stick to breastmilk, and pumped for three months and fed the milk to her baby in bottles]. I had one foot in breastfeeding and one foot in bottlefeeding. That's a real No-Woman's-Land, let me tell you.

—Donna

Why I chose the bottle from day one:

1. I was going back to work right away and knew that expressing milk at work would be difficult, if not impossible.
2. Family history. There are no allergies or other health problems in our backgrounds that might have given us an impetus towards breastfeeding [to prevent such things].
3. We'd engaged a baby nurse for two months and wanted her to be able to handle the night feedings and do bottle preparation.
4. I didn't want to exclude my husband from feeding the baby.

5. I didn't want to be a slave to breastfeeding. I believe many women choose it out of pressure, or because it's the fashionable thing. Bottlefeeding fit my lifestyle better. Women who breastfeed—if they go in for the full breastfeeding "thing"—are really supposed to keep it up for at least a year and do nothing but breastfeed. But for me there's more to life than feeding a baby.

—Barbara

I'm a pediatrician. While I encourage breastfeeding as the ideal, I'm aware that it isn't for everyone for a variety of reasons, be they cultural, economic, or personal preference. The tone of the discussion [on this e-mail medical forum] has been to tut-tut about those who choose not to breastfeed. For what it's worth, I don't think that's in anyone's best interest. [As to another e-mail writer's joke that] I can see the headlines in the future, "Child Sues Mother over Formula Fed to Her as Infant," the headline could just as easily read, "Mother Sues Lactation Consultant for Guilt Feelings Requiring Therapy." [Joking aside] we should work towards making breastfeeding comfortable and convenient for more mothers, instead of promoting it through formula-bashing and guilt-trips.

—a Canadian pediatrician voicing his concern about the anti-bottlefeeding attitudes expressed on-line

Scoring

For any question that is not applicable to your situation, score 0.

Part I: Physical Factors

Multiple Choice

1. A. = +2	**3.** A. = –2	**5.** A. = +1	**7.** A. = 0
B. = –1	B. = 0	B. = –1	B. = –20
C. = –2	C. = +2	C. = –2	C. = –20
D. = –4			D. = –10
E. = –3			

2. A. = +2	**4.** A. = –2	**6.** A. = +2	**8.** A. = 0
B. = +1	B. = +1	B. = 0	B. = –1
C. = –2	C. = –2	C. = –2	C. = +1
			D. = +3
			E. = –3
			F. = –2
			G. = +2
			H. = 0

True/False

1. T = +1	9. T = 0	17. T = +1	25. T = +1
F = −3	F = −6	F = 0	F = −1
2. T = +1	10. T = +1	18. T = +1	26. T = +1
F = −3	F = −6	F = 0	F = −1
3. T = +1	11. T = +1	19. T = +1	27. T = +1
F = −3	F = −2	F = 0	F = −1
4. T = +5	12. T = 0	20. T = +1	28. T = +3
F = 0	F = −1	F = −1	F = −1
5. T = +3	13. T = 0	21. T = +2	29. T = −5
F = 0	F = −8	F = −1	F = 0
6. T = +2	14. T =+10	22. T = +1	
F = −1	F = 0	F = −1	
7. T = +1	15. T = +1	23. T = +1	
F = 0	F = −1	F = −1	
8. T = 0	16. T = +1	24. T = +1	
F = −8	F = −1	F = −1	

30. F = 0. T = Consult your doctor. If told that you have a virus that presents a serious risk to your baby, plan to bottlefeed. If told that it is still safe to breastfeed because the virus does not present a risk to your baby, score 0. If told

that it will be safe to breastfeed after you have successfully completed treatment for the virus, score –3.

Part II: Attitudes

Multiple Choice

1. A. = +2	**5.** A. = +4	**9.** A. = +2	**13.** A. = –2
B. = +1	B. = +2	B. = +1	B. = –1
C. = 0	C. = 0	C. = 0	C. = 0
D. = –1	D. = –2	D. = –1	D. = +1
E. = –2	E. = –4	E. = –2	E. = +2
2. A. = +2	**6.** A. = +4	**10.** A. = +2	**14.** A. = –2
B. = +1	B. = +2	B. = +1	B. = –1
C. = 0	C. = 0	C. = 0	C. = 0
D. = –1	D. = –2	D. = –1	D. = +1
E. = –2	E. = –4	E. = –2	E. = +2
3. A. = +2	**7.** A. = +2	**11.** A. = +2	**15.** A. = +2
B. = +1	B. = +1	B. = +1	B. = +1
C. = 0	C. = 0	C. = 0	C. = 0
D. = –1	D. = –1	D. = –1	D. = –1
E. = –2	E. = –2	E. = –2	E. = –2
4. A. = +2	**8.** A. = +2	**12.** A. = +2	**16.** A. = +2
B. = +1	B. = +1	B. = +1	B. = +1
C. = 0	C. = 0	C. = 0	C. = 0
D. = –1	D. = –1	D. = –1	D. = –1
E. = –2	E. = –2	E. = –2	E. = –2

17. A. = +2	21. A. = +2	25. A. = −1	29. A. = +2
B. = +1	B. = +1	B. = 0	B. = +1
C. = 0	C. = 0	C. = 0	C. = 0
D. = −1	D. = −1	D. = +1	D. = 0
E. = −2	E. = −2	E. = +2	E. = 0

18. A. = +2	22. A. = +2	26. A. = +2	30. A. = −6
B. = +1	B. = +1	B. = +1	B. = −3
C. = 0	C. = 0	C. = 0	C. = 0
D. = −1	D. = −1	D. = −1	D. = +1
E. = −2	E. = −2	E. = −2	E. = +2

19. A. = +2	23. A. = +2	27. A. = +2	31. A. = +2
B. = +1	B. = +1	B. = +1	B. = +1
C. = 0	C. = 0	C. = 0	C. = 0
D. = −1	D. = −1	D. = 0	D. = −1
E. = −2	E. = −2	E. = −1	E. = −2

20. A. = −1	24. A. = −1	28. A. = −1	32. A. = −2
B. = 0	B. = 0	B. = 0	B. = −1
C. = 0	C. = 0	C. = 0	C. = 0
D. = +1	D. = +1	D. = +1	D. = +1
E. = +2	E. = +2	E. = +2	E. = +2

33. A. = –2
    B. = –1
    C. = 0
    D. = +1
    E. = +2

34. A. = –1
    B. = 0
    C. = 0
    D. = +1
    E. = +2

35. A. = +2
    B. = +1
    C. = 0
    D. = 0
    E. = –1

36. A. = –1
    B. = 0
    C. = 0
    D. = +1
    E. = +2

37. A. = +2
    B. = +1
    C. = 0
    D. = 0
    E. = –1

38. A. = +2
    B. = +1
    C. = 0
    D. = 0
    E. = –1

39. A. = +2
    B. = +1
    C. = 0
    D. = 0
    E. = –1

40. A. = –1
    B. = 0
    C. = 0
    D. = 0
    E. = +1

41. A. = +2
    B. = +1
    C. = 0
    D. = 0
    E. = –1

42. A. = +2
    B. = +1
    C. = 0
    D. = 0
    E. = –1

43. A. = –1
    B. = 0
    C. = 0
    D. = +1
    E. = +2

44. A. = –1
    B. = 0
    C. = 0
    D. = +1
    E. = +2

45. A. = +1
    B. = 0
    C. = 0
    D. = 0
    E. = –1

46. A. = +2
    B. = +1
    C. = 0
    D. = 0
    E. = –1

47. A. = +2
    B. = +1
    C. = 0
    D. = 0
    E. = –1

48. A. +1
    B. = 0
    C. = 0
    D. = 0
    E. = –1

49. A. = +2
    B. = +1
    C. = 0
    D. = 0
    E. = −1

50. A. = −1
    B. = 0
    C. = 0
    D. = +1
    E. = +2

51. A. = +1
    B. = 0
    C. = 0
    D. = 0
    E. = −1

52. A. = +2
    B. = +1
    C. = 0
    D. = 0
    E. = −1

53. A. = +2
    B. = +1
    C. = 0
    D. = 0
    E. = −1

54. A. = −1
    B. = 0
    C. = 0
    D. = +1
    E. = +2

55. A. = +2
    B. = +1
    C. = 0
    D. = −1
    E. = −2

Multiple Choice

1. A. = +5
   B. = 0
   C. = −5

2. A. = +5
   B. = +2
   C. = 0
   D. = −5

3. A. = +5
   B. = 0
   C. = −5
   D. = −3

4. A. = +3
   B. = 0
   C. = −3

5. A = +3
   B. = +1
   C. = 0
   D. = −1

Part III: Work and Childcare
Multiple Choice

1. A. = 0
   B. = +1
   C. = +1
   D. = 0
   E. = +2
   F. = −1

2. A. = 0
   B. = −1
   C. = 0
   D. = −1
   E. = −2

3. A. = −3
   B. = −2
   C. = −1
   D. = 0
   E. = +1
   F. = +2
   G. = +3
   H. = +2

4. A. = +2
   B. = +2
   C. = +1
   D. = −3

5. A. = −1
   B. = −1
   C. = −2
   D. = +2

6. A. = +2
   B. = +1
   C. = 0
   D. = −1

7. A. = +1
   B. = −1
   C. = 0
   D. = +1
   E. = +1
   F. = +1

Interpreting Your Score

-140 to -51 Bottlefeeder   From your responses you seem highly disposed toward bottlefeeding from day one. You are attracted to the freedom and convenience of being able to share feeding duties with others. You don't relate to the earth-mother image; just because something is natural doesn't mean it's necessarily best. You have confidence in formula as a product, and don't see breastmilk as a magical, mystical bonding agent. You are rational, highly organized, and your work may be as much a part of who you are as your family relationships. You look at the previous bottle-dependent generation and think, that worked fine for all those babies who are now adults, and you don't see any reason to try something that may be tiring and difficult when you know there is another way that's easy and has worked well for millions of parents and their babies.

-50 to +19 Flexible   You are not set on handling your infant feeding one way or another. You're open-minded and adaptable, and will probably wait until your baby is born and see how things strike you then. You may give breastfeeding a try, but you are not wedded to the idea; if it doesn't work out for you, your baby, or the rest of your family, you can switch without agonizing over the decision. You know there are health benefits to nursing and you hope the practice will be soothing and enjoyable, but you know many people who have raised perfectly fine children on the bottle, and you also know of mothers who stuck with breastfeeding despite pain and misery, whose children appeared to suffer from their mother's inflexibility.

+20 to +100 Strongly Motivated Breastfeeder You are oriented toward breastfeeding and will try your best to make it work. You believe in the benefits and are looking forward to the experience, which you hope will be rewarding and special. But you are not absolutist in your views. You see that there are advantages to the bottle in some situations (perhaps you will wean when you go back to work full time). You may try offering a bottle at times, so you can leave your baby with your husband or a sitter when the need arises. If you do run into difficulties in the nursing relationship, after you have done your best to try to overcome them, you would accept the bottle. You might feel disappointment that the nursing did not go on as long as you'd hoped, but you would not be consumed by guilt.

+101 to +170 Breastfeeding Absolutist You are a mother who attaches great importance to the establishment of a good breastfeeding relationship with your baby. While the odds are in your favor that you will be able to initiate and maintain lactation, if you encounter difficulties, you will be determined to take whatever measures are recommended by experts to keep on nursing (even if it means your own discomfort). Should it come to pass that breastfeeding, despite your best efforts, becomes impossible, you might find that outcome hard to accept; you might feel that you have failed your baby or failed as a woman. Continue to think positively about the nursing role you intend to play, but keep in mind that when it comes to infants, things don't always go according to our preset ideals. Should you unexpectedly find yourself having to use the bottle, you may need to revise your vision of what's right for *your* baby, and for the both of you at the moment. Don't let anyone else try to make you feel guilty, whatever happens!

Resource Guide

Product Information

Formula Brands

Bonamil	800-999-9384
Enfamil	800-BABY-123
Similac	800-550-7677
Isomil	800-550-7677
Lactofree	800-BABY-123
Carnation Good Start	800-782-7766
Carnation Follow-up	800-242-5200
Nursoy	800-999-9384
Prosobee	800-BABY-123
Gerber	800-828-9119
SMA	800-999-9384
Next Step	800-BABY-123
Soyalac	800-932-5525
I-Soyalac	800-932-5525
Alimentum	800-550-7677
Nutramigen	800-BABY-123

Equipment Information: Bottles, Nipples, Breastpumps

Evenflo bottles and nipples	800-356-BABY
Playtex Nursing Systems	800-222-0453
Johnson & Johnson Healthflow bottles	800-5-HEALTHY
Nuk/Gerber bottles and nipples	800-828-9119
Pur/Playskool nipples	800-PLAYSKL
Cherubs bottles and nipples	800-222-0453
Munchkin bottles and nipples	800-344-BABY
Kindergrips bottles and nipples	800-222-0453
Ameda Egnell electric breastpumps	800-323-8750
Medela breastpumps, SNS	800-TELL-YOU
Lact-Aid Nursing System	615-744-9090

Mail-order catalogs: Bottlefeeding and Breastfeeding Supplies

The Right Start	800-548-8531
One Step Ahead	800-274-8440
Hand in Hand	800-872-9745
The Orange Elephant	800-467-5597
Motherwear	800-633-0303
Mother Nurture	708-420-4233
Loving Moms	800-568-4648
Natural Choice Co.	800-528-8887
The Natural Baby	800-388-BABY
Ecobaby	800-596-7450

Formula Clubs

Ross Pediatrics' Welcome Addition Club
800-BABYLINE
Free formula samples, teddy bear, discount coupons, and
newsletter

Gerber Baby Club
800-828-9119
Free formula samples, discount coupons, educational pamphlets, and parenting tips

Carnation Special Delivery Club
800-826-1100
New baby book, discount coupons, various special offers

Wyeth Laboratories, SMA/Nursoy Discounts
800-999-9384
Voice-mail system for registering to receive discount coupons on powdered, concentrated, or ready-to-feed formulas

Endnotes

Introduction

1. Thirty-one out of the sixty-four women who responded to my newspaper notice expressed either relief at finding someone to talk to about their guilt feelings, or frustration at the widespread assumption that bottlefeeding mothers are not as committed to nurturing their babies as breastfeeding mothers are.

2. Much of what I have learned about the use of wet-nurses comes from two meticulously researched histories, one by English social historian Laurence Stone (*The Family, Sex, and Marriage in England, 1500–1800*, Harper Torchbooks, 1977), the other by a French academic, Elisabeth Badinter (*Mother Love, Myth and Reality: Motherhood in Modern History*, Macmillan, 1980). On wet-nurse's neglect of their own infants in order to feed their upper-class charges, Badinter says this: "Until the end of the sixteenth century it appears that hiring wet-nurses was common only among the aristocracy. Thus, it was to the noblewomen that Vives and Erasmus address their reproaches. But these rich women had nurses come to their homes, depriving other children—the nurses'—of their mothers. Consequently, every time an aristocratic mother refused to nurse her baby, *two* children were deprived of mother's milk. Montaigne already laments this fact in his essays, written between 1580 and 1590: 'Moreover, it is easy to see from experience that the natural affection to which we give such authority has very frail roots. Every day we snatch children from the arms of their mothers, and put our own in their charge for a very small payment. We force them to give theirs over to some wretched nurse, with whom we will not trust our own, or to a she-goat.'" (p. 41)

3. Badinter makes clear that great social pressure was brought
    to bear against the upper-class woman thinking of nursing
    her baby herself. "In the name of decency, nursing was de-
    clared ridiculous and disgusting. The word 'ridiculous' turns
    up quite often in letters and memoirs. Mothers, mothers-in-
    law, and midwives all did their best to dissuade the young
    mother from nursing, a task not sufficiently noble for a lady
    of quality. It was not seemly to expose the breasts. Beyond
    the fact that it would encourage an animalistic image of the
    woman as milk-cow, it was considered immodest. This was
    not to be taken lightly in the eighteenth century. Modesty
    was a real feeling that must be taken into consideration if we
    are to understand the refusal to breastfeed. If the mother
    nursed, she had to hide from the world, and that in turn
    interrupted for a long time both her social life and her hus-
    band's." (*Motherhood, Myth and Reality: Motherhood in
    Modern History*, pp. 69–70)
         Stone tells how some members of the medical profession
    in the seventeenth century sought to encourage nursing among
    upper-class women, but adds, "It is significant that those
    mothers who fed their own children regarded it as something
    to boast about, as it was an unusual occurrence. There is also
    some indication that it was the more puritanically inclined
    mothers who were the first from well-to-do families to try to
    nurse their own children. . . . In the early eighteenth century,
    the propaganda in favor of mothers nursing their own chil-
    dren was powerfully reinforced by a fierce attack in *The
    Spectator* on so inhumane and physically dangerous a prac-
    tice as handing children over to slovenly and dirty wet-nurses,
    even if they did only cost between three and six shillings a
    week. . . . In 1716 even so independent a woman as Lady
    Mary Wortley Montagu was against maternal breastfeeding:
    'I grant that Nature has furnished the mother with milk to
    nourish her child; but I maintain at the same time that if she
    can find better milk elsewhere, she ought to prefer it without
    hesitation.' . . . The conclusion seems to be, therefore, that
    the practice of using wet-nurses was largely confined to the
    wealthy classes. Although the proportion may have been
    declining, it seems that the majority of mothers, even devoted

and child-oriented ones, were still not feeding their own children well into the middle of the eighteenth century." (*The Family, Sex, and Marriage in England, 1500–1800*, p. 271)

4. Indeed, before 1972 the idea of "bonding" as a scientific construct was unknown. In that year two pediatricians, John Kennell and Marshall Klaus, published an enormously influential study defining and explaining the concept that the mother and baby must not be separated in the first hours after childbirth or else they will not "imprint" upon one another, leading to a wide variety of dysfunctional behavior (including, in extreme cases, delinquency and social maladjustment in the child, and abusive behavior toward the child by the mother). In her fascinating history *Mother Infant Bonding: A Scientific Fiction,* (Yale University Press, 1992), author Diane E. Eyer shows how the Kennell-Klaus study, though fundamentally flawed, caught on among various organizations and advocacy groups, who used it to advance their own agendas. Right wing and religiously conservative groups pushed the bonding theory because it lent scientific support to the belief that the mother should remain with her child at home rather than seek equal treatment with men in the workplace. Freudians endorsed bonding because it went hand in hand with their psychological theory that birth of a son is the woman's proper way of relieving the neurosis of penis-envy; by "bonding" with her son right after birth she experiences, at least vicariously, the possession of a penis. Hospital personnel also had a strong motive to promote the concept of bonding, because it encouraged new parents to express interest in the day-to-day care of extremely premature or ill newborns (the tendency before bonding research was for parents not to become too attached to a baby who might die).

5. For example, Stone asserts that in the 1640s, "The average recorded mortality rate in the first year in France was between fifteen and thirty percent, with the mean at twenty-one percent, but the real rate must have been much higher due to unrecorded deaths of children who died in the first few days or weeks of life." (p. 55) Badinter says that the rate of death

for French infants under one year was "consistently well above 25 percent." (p. 109)

6. Francine Du Plessix Gray, in her Foreword to Badinter's work, concisely summed up premodern attitudes towards infant death this way: "She [Badinter] forces us to realize that until the late eighteenth century a newborn was not the beloved person we now welcome into the world, but a marginal creature alarmingly replete with error and original sin. As late as the seventeenth century, such theologians as Pierre de Berulle and the soft-hearted Francois de Sales described infancy as a 'beastlike state deprived of reason and judgment,' 'the most vile and abject state of human nature, second only to death.' Barely possessing a soul of his own, the child came at the will of God, departed at His behest, and during his short sojourn on earth (which tended to be preceded and succeeded by the birth of innumerable siblings) deserved little sympathy and affection. It is in the context of this negative theology, and of a widespread lack of mourning for children being born in often undesirable abundance, that one hears the cool words of the great humanist, Michel de Montaigne: 'I lost three children during their stay with the wet-nurse—not without regret, mind you, but without any great vexation.'" (p. xii)

7. This figure was reported by Dr. Marianne Neifert, medical director of the lactation program at Presbyterian-St. Luke's Medical Center in Denver, who has conducted studies of the problem of insufficient milk production. Her findings were summarized in an article in *Time* magazine, August 22, 1994, "When Breastfeeding Fails."

8. Gabrielle Palmer in her book *The Politics of Breastfeeding* (Pandora Press/HarperCollins, 1988) provides perhaps the fullest explication found in the breastfeeding literature of the thesis that formula companies in the 1950s, '60s and '70s deliberately conspired to sabotage the practice of breastfeeding worldwide. In three full chapters of her book (pp. 199–302), Palmer analyzes the economic imperatives of capitalism that in her view led manufacturers to engage in their anti-breastfeeding campaigns and then details the methods the companies employed to undermine the practice and the

resulting damage she believes was wrought upon infants and mothers internationally, as a consequence.

9. I list a wide range, 75 percent to 90 percent for breastfeeding among educated women, because different sources give different statistics. *The New York Times*, April 5, 1994, reported that "In the United States an estimated three quarters of middle and upper income women nurse their infants" ("Quebec Bets on Subsidized Milk, Mother's Kind"); in the *Washington Post*, November 6, 1993, a high of 86 percent was given for nursing among new mothers at one hospital located in a high-income neighborhood of Washington, D.C. In her book, *Mothering the New Mother* (Newmarket Press, 1994), author Sally Placksin quotes an Upper East Side Manhattan pediatrician as reporting breastfeeding rates of up to 90 percent for the infants in her care. (p. 111)

10. According to *Child* magazine (December/January 1995, p. 28), the six states that protect the mother's right to breastfeed in public are: Florida, Illinois, Michigan, New York, North Carolina, and Virginia. New York's law is especially tough on anyone who would interfere with the mother's right to breastfeed, providing fines of $1000 to $5000 or prison sentences of one to five years for violators (SOURCE: *Mothering* magazine, Spring 1995, p. 31)

11. In my interviews I asked bottlefeeding mothers for their comments on cases involving breastfeeding rights, such as the right to be accommodated on the job so that milk may be expressed, or the right to feed in a restaurant or other public place. Not one of the mothers wanted to see breastfeeding restricted in any way, and quite a few made the point that anything that expanded the choices available to new mothers was to the advantage of society in general. (For more on bottlefeeding mothers' views about the rights of breastfeeding women, see "Mothers Talk" in chapter 5.)

Chapter 1

1. La Leche League International, *The Womanly Art of Breastfeeding*, Plume/Penguin Books, revised edition 1991 (fifth update of the original 1958 edition), p. 7.

2. Pryor, Karen, and Gale Pryor, *Nursing Your Baby,* Pocket Books, third edition, 1991 (originally published in 1963), p. i.

3. Eisenberg, Arlene, Heidi E. Murkoff, and Sandee E. Hathaway, *What to Expect When You're Expecting,* Workman Publishing, 1984, p. 390.

4. Nursing Mothers' Council for the Boston Association for Childbirth Education, *Breastfeeding Your Baby,* Avery Publishing Group, 1989, p. 93.

5. La Leche League International, "Establishing Your Milk Supply" (pamphlet, reprint No. 81), January 1989.

6. "Dying for Milk: Some Mothers, Trying in Vain to Breastfeed, Starve Their Infants," *The Wall Street Journal,* Kevin Helliker, July 22, 1994. "When Breastfeeding Fails," *Time* magazine, by Christine Gorman, August 22, 1994. "Check in, deliver, go home—Hospitals are hustling new mothers out in a day or less. Is it risky?" *U.S. News & World Report,* December 5, 1994. "Mother's Milk," ABC's *Primetime Live,* August 4, 1994.

7. "La Leche League International Answers Concerns Regarding Inadequate Milk Supply," press release dated August 2, 1994, Schaumberg, Illinois.

8. Facts reported in *Child* magazine's "Nursery News" column, December/January 1995.

9. Kleiman, Karen R. and Valerie D. Raskin, *This Isn't What I Expected: Recognizing and Recovering from Depression and Anxiety after Childbirth,* Bantam, 1994, p. 2.

10. La Leche League International, *The Womanly Art of Breastfeeding,* (Plume/Penguin Books, revised edition 1991) p. 234.

11. "Children of Smoking Mothers Show Carcinogens in Blood," *The New York Times,* September 21, 1994. The article reported the results of a study by Doctors Frederica Perera, Regina Santella, Jack Mayer and Florence Crawford, all of Columbia University, which found a variety of adverse effects from maternal smoking. The study included mothers who were light smokers, averaging ten cigarettes a day.

12. La Leche League International, *The Womanly Art of Breastfeeding,* pp. 321–322.

13. Pryor, Karen and Gale Pryor *Nursing Your Baby,* Pocket Books, third edition, 1991, pp. 171–172.

14. "Congress Moves to Limit Early Discharges After Childbirth," by Sandra G. Boodman, *The Washington Post,* July 4, 1995.

15. For example, here's a bit of the advice in the La Leche League's pamphlet, "Newborn Jaundice" (Publication No. 25, November 1989): "In addition to nursing early and often, a mother can help prevent jaundice in her baby by avoiding glucose water supplements, which are offered routinely at many hospitals." (p. 4) And "If a baby shows signs of physiologic or pathologic jaundice, continued and frequent breastfeeding can often help the baby clear the bilirubin from his system. In my case [the pamphlet's author gives her own child's bout with jaundice as an example] once Sadie's jaundice became evident, I could have insisted that I be allowed to try to nurse her during her few naturally occurring wakeful periods, and at the beginning when she was not nursing well, I probably should have used a breast pump to stimulate my milk." (p. 5)

16. "Newborn Jaundice" goes on to criticize doctors for being too quick to suggest a switch to the bottle. "Some doctors who are anxious to speed up the process [of elimination of bilirubin from the infant's bloodstream], perhaps because they feel the bilirubin level is becoming dangerously high or rising too rapidly, will suggest a temporary substitution of treated breast milk, donor milk from another mother, or formula." (p. 6) The pamphlet goes on to suggest ways for the mother to counter the doctor's advice: "If a doctor insists upon an approach that will negatively affect breastfeeding, saying 'La Leche League believes . . .' is unlikely to persuade a doctor to change his or her mind. But if a mother says, 'I have read about other approaches to treating jaundice and I have a couple of references to articles in medical journals, could we look at them together?' her doctor may be willing to listen." (p. 9)

17. La Leche League International, "Nursing Your Adopted Baby," Publication No. 55, May 1986, p. 3.

18. Dr. Neifert's finding were reported in the August 22, 1994 issue of *Time* magazine, "When Breast-feeding Fails," by Christine Gorman.

Chapter 2

1. From study abstract reported in *Medical Abstracts* Newsletter, March 1994. Original study published in the *Journal of American Dermatology*, 30:35, by J. Kay et. al., Jan. 1994.

2. *The New York Times*, "2 Healthful Bacteria Are Proved to Ward Off Diarrhea in Infants," by Warren E. Leary, Oct. 14, 1994.

3. *Washington City Paper*, "Milk Duds," by Clara Jeffrey, June 17, 1994.

4. Statistic cited in *The New York Times*, "Quebec Bets on Subsidized Milk, Mother's Kind," by Clyde H. Farnsworth, April 5, 1994. However, in some upper middle class areas the breastfeeding rate may be as high as 90 percent. In the book *Mothering the New Mother*, (Newmarket Press, 1994), author Sally Placksin quotes an OB-GYN in Manhattan who says that up to 90 percent of her patients breastfeed. (p. 111)

5. *The Washington Post*, "When Nursing Moms Go Back to Work," by Marylou Tousingnant, November 6, 1993. According to figures in the article, the mother who stays at home is twice as likely to be breastfeeding her 5- to 6-month old baby as one who works full time.

6. Asthma increased by 40 percent during the ten-year period from 1982 to 1992, according to the Centers for Disease Control in Atlanta (reported in the *The New York Times*, Jan. 7, 1995); among the factors cited by the CDC as contributing to the rise in asthma were unclean living conditions, environmental triggers such as cat danders and pollens, and poor access to health care—with no mention of bottlefeeding as being suspect in any way. The breastfeeding rate was cited by Jane E. Brody in her "Personal Health" column in *The New York Times*, April 6, 1994.

7. The possible link between diabetes and cow's milk or milk-based formulas was the subject of articles in many newspa-

pers the first weeks of September, 1994. Typical was this one by Thomas H. Maugh in the *Los Angeles Times,* Sept. 8, 1994: "Cluster of Genes Linked to Common Type of Diabetes," which noted, "The presence of the genes alone does not necessarily mean that the individual will develop the disease, but only that he or she is predisposed to developing it. The individual must be exposed to a trigger in the environment—a virus or a protein in cow's milk, in the case of diabetes—before the disease occurs."

8. Only a few months after the first articles appeared linking diabetes to cow's milk came more reports that the findings may have been in error. From the December 16, 1994 *Los Angeles Times* came this article compiled from wire service reports: "Study Rebuts Milk, Diabetes Link," which opened with the line, "Earlier reports that drinking cow's milk may trigger the onset of juvenile diabetes in susceptible people may be wrong, Florida researchers report today." All right, whom should we believe?

9. La Leche League, "Facts about Breastfeeding," leaflet, 1994.

10. Study by Mary Fran R. Sowers, et al., at the University of Michigan, reported in *Science News,* June 26, 1993, based on the June 23/30 *Journal of the American Medical Association.*

11. Prodigy News Service, "Pre-Menopause Cancer Risk Cut," Jan. 12, 1994.

12. In an on-line questionnaire, breastfeeding women were asked how many months they had breastfed (without formula supplementation) before their periods returned. The respondents' answers averaged out to eight and a third months, with the shortest time being 6 weeks and the longest, 24 months.

13. This figure was cited on-line by a lactation consultant for the Texas hospital in which she worked. Neither the Center for Health Statistics nor Ross Laboratories, both of which have compiled breastfeeding statistics, appeared to have collected figures on the breastfeeding drop-off rate at three months postpartum.

14. For much of my recounting of the battle against Nestle and other infant formula companies I am indebted to the article "Milk Duds" that appeared in *Washington City Paper,* June

17, 1994. Writer Clara Jeffreys presents a concise history of both the expansion of world formula markets and the rise of the anti-formula movement.

15. My knowledge of the controversy surrounding the AAP's voluntary ad-ban is largely taken from an article that appeared in *The New York Times,* June 15, 1993, "Battle for Baby Formula Market," by Barry Meier.

16. Quoted from the *New York Times* article, cited in footnote 16, above.

Chapter 3

1. As the Foreword to the third edition (1981) puts it: "In addition, La Leche League gave the new mother (as well as the old) a bible, *The Womanly Art,* an invaluable resource for the breastfeeding woman." Foreword by Dr. Herbert Ratner, reprinted in the fifth edition (1991), p. xx.

2. La Leche League sells the works of all of these experts through its catalog, but gives special prominence—a two-page spread—to the books of Dr. William Sears (with sometime co-author, Martha Sears, R.N.) Some of his most influential works—the ones that the breastfeeding militants on computer networks tend to tout most highly—include: *The Baby Book* (described in the catalog as the book that "emphasizes a baby's basic needs and helps new parents to meet those needs through the loving, nurturing, attachment-style of parenting."); *The Birth Book: Everything You Need to Know to Have a Safe and Satisfying Birth; Nighttime Parenting: How to Get Your Baby and Child to Sleep through the Night* (advocating unrestricted nighttime nursing for babies and toddlers and sleeping in the parents' bed); *The Fussy Baby: How to Bring Out the Best in Your High Need Child* (promoting "back to the womb" techniques, such as constant mother-baby skin contact and round-the-clock nursing on demand; and *Creative Parenting* (in which, according to the catalog copy, you will "learn the concept of continuum parenting, in which family members enjoy and respect one another and parents feel confident in trusting their instincts.")

3. See, for example, the very first of the "Ten Commandments of Lactation," page 116. See also the quotation from *The Womanly Art,* p. 73, about the unimportance of keeping track of the time spent breastfeeding, just as the mother needs not keep count of the number of kisses she bestows.

4. *WomanWise,* the Journal of the Concord [N.H.] Feminist Health Collective, published the contents of back issues for a five year period, with articles on nearly all of the breastfeeding cult's favorite issues. Here is just a small sampling of what that magazine has covered: anti-C-section, Winter/Spring 1979; childbirth at birthing centers instead of hospitals, Spring 1981; natural birth control methods, holistic healing, both in the Fall 1981 issue; the Nestle boycott, Spring 1982; infant formula abuse, Summer 1982; articles opposing the therapeutic use of sex hormones, and advocating "healing through imagery," both in Fall 1982; against reproductive technologies, Winter 1984; Native American healing methods, Spring 1985; diseases spread by hospitals, Summer, 1985; veganism, Fall 1986; midwives and child health nurses, Fall 1987; herbal healing, Winter 1988; review of the book *Babies, Breastfeeding, and Bonding* by Ina May Gaskin, Spring 1988; linking breast cancer and modern technological society, and the hazards of processed foods, both in the Fall 1988 issue; articles against drinking cow's milk and for alternative healing methods for fibroids and cysts, both in Winter, 1990; natural fertility monitoring, Summer 1991; against animal product testing, Fall 1991; naturopathy, herbalism, homeopathy, and other holistic therapies, Spring 1993; against reproductive technologies, Spring 1994.

5. In an advertising flyer seeking new subscribers, *The Nurturing Parent* defines itself as the magazine committed to a "philosophy based upon the wisdom and experience of authors such as Dr. William Sears and Martha Sears, R.N., who advocate such practices as birth-bonding, sharing sleep, unrestricted, extended breastfeeding, baby-wearing, openness to baby's cues, prompt response to cries, father involvement, and spousal commitment." The flyer also carried these words of praise from a reader: "It is heartening to know that there is indeed a desire and a need for your publication. . . . When

parenting 'attachment style,' it is often very lonely." And this: "We often wonder, 'Are we nuts nursing our two-year-old to sleep and never leaving him with any old sitter?' Then a gem of encouragement is published and we are encouraged." And this: "I like to hear about others who carry their babies all day . . . even heavy ones. I don't want to hear another person say, 'Just put your baby down!' "

Apparently, some cultists are sensitive to others' reactions to certain aspects of their lifestyle; if only they could stop and think how bottlefeeding women must feel when criticized for *their* mothering choices!

6. The ad for *Mothering* magazine inserted in the Ecobaby catalog contained this self-description: "*Mothering* advocates breastfeeding, natural health, demedicalized childbirth, involved fathers, cloth diapering, and more. Articles on immunizations, diapers, breastfeeding, pregnancy, childbirth, babies, children, and family dynamics are common in *Mothering*." There follows an offer for a free issue, the cover of which promises an article on "The Dangers of Prenatal Testing."

7. Ecobaby is really more than a product sales catalog. Its founder refers to it, quite appropriately, as a "magalog," since the write-ups for the items featured are intended to promote a point of view every bit as much as to sell the product. For example, the page with breastfeeding supplies begins with the title "Breastfeeding—Nature's Way," followed by a quarter-page account of why breastfeeding is best. Sprinkled throughout the Spring 1995 issue are mini-articles devoted to the health and environmental benefits of cloth diapering, the need of babies to learn from high-contrast pictures, and the benefits of clothing made only of organic, untreated cotton— all of these subjects very much in line with cult views.

8. There are three different books in the La Leche League catalog devoted to stay-at-home mothering: *Staying Home Instead: Alternatives to the Two-Paycheck Family*, by Christine Davidson; *What's a Smart Woman Like You Doing at Home?* by Linda Burton, Janet Dittmer, and Cheri Loveless; and *Sequencing* [a book proposing that women put their careers on hold during their children's younger years] by Arlene Rossen Cardozo.

9. Both the La Leche League and the Natural Baby catalogs feature books promoting natural childbirth. Both sell *A Good Birth, A Safe Birth: Choosing and Having the Childbirth Experience You Want*, by Diana Korte and Roberta Scaer. Here is the Natural Baby Catalog's write-up of this book: "Prevent unnecessary obstetrical interventions by arming yourself with the scientific studies which prove they are unnecessary and dangerous. I *insist* my friends read this book." Natural Baby also promotes the video *A Gentle Birth*, showing midwife assisted home births, including a water birth, childbirth witnessed by the mother's other children, and a VBAC (vaginal birth after Cesarean). The La Leche League catalog additionally offers *Natural Childbirth the Bradley Way*, by Susan McCutcheon-Rosegg and Peter Rosegg, and *Methods of Childbirth*, by Constance Bean, which, according to the catalog description, features sections on "home or midwife assisted birth."

10. The clothing, both for nursing mothers and babies, sold through The Natural Baby, Motherwear, and Ecobaby catalogs is, of course, only of natural fibers, much of it in peasanty-patterns or cutesy prints. But for the true organic purist, the Natural Baby catalog offers clothing and bedding made only of "green" cotton, which comes in just one shade, its natural, unprocessed color, off-white. As the catalog explains, "Cotton is the most pesticide-laden crop grown in the USA. The bleaching, processing, and dyeing of cotton adds even more toxic chemicals to the environment. . . . These green products are made just like our regular cotton items but we use cotton that is totally unprocessed and free from harmful chemicals. Sometimes we can even obtain organically-grown green cotton. When we can get it, these products will be made from it."

And lest the all-natural breastfeeding mom worry about toxins in her children's toys, she can buy all-natural wooden toys from the Natural Baby catalog, which, the catalog's copy suggests, will also contribute to a calmer personality: "Wild synthetic colors don't seem as peaceful for children as natural ones. Modern toys seem to try to pull the child out of their inner peaceful world and awaken them prematurely to our busy world. What's the rush?"

11. As long as she subscribes to a nursing journal or is on the mailing list of a breastfeeding supply house, the mother who believes in as little physical separation as possible will have no trouble getting hold of a baby sling or front carrier. The Natural Baby Catalog offers slings in three different styles and Motherwear offers two styles, plus a woman's winter coat designed to zip up around a baby in a front carrier, so that the baby will not have to wear its own separate coat. I also noted the ubiquity of ads for slings and front carriers in each of the mothering/breastfeeding magazines I collected.

12. La Leche League promotes reliance on natural methods of birth control through its pamphlet "Breastfeeding and Fertility," that "tells how and why breastfeeding delays the return of fertility when mothers don't introduce formula or other foods in the early months;" The LLL catalog also sells a book titled *Your Fertility Signals: Using Them to Achieve or Avoid Pregnancy Naturally*, by Merryl Winstein.

13. *The Womanly Art of Breastfeeding*, page 399. All other biographical information about the founders can be found on pp. 397–403. Incidentally, let me add a bit of information about Mary Ann Cahill's family: she gave birth to only nine children; the tenth is a foster child who lived with the family for several years and still attends all family gatherings. I included her in the count so as not to imply that a foster child is somehow less "real" than a biological child.

14. When it comes to the natural medicine issues, two breastfeeding/baby-supply catalogs, Motherwear and Natural Baby, have the most extensive offerings. Motherwear sells a complete "homeopathic kit"of natural healing substances, as well as some separately offered natural remedies for sore nipples, and baby's teething pain. Motherwear also offers a book called *Homeopathic Medicine at Home*. But by far the "purest" source of products for the mother intent on bringing up children free from synthetic milk, synthetic drugs, synthetic fibers, and other manufactured substances is the Natural Baby Catalog. It is a breastfeeding cultist's treasure-house, filled with both literature and supplies. There are books questioning modern pediatric practices (such as

How to Raise a Healthy Child in Spite of Your Doctor, by Robert Mendelsohn,) and books promoting "appropriating therapies—herbal, homeopathic, accupressure, nutritional, and others"—such as *Your Healthy Child: A Guide to Natural Health Care for Children,* by Dr. Duncan, *Everybody's Guide to Homeopathic Medicines: Taking Care of Yourself and Your Family with Safe and Effective Remedies,* by Stephen Cummings and Dana Ullman, and *An Alternative Approach to Childhood Ear Infections,* by Dr. Michael A. Schmidt. Natural Baby also sells what it calls natural remedies for all kinds of childhood ills, including colic, teething pain, fever, earache, stomachache, colds and stuffy noses, headache, poison oak and ivy, coughing, lung problems, bedwetting, and many, many others. The catalog copy assures the consumer that these herbal or other alternative medicines have "no side effects or toxicity like ordinary drugs," which "may do more harm than good." (If exclusively breastfed children are all so healthy, then who's buying all these herbal cures?) The breastfeeding cultist may also be attracted to the line of all-natural baby soaps, creams, and shampoos, because, as the catalog copy puts it "we believe strongly that it is unhealthy and unwise to expose your baby's body—externally or internally, to potentially harmful chemicals. Remember, the body does absorb chemicals through the skin."

15. Citations for anti-circumcision materials from breastfeeding cult journals have been combined with citations of anti-vaccination materials in note #16.

16. The Natural Baby catalog includes materials opposing circumcision, including the book, *Circumcision: What Every Parent Should Know,* by Anne Briggs, and the booklet, "Caring for Your Intact Little Boy," by R. Romberg, which, as the catalog tells it, covers "all issues pertaining to circumcision." Presenting the case against vaccination is a book, *The Immunization Decison,* also found in the Natural Baby catalog.

The Ecobaby catalog is even better stocked when it comes to anti-vaccination materials. Although it carries only one book opposing circumcision (*Say No to Circumcision,* author not named), it lists seven different books or pamphlets opposing vaccination. One of the books, titled *Vaccination:*

100 years of Orthodox Research Shows Vaccines Represent a Medical Assault on the Immune System, by Viera Scheibner, Ph.D., receives a half-page write-up in the catalog, in which it is explained that research has proven a link between SIDS and vaccination, as well as the rise in "asthma, childhood leukemia and cancer, the enormous upsurge in cerebral palsy and infantile convulsions." The catalog copy asserts that "Vaccines are highly noxious. They contain formaldehyde, aluminum phosphate, thimerosol (a mercury compound), foreign proteins, and contaminating animal proteins and viruses" and that "Infectious diseases of childhood are beneficial, and when contracted at a suitable age and allowed to run their natural course, these diseases serve to prime and mature the immune system of children." Another book from Ecobaby's list, *Vaccination, Social Violence and Criminality* (author's name given as Coulter) "considers the relationship of vaccination to autism, hyperactivity, allergies, autoimmune diseases, and learning disabilities" and suggests "a connection between neurological damage and the present high level of criminality in American society."

This catalog also carries a warning that rubber nipples and pacifiers are toxic, because of the nitrosomines contained in latex that "can cause cancer, tumors, and have been linked to Kaposi's Syndrome." But few consumers on the mailing list for this catalog would be likely to use bottles or pacifiers. They would be far more interested in the breastfeeding supplies, cloth diapers made of organically grown cotton, matching mother-baby outfits, or the large selection of books on such subjects as: the benefits of sharing a family bed, the dangers of modern pediatric practices, how to use homeopathic medicines, how to cook organically, or why all processed foods are slowly poisoning most Americans.

17. The Ecobaby catalog offers several choices of books promoting homeschooling, including: *The How and Why of Home Schooling, The Big Book of Home Learning (Volumes I and II),* and *You Are Your Child's First Teacher* (no authors' names listed in the catalog for any of these books).

Chapter 5

1. In an article, "Breastfeeding and Work," in the November 1994 issue of *American Baby* magazine, a researcher for the magazine checked out daycare centers and found that many were unwilling to cooperate with nursing mothers' requests to handle bottled breastmilk—some refusing to thaw frozen breastmilk, while others declining responsibility for ensuring that the baby got only its own bottle. To deal with the problem, *American Baby* suggests that breastfeeding mothers use only a one-on-one daycare provider—a solution that would be too expensive for many mothers.

2. La Leche League's *Breastfeeding Rights Packet* is a compilation of quotations and excerpts from different child psychologists and childcare authors, whose views first appeared elsewhere. Dr. Shaywitz's quotation originally appeared in an article in *The New York Times Magazine*, dated March, 1973.

3. Less than one percent of fathers (77,000 out of 25 million families) assume primary childcare responsibilities while the wife works, according to *The Washington Post*, April 28, 1987 ("Fathers Raising Kids—What Happens When Mom Goes to Work and Dad Stays Home," by Abigail Trafford).

4. The paragraph reprinted in the *Breastfeeding Rights Packet* originally appeared in an article in the *Chicago Tribune*, April 16, 1979, by Donna Joy Newman.

Chapter 6

1. *The New York Times*, "2 Healthful Bacteria Are Proved to Ward Off Diarrhea in Infants," by Warren E. Leary, October 14, 1994.

2. *The Washington Post*, "Drug Will No Longer Be Sold to Stop Breast Milk," by Rick Weiss, August 23, 1994.

Index

About the Author

Peggy Robin is the author of five books and the mother of two daughters. She had her first child, conceived with the help of fertility treatment, in 1990. After breastfeeding contentedly for seven months, Peggy weaned in order to resume fertility treatment in the hope of having a second child. Her experience in treatment gave impetus to her 1993 book, *How to Be a Successful Fertility Patient*. The treatment also resulted in the conception of her second daughter, born in the same year.

Though she intended to breastfeed the second time around, a postpartum infection led to a three-day hospital stay, during which the baby was kept at home and put on the bottle. After returning home, Peggy spent several stressful weeks attempting to return to breastfeeding before concluding, at first reluctantly, to stick with what seemed to work best for the baby: the bottle.

Though her bottlefed daughter was happy and thriving, Peggy quickly discovered how often the bottlefeeding mother is criticized for her choice, told by friends, acquaintances, or even strangers on the street that "breast is best." She wrote *Bottlefeeding Without Guilt* to reassure all new parents that loving and caring come from the heart, not from the type of nipple we use.

Peggy and her husband, Bill Adler, Jr., live in Washington, D.C.